International Perspectives on Materials in ELT

Edited by

Sue Garton
School of Languages and Social Sciences, Aston Univ

and

Kathleen Graves
School of Education, University of Michigan, USA

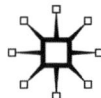

First published 2014 by
PALGRAVE MACMILLAN

Palgrave Macmillan in the UK is an imprint of Macmillan Publishers Limited, registered in England, company number 785998, of Houndmills, Basingstoke, Hampshire RG21 6XS.

Palgrave Macmillan in the US is a division of St Martin's Press LLC, 175 Fifth Avenue, New York, NY 10010.

Palgrave Macmillan is the global academic imprint of the above companies and has companies and representatives throughout the world.

Palgrave® and Macmillan® are registered trademarks in the United States, the United Kingdom, Europe and other countries

ISBN: 978–1–137–02329–2 (hardback)
ISBN: 978–1–137–02330–8 (paperback)

This book is printed on paper suitable for recycling and made from fully managed and sustained forest sources. Logging, pulping and manufacturing processes are expected to conform to the environmental regulations of the country of origin.

A catalogue record for this book is available from the British Library.

A catalog record for this book is available from the Library of Congress.

International Perspectives on Materials in ELT

International Perspectives on English Language Teaching

Series edited by **Sue Garton** and **Keith Richards**

Titles include:
Ema Ushioda (*editor*)
INTERNATIONAL PERSPECTIVES ON MOTIVATION

Sue Garton and Kathleen Graves (*editors*)
INTERNATIONAL PERSPECTIVES ON MATERIALS IN ELT

Forthcoming titles in the series:

Sarah Rich (*editor*)
INTERNATIONAL PERSPECTIVES ON TEACHING ENGLISH TO YOUNG LEARNERS
New Language Learning and Teaching Environments

International Perspectives on English Language Teaching
Series Standing Order ISBN 978–0–230–30850–3 (hardback)
                                    978–0–230–30851–0 (paperback)
(*outside North America only*)

You can receive future titles in this series as they are published by placing a standing order. Please contact your bookseller or, in case of difficulty, write to us at the address below with your name and address, the title of the series and one of the ISBNs quoted above.

Customer Services Department, Macmillan Distribution Ltd, Houndmills, Basingstoke, Hampshire RG21 6XS, England

---

Also by Sue Garton

FROM EXPERIENCE TO KNOWLEDGE IN ELT (*co-author*)

PROFESSIONAL ENCOUNTERS IN TESOL
Discourses of Teachers in Teaching (*co-author*)

Also by Kathleen Graves

DESIGNING LANGUAGE COURSES
A Guide for Teachers

DEVELOPING A NEW CURRICULUM FOR SCHOOL-AGE LEARNERS (*co-editor*)

ICON-ENGLISH FOR INTERNATIONAL COMMUNICATION (*co-author*)

TEACHERS AS COURSE DEVELOPERS (*editor*)

Contents

List of Figures

List of Tables

Series Editors' Preface

Anyone looking back on the history of English language teaching could be forgiven for thinking that teaching materials are the flotsam and jetsam of our profession, floating on the tides and currents of ELT fashion. Every so often some enterprising beachcomber in search of littoral treasure holds them up for inspection and we are reminded of their value, but our attention is soon drawn back to the navigational challenges of our profession and we sail on by.

This is a pity because as the editors of this volume, drawing on Richards, make clear at the outset, much teaching depends on materials; they are part of the waters on which we move. This is of fundamental importance, for as long as we see materials as mere objects available for our use and, if necessary, analysis, we deny ourselves the opportunity of understanding their place in our pedagogic world. What makes this collection distinctive is its focus on materials *in situ*: on the relationships between teachers and their materials; on the challenges of using, adapting and creating materials; and on their developmental potential.

In keeping with the theme of this series, the relationship between local and global emerges strongly in the collection, but it also includes López-Barrios and de Debat's (Argentina) provocative challenge to the relevance of the distinction itself. Ultimately, responses to this challenge must be formulated not just in terms of local contingencies but in the connection between teacher and students realised through the design and use of relevant materials. Igielski (US) touches on the essence of this relationship in her engaging chapter on designing culturally and linguistically sensitive materials: 'My prior knowledge of the students as learners at school and my willingness to recognize them as possessors of valuable cultural capital were the building blocks of the unit's design.'

At one level, this demands of the teacher sensitivity to local constraints and opportunities, and a willingness to design or adapt materials accordingly. We see in this collection the various ways in which teachers have responded to this, whether wrestling with the challenges of the cultural adaptation of existing materials (Messekher, Algeria), developing supplementary materials (Nuangpolmak, Thailand), or seizing opportunities offered by new technologies (Rahman and Cotter, Bangladesh). At another level, however, teaching materials raise profound questions about the nature of pedagogy and its place within political and ideological systems. They can be facilitators of change (Humphries, Japan) but also instruments of control, representing the imposition of potentially alien approaches, as Seferaj (Albania) indicates.

If we narrow our view of materials to embrace only issues of design, evaluation, and application, we obscure their indexical significance and may thereby fail to appreciate their potential. We believe that this collection offers a broader perspective and that it represents an opportunity to think differently about materials and their place in our pedagogic world.

Acknowledgements

We would like to thank the following for permission to reproduce copyright material:

The Ministry of National Education of the Democratic Republic of Algeria for permission to reproduce page 13 from *Spotlight on English*, Middle School, Year Two and page 21 from *On the Move*, Middle School, Year 4.

Adam Cadre for permission to use a screen shot from *9:05*.

Emily Short for permission to use a screen shot from *Bronze*.

CNA, Brazil for permission to use excerpts from *Step Ahead 1* by S. Cunningham and P. Moor.

We would also like to thank the BBC Janala project for their contribution to the volume.

Notes on Contributors

Denise M. de Abreu-e-Lima is an associate professor at Universidade Federal de São Carlos (UFSCar-Brazil). She has taught English for 25 years and has worked as a teacher educator in the undergraduate program since 1994. She is also coordinator of Distance Education Programs at UFSCar. Her research interests include teacher education, feedback processes, and using technology for teaching.

Sahar al Majthoob is the Head of the Languages and Humanities Section at the Curricula Directorate in the Ministry of Education in Bahrain. She started her career as an English teacher then moved to the field of curriculum. She supervises and participates in the materials selection and development. Her interests include first and second language literacy processes.

Eliane H. Augusto-Navarro is an associate professor at Universidade Federal de São Carlos (UFSCar-Brazil). She has taught English for over 20 years and has worked as a teacher educator in the undergraduate (since 1996) and graduate (since 2005) programs at UFSCar. Her research interests include teacher education, grammar(ing) as skill, ESP/EAP, genre analysis, and teaching materials.

Esther G. Bosompem is a lecturer at the Ghana Institute of Languages, Ghana, and has been engaged in the teaching of English as a foreign language for more than ten years. She holds an MA in TESOL and Translation Studies from Aston University, UK. Her main research interest is ELT materials use and development.

Maurizia Cherubin is a high school teacher of English in Vittuone, Italy. She is interested in ICTs and CLIL, and is an IWB tutor and coach. She holds three masters degrees: teaching foreign languages and communication; teaching English as a foreign language; communication with IWB. She also has a TKT CLIL certificate.

Tanya Cotter has worked in a variety of ELT roles in Europe, Asia, and North Africa since 1991. She was the ELT Editor for BBC Media Action on the BBC Janala project from 2010 to 2012. She is currently English for the Future Manager for the British Council in Libya.

Enrique García Pascual is Professor and Dean of the Faculty of Education at the University of Zaragoza, Spain, and a member of the School Board of Aragon. He has published books and articles about adult education, CLIL, the role and responsibilities of teachers, and the use of ICTs in teaching and research. He has participated in Comenius, Grundtvig, Minerva, and Erasmus European projects.

Sue Garton is Director of Postgraduate Programmes in English at Aston University, UK, where she tutors on postgraduate programmes in TESOL. She has written and edited books and articles for teachers including *From Experience to Knowledge in ELT* with Julian Edge and *Professional Encounters in TESOL* with Keith Richards.

Kathleen Graves is Associate Professor of Education Practice at the University of Michigan, USA. She has written and edited books and articles on curriculum development including *Teachers as Course Developers, Designing Language Courses: A Guide for Teachers,* and, with Lucilla Lopriore, *Developing a New Curriculum for School Age Learners.*

Josie Guiney Igielski teaches in Madison, Wisconsin, USA. She taught Kindergarten for three years in an English Learner clustered classroom. For the last four years she has taught fourth grade to a diverse group of learners. She has a BA in Education and a masters in Curriculum and Instruction from the University of Wisconsin, Madison.

Simon Humphries holds a PhD in Linguistics from Macquarie University and an MSc in TESOL from Aston University. His recent publications focus on action research, classroom interaction, the analysis of EFL materials, issues in CLT implementation and classroom observation. He is currently an associate professor in the Faculty of Foreign Language Studies at Kansai University in Osaka, Japan.

Mario López-Barrios is Professor of Foreign Language Teaching at the School of Languages, Universidad Nacional de Córdoba, Argentina. His research interests include second language acquisition, materials development, and research methods in applied linguistics.

Fabrizio Maggi is a high school teacher, an EFL and ICT teacher trainer, and trainer of trainers. He has been involved in CLIL projects since the mid-1980s and has developed language courses and educational software. He is also a lecturer of English Language at the University of Pavia, Italy, and has organized Comenius and Leonardo European projects.

Hayat Messekher is an assistant professor of English at the Ecole Normale Supérieure de Bouzaréah in Algiers. Her research interests include teacher education, critical pedagogy, critical discourse analysis, and linguistic landscapes.

Apiwan Nuangpolmak is a lecturer at Chulalongkorn University Language Institute (CULI) in Bangkok, Thailand. She obtained her Master of Applied Linguistics (TESOL) and Doctor of Philosophy (Linguistics) from Macquarie

University, Australia. Her research interests include materials development, motivational strategies, fostering learner autonomy, and writing instruction.

Luciana C. de Oliveira is an associate professor of TESOL and Applied Linguistics at Teachers College, Columbia University, New York City. Her research focuses on issues related to teaching English language learners (ELLs) at the K-12 level, including the role of language in learning content areas and teacher preparation for ELLs.

Patricia Pashby has taught in university settings in the US and Thailand for 25 years. Her work with in-service teacher training includes K-12 teachers from Brazil, South Korea, and Taiwan. She currently teaches in the Language Teaching Specialization programme at the University of Oregon.

Joe Pereira is an EFL teacher at the British Council in Porto, Portugal, and has a deep interest in digital game-based learning. He actively researches and promotes the use of parser-based Interactive Fiction as a language learning tool, mainly through his blog, 'IF Only: Interactive Fiction and Teaching English a Foreign Language', which can be found at http://www.theswanstation.com.

Arifa Rahman is an English language teacher and teacher educator in Bangladesh with experience in educational research, materials development, assessment, and programme evaluation. A reviewer for academic journals, she has published widely. She has also been an educational consultant with BBC Media Action, the British Council, and the European Union.

Jack C. Richards has taught in universities in New Zealand, Canada, the USA and Hong Kong and is currently based mainly in Sydney, Australia. He has published widely on methodology and teacher training, and has also written many popular classroom texts, including the *Interchange* and *Four Corners* series.

Kristjan Seferaj is currently a doctoral candidate at Aston University, UK, and his chapter is based on his doctoral dissertation. He has taught general, academic English, and EFL teacher training courses in East Europe, West Europe, and North America. His research interests are teacher thinking and EFL methodology.

Bonny Tibbitts has worked in TESL for 35 years, teaching middle school English in Kenya, professional English at Rice University, and intensive and academic ESL at the University of Oregon. She consults and facilitates workshops on vocabulary acquisition, teaching reading, and using authentic materials to teach grammar, vocabulary, and reading strategies.

Elba Villanueva de Debat teaches EFL Methodology at the Universidad Nacional de Córdoba, Argentina. She served as ACPI President (Córdoba EFL Teachers´ Association). She has presented at conferences in Latin America, Europe, and the USA. Her research interests include materials development and teacher education.

1
Materials in ELT: Current Issues

Sue Garton and Kathleen Graves

Overview

Materials in general, and commercial materials in particular, play a central role in language learning and teaching. As Richards (2001: 251) notes 'Much of the language teaching that occurs throughout the world today could not take place without the extensive use of commercial materials.' Yet, until relatively recently, this was a neglected area in English Language Teaching (ELT) research and publication. Tomlinson (2012) identifies the early nineties as the decade in which serious attention began to be shown towards materials development. Fortunately, the last few years have seen an increase in this attention with a number of new publications, including Harwood (2010), Tomlinson (2008), Tomlinson and Masuhara (2010a), Tomlinson (2013), as well as new editions of previous publications (McDonough and Shaw, 1993, 2003; McDonough, Shaw and Masuhara, 2013; Tomlinson, 1998, 2011). An important contribution to the field has also come from Tomlinson's (2012) state-of-the-art review of materials development.

Two things are noticeable about the majority of these publications, however. First, the field is generally under-researched. Many of the books published are 'how to' books, with advice for teachers (see for example McDonough, Shaw and Masuhara, 2013; McGrath, 2002; Tomlinson, 2003, 2011). These books may draw on research and theory, especially in Second Language Acquisition (SLA), but they are not based on research studies into materials. Most certainly such volumes have an important role to play but we think it is fair to say that the field is generally lacking in empirical studies, a point also made by Chapelle (2009) in relation to materials evaluation and Tomlinson and Masuhara (2010b) in relation to materials development. Three notable exceptions are the edited collections by Harwood (2010), Tomlinson and Masuhara (2010a) and Tomlinson (2013). The chapters in these volumes generally take a more theoretical perspective in looking at what underlies the development of

ELT materials, although they tend again to be based on relating theories of language and language learning to materials development rather than research into the materials themselves or their use.

The second point to be made is that the majority of previous publications focus primarily on certain aspects of ELT materials. Thus we find books and chapters on materials design and development (Harwood, 2010; Jolly and Bolitho, 2011; McGrath, 2002), materials evaluation and adaptation (Islam and Mares, 2003; Littlejohn, 2011; McDonough, Shaw and Masuhara, 2013; McGrath, 2002; Nation and Macalister, 2010; Richards, 2001), the materials writing process (Bell and Gower, 2011; Mares, 2003; Maley, 2003) and types of materials (Tomlinson, 2008).

Tomlinson's (2012) review, for example, is concerned with 'materials development', which he sees as both practical and a field of academic study. From a practical point of view, 'it involves the production, evaluation and adaptation of materials' (p. 144), while as an object of study, the focus is on 'the principles and procedures of the design, writing, implementation, evaluation and analysis of materials' (p. 144). There seems to be, however, a curious omission from these definitions – that of use. Any view of materials that neglects their actual use by teachers and/or learners can, in our view, only be partial, and yet none of the recent publications listed above (and indeed earlier ones such as Cunningsworth, 1995; McDonough and Shaw, 1993; Tomlinson, 1998) focus on this aspect, although Tomlinson (2012) does say that investigations into materials should ideally inform and be informed by their use.

This volume therefore focuses not only on materials but on their use, not only by teachers but also by learners. Where it is original is in the number of chapters written either by or about practitioners and based on research into the preparation and use of materials in everyday teaching in a variety of contexts around the world.

The field of materials is vast and cannot possibly be covered in one introductory chapter. What follows will focus on the areas identified by the contributors to this volume as important in their work. As such, it will examine aspects of materials that have been neglected, as well as look at more common aspects from new perspectives.

The coursebook

Current developments in materials, particularly in the use of technology (see for example, Macaro, Handley and Walter, 2012; Maggi, Cherubin and Garcia Pascual, Chapter 12; Pereira, Chapter 11; Rahman and Cotter, Chapter 10), challenge traditional definitions. Harwood (2010: 3) uses the term materials to include texts in all forms (paper, audio, video) and language learning tasks, with the expressed intention of including everything from teacher handouts to global coursebooks[1]. Tomlinson (2011: 2) gives an even broader definition when he states that materials are 'anything which is used by teachers or learners to facilitate the learning of a language'. His list of examples ranges from videos, emails and YouTube to grammar books, food packages and instructions given by the teacher.

Yet in spite of the broad definitions of materials that are now generally accepted, the coursebook is still ubiquitous and plays a fundamental role in ELT around the world (Littlejohn, 2011; Richards, Chapter 2; Tomlinson, 2003), as can be seen in the number of chapters in this volume that focus on some aspect of it. Thus we find discussions of different types of coursebooks (Lopez-Barrios and Villanueva de Debat, Chapter 3; Richards, Chapter 2); of how coursebook materials are developed to meet local conditions (al Majthoob, Chapter 4) and of cultural content (Messekher, Chapter 5). Other chapters focus on how teachers use coursebooks and factors affecting their decisions (Bosompem, Chapter 7; Humphries, Chapter 15; Seferaj, Chapter 6) or how they can be used in teacher education (Augusto-Navarro, de Oliveira and Abreu-e-Lima, Chapter 14).

The global coursebook

The advantages and disadvantages of global coursebooks are well documented in the literature, as well as being experienced by teachers in their daily professional practice. Below is a list that some of Garton's students on a graduate TESOL programme drew up when asked why they would or would not want to use a coursebook in their teaching:

Why use a coursebook?

1. It gives structure to lessons and to a course.
2. It saves time – teachers are too busy to prepare their own materials.
3. It gives a sense of security – teachers feel they know what they are doing.
4. It promotes autonomy as learners can use and refer to it outside the classroom.
5. It is reliable as it is written by experts and published by well-known publishers.
6. It gives a sense of professionalism in the way it is presented.
7. It offers different perspectives as it focuses on different cultures and different places.

Why not use a coursebook?

1. It cannot meet the needs of a particular group of learners.
2. The language taught might not be appropriate.
3. It might not be culturally appropriate.
4. It is outdated.

5. It is not authentic.
6. It is not representative of the local context.
7. It takes away the teacher's creativity.

Perhaps unsurprisingly, this list is very similar to those in the literature (see for example, Masuhara and Tomlinson, 2008; McGrath, 2002; Richards, 2001, Chapter 2).

Different views of coursebooks were also noted by McGrath (2006) in the metaphors that teachers use to describe them. McGrath (2006: 174) categorised these metaphors into four groups, on a continuum from dependence to independence, the first three of which demonstrated a relatively positive attitude: Guidance (map, compass); Support (anchor, petrol); Resource (convenience store, menu); Constraint (millstone, straightjacket). Although this study, and the list above, show that teachers generally have quite favourable views of coursebooks, they also underline a certain ambivalence and highlight a number of issues.

In-depth reviews by Tomlinson, Dat, Masuhara and Rubdy (2001) and Masuhara, Hann, Yi and Tomlinson, (2008) have revealed perhaps less obvious issues with the global coursebook. For example, overall Tomlinson, Dat, Masuhara and Rubdy (2001) found that the coursebooks they reviewed did not encourage adaptation or facilitate the tailoring of the materials to learners' needs or to local contexts. Moreover, Masuhara, Hann, Yi and Tomlinson (2008) found a lack of suggestions for personalisation, localisation and mixed-level classes. They also found that topics were generally banal and that there was a focus on politeness rather than conflict and competition. Yet most of the above are issues that have long been recognised as key principles that should underlie successful materials (see, for example, Tomlinson, 2008, 2011, 2012).

Critical views

In the wake of critical approaches to TESOL (see, for example Block, Gray and Holborrow, 2012; Edge, 2006) global coursebooks have also come under more critical scrutiny. At its most basic this can be seen in the open acknowledgement that global publishing is a multi-million pound business (Masuhara and Tomlinson, 2008), a realisation that is often something of a surprise to graduate students and teachers. Masuhara and Tomlinson (2008) point out that, in an attempt to maximise profits, global coursebooks for general English are aimed at the dual markets of language courses in English-speaking countries and in English as a Foreign language contexts. The result is that they may not satisfy the needs of learners and teachers in either (Masuhara et al. 2008: 310) and al Majthoob (Chapter 4) makes a strong case for materials that reflect different realities.

Tomlinson (2008) even goes so far as to assert that coursebooks are at least partly to blame for the failure of learners to learn in that they conform to the expectations of stakeholders and the demands of the market rather than to what we know about language acquisition and the learning process. Underlying Tomlinson's criticism are pedagogical premises, which still view materials as 'curriculum artefacts' (Apple and Christian-Smith, 1991: 4 as cited in Gray, 2010: 2). However, Gray (2010, 2012), building on the work of critical applied linguists such as Pennycook (1994) and Phillipson (1992, 2009) makes a compelling case for considering the global coursebook as a cultural artefact which presents a particular view of reality and is value laden. He describes how ELT publishers focus on 'aspirational content' with frequent use of topics around personal and professional success, celebrities, cosmopolitanism and travel, all of which are believed to be motivating for language learners (Gray, 2012: 87) and with the underlying message that English equates with success (Gray, 2012: 104). However, such images may not be motivating and may be resisted by learners (Canagarajah, 1993) or may leave them feeling inadequate (Masuhara and Tomlinson, 2008: 19).

The values portrayed by coursebooks are also inscribed in the methodological approaches they adopt (Prodromou and Mishen, 2008). Global coursebooks tend to be based on approaches developed in western academic departments, exhibiting what Prodromou and Mishen (2008: 194) call 'methodological correctness'. They define methodological correctness as:

> a set of beliefs derived from prestigious but incomplete academic research in the Anglophone centre that influence the decisions one makes regarding materials and methods in the classroom, even if those decisions are incon-sistent with the local context and particular needs and wants of the students. (ibid.: 194)

The effects of the introduction of western methodological approaches, and the pressure it may put on teachers who are expected to use new approaches and materials, are well documented (see Garton, Copland and Burns, 2011 for a summary of the issues).

Gray (2012: 111) calls for alternative articulations of English, a call that is reflected in alternative approaches such as that outlined by Guiney Igielski (Chapter 9) through the development of materials that are based in culturally and linguistically responsive pedagogy.

However, in spite of criticisms, teachers and learners themselves may generally view global coursebooks favourably, albeit with a healthy lack of idealism (Yakhontova, 2001; Zacharias, 2005). This is far from the view of teachers and learners as unquestioning consumers, which sometimes seems to emerge from more critical approaches to materials.

Global vs. local coursebooks

An alternative to the global coursebook lies in books that are produced for specific countries or regions. In some cases these are local versions of global books; in others they are books written especially for a particular country, either by 'experts' from English-speaking countries, or by local writers, or in collaboration. The solution in China has been to use cooperation between local education departments, local publishers, overseas publishers and textbook writers (Hu, 2005). Al Majthoob (Chapter 4) provides an excellent example of how a local version of a coursebook can meet the needs of learners in a specific context far more effectively than any global coursebook.

However, these books do not necessarily address the issues raised above in relation to global coursebooks. As Hoque (2009) points out, in Bangladesh, for example, textbook writing committees are led by academics with little experience of teaching in schools. Taking the case of Algeria, Messekher (Chapter 5) notes how, even in locally produced coursebooks, the culture of Inner Circle (Krachu, 1985) countries may still predominate, and even where local culture is included, it may be in a diluted form. Moreover, the approach taken to culture is one of acritical information-giving, which does little to develop the intercultural awareness needed by learners who are more likely to be using English to communicate with other 'non-native speakers' than with 'native speakers'[2]. As Graves and Garton note (Chapter 16) 'localizing content enables learners to talk and write about their own experiences, concerns and culture through English'. Producing local textbooks that do not reflect local contexts seems like a missed opportunity to promote positive attitudes towards both local culture and English.

Interestingly, Chapelle (2009) points to US national guidelines that state the focus of materials should be on contexts where language is used. Given that, in the case of English, that now means everywhere in the world, all materials should be taking an awareness-raising approach to language and culture (see Graves and Garton, Chapter 16).

However, local publishers can also have a positive influence on their global counterparts. Prodromu and Mishen (2008) look at the example of Greece as what they call (ibid.: 203) 'an interesting example of the local determining the global, the periphery fighting back against the centre'. In response to local demands, Greek publishers produced coursebooks that introduced a stronger form-focused element, which was not only more suited to local 'cultures of learning' (Jin and Cortazzi, 2006) but also went some way to reinstating practices that had long fallen out of favour, such as use of the L1 and grammar explanations. As a result, this 'hybrid' approach has now become the norm in materials published for the Greek market.

It is worth noting that such hybrid practices have probably always been very much alive in the majority of English classrooms around the world, as teachers adapted global materials to their own contexts (see Humphries,

Chapter 15; Seferaj, Chapter 8). However, at least with the advent of more hybrid practices in published coursebooks, such practices can again be considered respectable.

Materials and their users

We made the point in the introduction that there is surprisingly little written about materials users and so far, in this chapter, we have considered the coursebook as a tool. Yet any discussion that sees materials independently of their users, the learners and teachers in a variety of learning contexts, can only be partial. As Edge and Garton (2009: 55) put it:

> the teacher's purpose is not to teach materials at all: the purpose is to teach the learners and the materials are there to serve that purpose.

They go on to note (ibid.: 60) that what published materials cannot provide are *insights* into the needs and interests of particular groups of learners and *decisions* about how best to use the materials. It is precisely how teachers use materials to serve the purpose of teaching learners, their insights and decision-making, as well as learners' attitudes towards, and use of materials, that is currently missing from the literature. As Moulton (1997: vii quoted in Opoku-Amankwa, 2010: 162) noted:

> It is difficult to find out how teachers use textbooks without actually observing them...what they think about their use without actually asking them...Observing how teachers use textbooks and asking them why they use them as they do will reveal significant information about the learning-teaching process and how it can be improved.

Moreover, the continued separation of materials and their actual use risks entrenching the old theory/practice divide that Clarke was problematising twenty years ago (Clarke, 1994).

One notable exception is Opoku-Amankwa (2010), whose ethnographic study looked at the interaction between teachers, learners and textbooks in an urban primary school in Ghana. Opoku-Amankwa (2010) identified a number of factors that influenced students' access to and use of textbooks, including class size, seating arrangements and teachers' interpretation of policy concerning student access to textbooks. He concluded that there was a discrepancy between the availability of materials and students' access to and use of them and that this could have a negative impact on literacy development. This study underlines the importance of looking at the role materials play in actual classroom contexts.

Studies such as this, together with those looking at teachers' beliefs and attitudes towards materials (see, for example, Lee and Bathmaker, 2007; Zacharias, 2005), learners' attitudes (Yakhontova, 2001) and those comparing teachers' and learners' attitudes (see, for example, McGrath, 2006; Peacock, 1997) offer an important insight into materials and their users.

A number of chapters in this volume go some way to addressing this gap in the literature and from a variety of perspectives. Seferaj (Chapter 6) and Humphries (Chapter 15) both report on teachers' actual classroom practices in using materials, while Bosompem (Chapter 7) shows how a group of teachers in Ghana actually adapted their materials and also examines their motivations for doing so. What is also interesting about Bosompem's chapter is the attention it draws to the power of the coursebook in some contexts as her teachers, far from seeing adaptation as necessary for learners and the sign of a good teacher, felt guilty and inadequate. Detailed and personal accounts of materials adaptation to suit a particular context are given by Nuangpolmak (Chapter 8) and Guiney Igielski (Chapter 9), both of whom are responding to issues that have been identified in the literature. By focusing on materials for mixed levels, Nuangpolmak addresses a problem that has not only been raised by Masuhara, Hann, Yi and Tomlinson (2008) in regard to coursebooks, but which is also seen by English teachers, at least at primary level, as their biggest challenge (Garton, Copland and Burns, 2011). Guiney Igielski's focus on culturally and linguistically responsive pedagogy is an effective contribution to the debates around how best to value the multilingual and multicultural experiences of learners in the language classroom.

However, most of the chapters in this book address materials use from the teacher's point of view, rather than from that of the learners. Tomlinson and Masuhara (2010b) note that investigations into the effects of materials on language learning would be desirable, but that there are practical difficulties to carrying out such studies: they would have to be longitudinal, requiring considerable resources; and it would be extremely difficult to control for variables influencing acquisition in a classroom situation. This remains an area for research.

Materials use and change

As outlined above, one of the reasons for the popularity of coursebooks is that they are deemed to provide a clear set of activities and guidelines that both teachers and students can follow. Writers such as Hutchinson and Torres (1994), Masuhara and Tomlinson (2008) maintain that materials can support novice teachers or those who lack confidence.

It is also often argued that appropriate coursebooks can facilitate curricular change because they provide a visible framework that both teachers and students can follow (Rubdy, 2003) and they help teachers to 'fully understand and "routinize" change' (Hutchinson and Torres, 1994: 323). However, it would seem this is often not the case.

In response to the perceived global demand for communication in English, new language curricula around the world have generally emphasised communicative competence. Recent curriculum changes at all levels, together with the introduction of English to primary schools, have created a series of challenges for teachers (see Garton, Copland and Burns, 2011 for a detailed discussion), and their use of materials, putting to the test the assertion that coursebooks can facilitate change.

First, while curricula may change, the books used may not. Thus in many countries, teachers have found themselves with a lack of suitable materials, either because materials are not available (Hoque, 2009; Hu, 2007; Mathew and Pani, 2009) or because those that are available do not reflect changes in the curriculum (Hu, 2007; İnal, 2009; Nunan, 2003).

Second, it may simply not be enough to give teachers a new book and expect them to change how they teach. As Nur (2003) notes, teachers may need training to use the new books, otherwise they continue to employ previous methods. While multimedia packages may offer support to teachers with low levels of English proficiency (Mitchell and Lee, 2003; Nunan, 2003), actually changing the way that teachers teach is far more complex, as Seferaj (Chapter 6) and Humphries (Chapter 15) both show. Humphries (Chapter 15) identifies a range of factors that influence the way that teachers use coursebooks and shows that simply changing a coursebook will not necessarily change the way a teacher teaches. Seferaj's teacher informant also raises the question as to what extent teachers should be expected to change the way they teach and brings us back to Prodromou and Mishen's (2008) idea of methodological correctness. As Seferaj's (ibid.) teacher shows, teachers demonstrate a clear understanding of, and are able to clearly articulate, the very good reasons for adapting the new materials they are given rather than changing the way they teach. So, while governments mandate communicative language teaching, the typical pragmatic response from teachers is to interpret and adapt the approaches according to their local context (Littlewood, 2007).

It seems, therefore, that the introduction of new coursebooks alone may not lead to changes in practice. Although coursebooks may represent the new curriculum and provide some basic support when there is a shortage of qualified practitioners, the teachers may not understand the underlying principles (Nur, 2003). Moreover, beginning teachers do not always have the confidence to challenge the authority of the coursebook (Bosompem, Chapter 7; Gray, 2000) potentially leading to confusion and feelings of guilt.

Teacher education is necessary to help practitioners to understand materials better, together with how and whether to introduce changes inherent in new materials. Yet courses on materials evaluation, adaptation and design seem to be relatively rare on graduate programmes. Tibbits and Pashby (Chapter 13) and Augusto-Navarro, de Oliveira and Abreu-e-Lima (Chapter 14) show how teacher education programmes can ensure that teachers are informed users of materials rather than mere consumers.

Technology

No overview of materials in ELT can ignore the enormous impact that technology has had in recent years. It is no exaggeration to say that developments in digital technology have revolutionised language learning materials (see Macaro, Handley and Walter, 2012 for a review of Computer Assisted Language Learning in primary and secondary education).

On the one hand, technology has been embraced by publishers who now use it to accompany coursebooks, producing not only CD-roms and DVDs but also companion websites and versions of their materials for the Interactive Whiteboard (IWB). This is what we might call top-down uses of technology. However, perhaps the most exciting developments are the affordances given for the bottom-up development of materials by teachers and learners through the use of Web 2.0 tools. Thomas (2009) shows the range of possibilities afforded by these tools with chapters on Skype, mobile phones, Personal Learning Environments, social networking sites, podcasts and weblogs, to name just a few. Motteram (2011) also gives examples of how teachers can use technology to develop materials. The use of digital audio and video, the Internet, blogs, wikis, Virtual Learning Environments and so on has put 'the possibilities of the adaptation and creation of a broad range of language learning materials into the hands of the teacher, but also into the hands of the learners' (Motteram, 2011: 304).

This last point is important. Prensky (2001) calls the current generation of students, the first generation to have grown up with digital technology, *digital natives*. On the other hand, he calls their teachers *digital immigrants*, a group who needs to get used to a new way of thinking and learning and who have varying degrees of success. Therefore, the use of technology can place the learner squarely at the centre of materials in a way not always possible with traditional materials. Pereira's use of interactive fiction in language learning (Chapter 11) shows how learners can be active users of materials. The project described by Maggi, Cherubin and Garcia Pascual (Chapter 12) is a clear example of how learners can take control of the materials and of their own learning.

However, not all learners have the opportunity to become digital natives. Chapelle (2009) points out that the global spread of technology in language learning and the social, political and economic realities of learners around the world may not be compatible. However, Rahman and Cotter's experience (Chapter 10) shows that widely accessible and relatively low-cost technology, such as mobile phones, can be effective in language learning and actually has the potential to reach learners who may otherwise struggle to access English classes.

The example that Rahman and Cotter (Chapter 10) give is a very significant one. The use of mobile phones to deliver English courses in Bangladesh is an example of how technology contributes to clear pedagogical goals and enhances the learning experience. As Kervin and Derewianka (2011: 328) note, the concern should always be with the contribution that technology can make to learning, and they list a number of important pedagogical considerations (ibid.: 349) concerning how the electronic materials fit with learning aims and objectives as key. Unfortunately, this is not always the case. Mukundan (2008: 100) notes the money wasted on technology through investments such as language laboratories, leaving teachers to puzzle over how to fit new materials into existing practices and with the risk they will focus on technology and not on learners.

Conclusion

This introduction, and indeed this book cannot focus on every aspect of materials in ELT, which is a huge area. We have only very briefly mentioned well-covered ground such as materials development and evaluation. We have ignored aspects of the content of materials, such as gender, and the language used (see for example, Jones, Kitetu and Sunderland, 1997; Nguyen, 2011; Sunderland, 2000) as well as debates around authentic materials (see for example, Guariento and Morley, 2001; Gilmore, 2007; Peacock, 1997). We have also not mentioned the use of corpora in materials or as materials (see for example, Willis, 2011). Finally, we have also, to an extent, ignored learners, both from the perspective of learner-developed materials (see, for example, Maley, 2011; Willis, 2011) and the effects of materials on learners (but see Rahman and Cotter, Chapter 10). Tomlinson (2012) called for more research on the empirical effects of materials on SLA. Ellis (2011) also calls for evaluation based less on the appeal of materials and more on what learners do with them and what they learn. We would certainly endorse both these calls.

However, in this volume we have focused on the materials themselves and the way that teachers use them, relatively neglected areas to date. We see the underlying message of this introduction and of this volume as how materials need to be a fit with learning aims and objectives. Materials are fundamental to language learning and teaching (although see Thornbury, 2000 for an alternative view) but materials cannot be viewed independently of their users. What this volume does is look at how materials are actually used to fulfil the learning aims and objectives in a variety of local contexts and how these local experiences can resonate with practitioners around the world in order to help them become more effective materials users.

Notes

1. Throughout this volume, the terms coursebook and textbook will be used interchangeably.
2. We use these terms purely for convenience, fully aware of how problematic they are.

References

Bell, J. and Gower, R. (2011). Writing course materials for the world: a great compromise. In Tomlinson, B. (ed.), pp. 135–150.
Block, D., Gray, J. and Holborow, M. (2012). *Neoliberalism and Applied Linguistics*. London: Routledge.
Canagarajah, S. (1993). Critical ethnography of a Sri Lankan classroom: ambiguities in student reproduction through ESOL. *TESOL Quarterly*, 27(4): 601–626.
Chapelle, A.A. (2009). The spread of computer-assisted language learning. *Language Teaching*, 43(1): 63–74.
Clarke, M. (1994). The dysfunctions of the theory/practice discourse. *TESOL Quarterly*, 28(1): 9–26.
Cunningsworth, A. (1995). *Choosing your Coursebook*. Oxford: Macmillan Heinemann.
Edge, J. (ed.) (2006). *(Re)locating TESOL in an Age of Empire*. London: Palgrave.
Edge, J. and Garton, S. (2009). *From Knowledge to Experience in ELT*. Oxford: Oxford University Press.
Ellis, R. (2011). Macro- and micro-evaluations of task-based teaching. In Tomlinson, B. (ed.), pp. 212–235.
Garton, S., Copland, F. and Burns, A. (2011). *Investigating Global Practices in Teaching English for Young Learners: Project Report*. British Council.
Gilmore, A. (2004). A comparison of textbook and authentic interactions. *ELT Journal*, 58(4): 363–374.
Gilmore, A. (2007). Authentic materials and authenticity in foreign language learning. *Language Teaching*, 40(2): 97–118.
Gray, J. (2000). The ELT coursebook as cultural artefact. *ELT Journal*, 54(3): 274–283.
Gray, J. (2010). *The Construction of English: Culture, Consumerisim and Promotion in the ELT Global Coursebook*. Basingstoke: Palgrave Macmillan, pp. 1–20.
Gray, J. (2012). Neoliberalism, celebrity and 'aspirational content' in English teaching textbooks for the global market. In Block, D., Gray, J. and Holborrow, M. (eds), *Neoliberalism and Applied Linguistics*. Abingdon: Routledge, pp. 86–113.
Guariento, W. and Morely, J. (2001). Text and task authenticity in the EFL classroom. *ELT Journal*, 55(4): 347–353.
Harwood, N. (ed.) (2010). *English Language Teaching Materials: Theory and Practice*. Cambridge: Cambridge University Press.
Hoque, S. (2009). Teaching English in primary schools in Bangladesh: competencies and achievements. In Enever, J., Moon, J. and Raman, U. (eds), *Young Learner English Language Policy and Implementation: International Perspectives*. Reading, England: Garnet Education, pp. 61–69.

Hu, G. (2005). Contextual influences on instructional practices: a Chinese case for an ecological approach to ELT. *TESOL Quarterly*, 39(4): 635–660.

Hu, Y. (2007). China's foreign language policy on primary English education: what's behind it? *Language Policy*, 6: 359–376.

Hutchinson, T. and Torres, E. (1994). The textbook as agent of change. *ELT Journal*, 48(4): 315–328.

İnal, D. (2009). The early bird catches the worm: the Turkish case. In Enever, J., Moon, J. and Raman, U. (eds), *Young Learner English Language Policy and Implementation: International Perspectives*. Reading, England: Garnet Education, pp. 71–78.

Islam, C. and Mares, C. (2003). Adapting classroom materials. In Tomlinson, B. (ed.), London: Continuum, pp. 86–100.

Jin, L. and Cortazzi, M. (2006). Changing practices in Chinese cultures of learning. *Language, Culture and Curriculum*, 19(1): 5–20.

Jolly, D. and Bolitho, R. (2011). A framework for materials writing. In Tomlinson, B. (ed.), pp. 107–134.

Jones, M. A., Kitetu, C. and Sunderland, J. (1997). Discourse roles, gender and language textbook dialogues: who learns what from John and Sally? *Gender and Education*, 9(4): 469–490.

Kachru, B. B. (1985). Standards, codification and sociolinguistic realism: the English language in the outer circle. In Quirk, R. and Widdowson, H. G. (eds), *English in the World: Teaching and Learning the Language and Literatures*. Cambridge University Press for The British Council.

Kervin, L. and Derewianka, B. (2011). New technologies to support language learning. In Tomlinson, B. (ed.), pp. 328–356.

Lee, R. N. F. and Bathmaker, A. M. (2007). The use of English textbooks for teaching English to vocational students in Singapore secondary schools: a survey of teachers' beliefs. *RELC Journal*, 38(3): 350–374.

Littlejohn, A. (2011). The analysis of language teaching materials: inside the Trojan horse. In Tomlinson B (ed.), pp. 179–211.

Littlewood, W. (2007). Communicative and task-based language teaching in East Asian classrooms. *Language Teaching*, 40: 243–249.

Macaro, E., Handley, Z. and Walter, C. (2012). A systematic review of CALL in English as a second language: focus on primary and secondary education. *Language Teaching*, 45(1): 1–43.

Maley, A. (2003). Creative approaches to writing materials. In Tomlinson, B. (ed.), pp. 183–198.

Maley, A. (2011). Squaring the circle – reconciling materials as constraint with materials as empowerment. In Tomlinson, B. (ed.), pp. 379–402.

Mares, C. (2003). Writing a coursebook. In Tomlinson, B. (ed.), pp. 130–140.

Masuhara, H., Hann, N., Yi, Y. and Tomlinson, B. (2008). Adult EFL courses. *ELT Journal*, 62(3): 294–312.

Masuhara, H. and Tomlinson, B. (2008). Materials for general English. In Tomlinson, B. (ed.), pp. 17–37.

McDonough, J. and Shaw, C. (1993). *Materials and Methods in ELT*, 1st Edition. Oxford: Blackwell.

McDonough, J. and Shaw, C. (2003). *Materials and Methods in ELT*, 2nd Edition. Oxford: Blackwell.

McDonough, J., Shaw, C. and Masuhara, H. (2013). *Materials and Methods in ELT*, 3rd Edition. Oxford: Blackwell.

McGrath, I. (2002). *Materials Evaluation and Design for Language Teaching*. Edinburgh: Edinburgh University Press.

McGrath, I. (2006). Teachers' and Learners' images for coursebooks. *ELT Journal,* 60(2): 171–180.

Mitchell, R. and Lee, J. H. W. (2003). Sameness and difference in classroom learning cultures: interpretations of communicative pedagogy in the UK and Korea. *Language Teaching Research,* 7(1): 35–63.

Motteram, G. (2011). Developing language-learning materials with technology. In Tomlinson, B. (ed.), pp. 303–327.

Mukundan, J. (2008). Multimedia materials in developing countries: the Malaysian experience. In Tomlinson, B. (ed.), pp. 100–110.

Nation, I. S. P. and Macalister, J. (2010). *Language Curriculum Design.* New York: Routledge.

Nguyen, M. T. T. (2011). Learning to communicate in a globalized world: to what extent do school textbooks facilitate the development of intercultural pragmatic competence? *RELC Journal,* 42(1): 17–30.

Nunan, D. (2003). The impact of English as a global language on educational policies and practices in the Asia-Pacific region. *TESOL Quarterly,* 37(4): 589–613.

Nur, C. (2003). English Language Teaching in Indonesia: changing policies and practical constraints. In Ho, W. K. and Wong, R. Y. L. (eds), *English Language Teaching in East Asia Today: Changing Policies and Practices.* Singapore: Eastern Universities Press, pp. 163–172.

Opoku-Amankwa, K. (2010). What happens to textbooks in the classroom? Pupil's access to literacy in an urban primary school in Ghana. *Pedagogy, Culture & Society,* 18(2): 159–172.

Peacock, M. (1997). The effect of authentic materials on the motivation of EFL learners. *ELT Journal,* 51(2): 144–156.

Pennycook, A. (1994). *The Cultural Politics of English as an International Language.* London: Longman.

Phillipson, R. (1992). *Linguistic Imperialism.* Oxford: Oxford University Press.

Phillipson, R. (2009). *Linguistic Imperialism Continued.* London: Routledge.

Prensky, M. (2001). Digital Natives, Digital Immigrants. Available at http://www.marcprensky.com/writing/prensky%20%20digital%20natives,%20digital%20immigrants%20-%20part1.pdf [Accessed 31/05/13].

Prodromou, L. and Mishen, F. (2008). Materials used in Western Europe. In Tomlinson, B. (ed.), pp. 193–212.

Richards, J.C. (2001). *Curriculum Development in Language Teaching.* Cambridge: Cambridge University Press.

Rubdy, R. (2003). Selection of materials. In Tomlinson, B. (ed.), pp. 37–57.

Sunderland, J. (2000). New understandings of gender and language classroom research: texts, teacher talk and student talk. *Language Teaching Research,* 4(2): 149–173.

Thomas, M. (2009). *Handbook of Research on Web 2.0 and Second Language Learning.* New York: IGI Global

Thornbury, S. (2000). A Dogma for EFL. Available at http://www.thornburyscott.com/tu/Dogma%20article.htm [Accessed 31/05/13].

Tomlinson, B. (ed.) (1998). *Materials Development in Language Teaching.* 1st edition. Cambridge: Cambridge University Press.

Tomlinson, B. (ed.) (2003). *Developing Materials for Language Teaching.* London: Continuum.

Tomlinson, B. (ed.) (2008). *English Language Teaching Materials: A Critical Review.* London: Continuum.

Tomlinson, B. (2010). Principles of effective materials development. In Harwood, N. (ed.), pp. 81–108.

Tomlinson, B. (ed.) (2011). *Materials Development in Language Teaching,* 2nd Edition. Cambridge: Cambridge University Press.

Tomlinson, B. (2012). Materials development for language learning and teaching. *Language Teaching,* 45(2): 143–179.

Tomlinson, B. (ed.) (2013). *Applied Linguistics and Materials Development.* Bloomsbury.

Tomlinson, B., Dat, B., Masuhara, H. and Rubdy, R. (2001). EFL courses for adults. *ELT Journal,* 55(1): 80–101.

Tomlinson, B. and Masuhara, H. (eds) (2010a). *Research for Materials Development in Language Learning.* London: Continuum.

Tomlinson, B. and Masuhara, H. (2010b). Published research on materials development for language learning. In Tomlinson, B. and Masuhara, H. (eds), pp. 1–18.

Willis, J. (2011). Concordances in the classroom without a computer: assembling and exploiting concordances of common words. In Tomlinson, B. (ed.), pp. 51–77.

Yakhontova, T. (2001). Textbooks, contexts and learners. *English for Specific Purposes,* 20: 397–415.

Zacharias, N. T. (2005). Teachers' beliefs about internationally-published materials: a survey of tertiary English teachers in Indonesia. *RELC Journal,* 36(1): 23–37.

Part I
Global and Local Materials

2

The ELT Textbook

Jack C. Richards

Introduction

Despite the advances in technology and the role of the internet, coursebooks are the main teaching resource used by many of the world's English teachers. The extent of English teaching worldwide could probably not be sustained without the support of the many different kinds of textbooks and their ancillaries that are available to support English teachers (Tomlinson, 2003). In many schools textbooks provide the main basis for the curriculum (Richards, 1993). Appel (2011: 50–51) comments: 'In no other school subject do coursebooks exert a similar influence as in language teaching. The book is in fact often treated as the syllabus.' Coursebooks often determine the goals and content of teaching, as well as the methods teachers use. For both teachers and learners, the textbook provides a map that lays out the general content of lessons and a sense of structure that gives coherence to individual lessons, as well as to an entire course.

McGrath (2002: 8) presents a number of metaphors teachers use to describe the role of a textbook for them: recipe, springboard, straightjacket, supermarket, holy book, compass, survival kit, crutch. As these metaphors suggest, some teachers use textbooks as their primary teaching resource. The materials provide the basis for the content of lessons, the balance of skills taught, and the kinds of language practice students take part in. In other situations the textbook may serve primarily to supplement the teacher's instruction. For inexperienced teachers a textbook together with the teacher's manual may be an important source of training on the job. For learners a textbook and its audio or video components may provide the major source of English language input they receive, apart from that which they get from their teacher, serving both for class use and for self-study before and after lessons. A textbook can give learners a sense of independence, which reliance on daily or weekly teacher-prepared lesson handouts does not provide. Crawford (2002: 28) notes:

It may well be this sense of control which explains the popularity of textbooks with students. Consequently a teacher's decision not to use a textbook may actually be 'a touch of imperialism'...because it retains control in the hands of the teacher rather than the learner.

In this chapter we will explore the process of textbook development and issues involved in selecting and evaluating textbooks in language programs.

Types of published materials

A few minutes browsing in any ELT catalogue will reveal a wide range of textbooks and materials to support every type of teaching and learning situation. These include:

- Coursebooks for international markets;
- Materials for specific age groups – children, teenagers, adults;
- Materials for specific skills – reading, writing, listening, speaking;
- Materials for specific purposes – academic study, travel, business, law, engineering;
- Materials for exam preparation – TOEFL, TOIEC, IELTS, KET;
- Reference materials – dictionaries and grammars;
- Self-study materials;
- Readers.

Contemporary ELT materials generally reflect a large investment of time, effort, and financial resources by authors and publishers. They also reflect the fact that ESL learners are generally 'digital natives', often teenagers and young adults, who are interested in popular culture, often associate English with travel, consumerism, socialising, and expect their coursebooks to reflect their real or 'ideal' world. Textbooks are consequently design rich, in full colour and, rather than looking like classroom materials, often have a magazine-like appearance or resemble content seen on the internet. Their titles often make no reference to English language learning but reflect English as a cross-cultural or international experience or journey (Gray, 2010). Textbooks have multiple components such as workbooks, an assessment package, DVDs and CD-ROMs, and additional resources for teachers and students. Digital components are used increasingly, such as an e-book, online workbooks, and options for varying levels of blended use.

From concept to classroom

In the case of national textbooks, such as those used in public schools, they may be produced by the ministry or department of education, or written by freelance writers contracted by textbook publishers to write books for the national curriculum (Cheng, 2002). If commercially produced textbooks are used in public schools an approval process is normally in place and only books that are approved by the ministry of education can be used in schools. A chain of events takes place in which the ministry of education produces test formats or guidelines, publishers produce test formats to match the guidelines, school districts set in place procedures by which textbooks are reviewed and adopted, lists of approved textbooks are published, and teachers (or their supervisors) then select the textbooks they will use.

In some countries (e.g. Japan, China), groups of academics and teachers often work together to write textbooks according to the ministry of education guidelines. The guidelines include the exact number of words to be taught at each level, the verb tenses that are to be covered, the topics and type of classroom activities to be used, and assessment procedures. Selecting one or more of the textbooks from among the drafts submitted is a type of competition and the successful textbook series chosen through this process may sell in huge quantities. In this way the ministry of education controls the content that will be taught in its public schools.

Commercial textbooks for international or regional markets reflect a different publication process. Most textbooks are written by experienced teachers in cooperation with editors and consultants who guide the writers through the process of textbook development (Richards, 1995). Effective textbooks do many of the things a teacher would normally do as part of his or her teaching. They should:

- arouse the learners' interest;
- remind them of earlier learning;
- tell them what they will be learning next;
- explain new learning content to them;
- set clear learning targets;
- provide them with strategies to use in learning;
- help them get feedback on their learning;
- provide practice opportunities;
- enable them to check their progress.

While many teachers are successful in helping learners do these things in classroom-based learning, developing a book that does the same things calls upon a very different set of skills. As Byrd (1995: 7) observes:

> For the writer of textbooks, the most demanding of the differences between writing for a particular class and writing for publication is the search for coherence. At its best, a textbook is a unified, seamless whole rather than a random collection of materials. The creative energy demanded for writing

textbooks involves more than the ability to present language learning materials that are different in some way from those that have been published previously. Textbooks need to be different in conception and organization from previously published materials that all of us develop over the years as we teach our various ESL courses.

Another difference is that, in preparing materials for their own classes, teachers can draw on a great deal of knowledge about who the learners are, what their specific interests, needs, difficulties, and learning style preferences are, as well as the teachers' beliefs, principles, and assumptions about effective teaching. Much can be left unstated and filled in by the teacher during the process of teaching (Allwright, 1981). In writing materials for publication, however, the goal is to produce materials that can be used in many different circumstances and taught by teachers with widely different teaching styles and levels of training, so the goals of the materials and the activities they contain must be much more explicit (Cheng, 2002).

There are usually two approaches to publishing English language teaching materials, particularly those intended for a large market. Either a teacher or group of teachers develop a concept for a book based on their perception that the book they propose has some advantages or unique features that would make it appealing to both teachers and students. They then contact a publisher with their proposal. Alternatively a publisher might identify the need for a new book and identify teachers or writers who might be able to write it. Once a commitment is made to publish the book, the writers work with editors from the publishing company to develop the concept for the book project in more detail (Richards, 1995).

Questions such as the following will need to be addressed at this stage:

- What kind of teachers, learners and institutions is the book intended for?
- What features are they likely to look for in the book?
- What approach will the book be based on and what principles of teaching and learning will it reflect?
- How many levels will be involved and at what level will the book or books start and end?
- How will the material in the book be organised and what kind of syllabus will it be based on?
- How many units will the book contain and how many classroom hours will be needed to teach it?
- What ancillaries will be involved, such as teacher book, workbook, tests, audio component, video component, electronic and online components, and who will develop these?

- What will the format of units be and what kinds of exercises and activities will be used throughout the book?

As the answers to these questions are clarified the writer or writers will be in a position to develop a proposal for the book or book series, a preliminary syllabus and unit format for the book, and to develop some sample units. The publisher then arranges to have the sample materials reviewed by a range of people, both internally (i.e. editors) and externally (teachers and consultants). Often teachers will be brought together in focus groups to review the materials and may try it out with their students. This review process may repeat several times as different samples are drafted until the specifications for the book have been finalised. Only at this stage can writing begin in earnest. A writing schedule is developed so that the publisher can plan for the different stages of editing, design, and manufacturing that are involved in publishing a book.

Issues involved in evaluating English language textbooks

English language textbooks are a source of activities for teaching English. As such they provide information about English and examples of how English is used. They also contain real world information; the materials they make use of will, intentionally or unintentionally, present information about countries, cultures, people, lifestyles, beliefs, and values. Therefore textbooks raise two important issues: the authenticity of the language they contain, and the representation of the content they provide (Harwood, 2010).

Authenticity of language

There has been a great deal of discussion and debate in language teaching about the kind of language that is presented in textbooks and the role of constructed versus authentic language examples (Waters, 2009). Generally, authentic texts are recommended:

> Authenticity is felt to be important because it gives learners a taste of the real world, an opportunity to 'rehearse' in a sheltered environment, hence the less authentic the materials we use the less well prepared learners will be for that real word. (McGrath, 2002: 105)

Traditionally, the writers of textbooks generally employ their own intuition about language use as the basis for writing dialogue, developing scripts for listening texts, and creating reading passages. This was often justified on the grounds that using authentic texts taken from real life would expose learners to language that was unnecessarily complex and would not allow the writer to provide a specific language focus to texts that are designed to support instruction. This has sometimes resulted in the charge that textbooks that contain unnatural or 'artificial' language, such as we see in the following dialogue that introduced different forms of the verb *sing*:

A: When did you learn to sing?
B: Well I started singing when I was ten years old, and I've been singing everyday since then.
A: I wish I could sing like you. I've never really sung well.
B: Don't worry. If you start singing today, you'll be able to sing in no time.
A: Thank you. But isn't singing very hard?
B: I don't think so. After you learn to sing, you'll be a great singer.

(Saslow, no date)

Proponents of the use of authentic language in textbooks suggest that the linguistic information and grammar it contains is often based on author intuition and may not reflect the findings of research into how the language is really used. Jones and Waller (2011) compare information about conditionals in textbooks, where conditionals are typically divided into zero, first, second, and third conditionals, a distinction they find is not supported by corpus-based data on how conditionals are used in English. Similarly, Chan (2009: 11) compares the language presented for expressing functions in business English textbooks with the language used in actual business meetings and he notes that the textbook language is over explicit. This tends to suggest that there is a close relationship between function and form, whereas in real communication functions are realised in much more complex and subtle ways:

Table 2.1 A comparison of textbook and real-life language

Function	Examples from contemporary textbooks	Examples from real-life business meetings
Agreeing	You've got a point there I totally agree with you Absolutely/Precisely/Exactly	Mmm Implied by the function 'accept' (e.g. yes) Implied by not disagreeing Nods
Disagreeing	That's not right I don't agree I don't quite agree with that point because…	Well + comment But… Yes. But…

Continued

Table 2.1 Continued

Function	Examples from contemporary textbooks	Examples from real-life business meetings
Suggesting	I suggest that... I propose that... What about...?	We could... So, if... Imperative
Interrupting	Sorry to interrupt, but... If I may interrupt, could you...? Sorry, can I just say something?	Yes, but... But... Repetition of overlapping utterance (e.g. 'I got, I got...')

Since the 1980s there has been a movement towards the use of authentic language in textbooks, drawing on information derived from discourse and corpus analysis of authentic speech. Carter and McCarthy (1988: 369) comment:

> We know from our knowledge of our first language that in most textbook discourse we are getting something which is concocted for us, and may therefore rightly resent being disempowered by teachers or materials writers who, on apparently laudable ideological grounds, appear to know better. Information or knowledge about language should never be held back; the task is to make it available without artificial restrictions, in ways which answer most learners' needs.

No textbook writer or publisher, of course, would advocate the use of texts or language models that provide incorrect or inaccurate information about the use of English. The goal is to use texts and discourse samples that show how language is used and that also enable learners to use authentic cognitive, interactional, and communicative processes when carrying out activities. A dialogue in a textbook, or one prepared by a teacher, may have been constructed to reflect features of authentic conversational interaction. It is these features, rather than the text itself, that form the focus of classroom activities.

While the use of authentic texts in materials may be a desirable goal, it is not always feasible. McGraw (2002: 104–105) comments:

> Strictly speaking, an authentic listening text would be neither scripted nor edited; in practice, poor quality, length, and other pedagogical considerations lead to spoken texts being re-recorded and/or edited for use in classrooms. Written texts may similarly be retyped and edited.

When choosing texts for use in reading and listening textbooks some texts taken from real world sources may suit the writer's needs. However, it may not be possible to find texts that are of the right length, at the right level of difficulty, reflect the reading or listening skills that are being addressed, and are on a topic relevant to the unit. In this case the writer may adapt or create a text while making sure that it requires the use of the *processes* the text is intended to practise, such as listening to make inferences or reading to identify cause and effect. What is important here is *authenticity of process* rather than *authenticity of text*.

Representations of content

In writing textbooks the author has to create situations and choose texts that illustrate how language is used, and in so doing make decisions about what kinds of situations and texts will be used and who the participants are. Decisions have to be made concerning whose culture and values will be represented in the book. The choices the writer makes can send different kinds of messages to students. Gray (2010: 142, citing Brown, 1990) reports:

> The kind of English contained in coursebooks can be called 'cosmopolitan English' because it 'assumes a materialistic set of values in which international travel, not being bored, positively being entertained, having leisure, and above all, spending money casually and without consideration of the sum involved in the pursuit of ends, are the norm.

Two scholars who have examined the role of culture in language teaching from a cross-cultural perspective are Byram and Kramsch, who argue for the concept of 'intercultural competence' as a goal in teaching – and one that should also be reflected in textbooks. Language learning provides opportunities for learners to reflect on their own culture, as well as that which is embodied in the foreign language.

Gray (2010: 33) summarises the views of Byram and Kramsch on foreign language teaching and learning in this table:

Table 2.2 Two paradigmatic views of coursebooks

Dominant paradigm in foreign language teaching	Proposed educational alternative
– Language teaching as skills training	– Language teaching as education
– Impoverished and conservative	– Rich and critical
– Instructional and monologic	– Educational and dialogic
– Culture occupies the background	– Culture occupies the foreground
– Communicative competence the aim	– Intercultural competence the aim
– Native-speaker model	– Intercultural speaker model
– Aim to enable learners to survive as tourists/consumers	– Aim to create learners who are internationally socially aware
– Learners construed as skills acquirers	– Learners construed as apprentice ethnographers
– Textbook as carrier of superficial view of target culture	– Textbook as carrier of realistic view of target culture

Textbook writing thus involves more than making decisions about how to teach what English. It also involves consideration of how values are communicated through language. There are various ways in which messages may be communicated through the choice of content in textbooks. For example:

- the diversity of characters presented throughout the book: what ethnic groups will be represented?
- the treatment of gender: in what roles will male and female characters be presented?
- the treatment of age: will younger and older characters appear, and in what roles and situations?
- language varieties: what kind of accents will speakers use? Will English for both native and non-native speakers be presented? Will standard, regional, and social dialects be used and, if so, by whom?
- situations: in what contexts will characters be located?
- lifestyles: what kinds of lifestyles will be depicted?
- topics: what topics and issues will be explored throughout the book?
- art: what kinds of images will be used?

However, textbooks today are much more culturally sensitive than their predecessors. Publishers and writers seek to ensure that their textbooks reflect progressive and politically acceptable values. Efforts are made to avoid social bias and ethnocentrism, and to reflect universal human concerns, needs, and values in their content. Often guidelines are provided for authors. Part of one publisher's guidelines suggests maintaining a 50–50 balance between the sexes: numerically and in terms of the significance and prominence of the activity illustrated; within schools and across the series, to aim for a gender-neutral style of illustration; to use illustrations that include all physical types, with occasional evidence of physical disability; and to avoid images with a stereotypical association.

Despite these efforts the criticism is still made that textbooks often present an idealised view of the world or fail to represent real issues. In order to make textbooks acceptable in many different contexts, controversial topics are generally avoided, instead an idealised, middle-class view of the world is presented as the norm. Gray (2010: 3) describes the global coursebook in these terms:

> a carefully constructed artefact in which discourses of feminism, multiculturalism and globalization are selectively co-opted by ELT publishers as a means of inscribing English with a range of values and associations that include individualism, egalitarianism, cosmopolitanism, mobility and affluence, in which students are increasingly addressed as consumers.

However the comments of Jose Lema, an English teacher and teacher trainer from Ecuador, reflect a different point of view:

> My students have busy stressful lives and as often as not what they seem to want from English classes is an exposure to 'the brighter side of life'. They don't really come to class to try to solve the problems of the world but want to have a chance to socialize with their friends and have fun. Their own lives are often quite a struggle and the English class is a time to enter a different imaginary world.

Choosing textbooks

When looking at the book in relation to the teaching context we find that some teachers choose their own textbooks; for others, as with the example above, they are chosen for them by coordinators or other teachers. Several levels of review are involved in choosing textbooks (Cunningsworth, 1994, 1995). Apart from the content and quality of books themselves, the choice of textbooks will reflect institutional, teacher, and learner factors. Let us consider these issues first.

Institutional factors include:

- the type of curriculum and tests in place in the school;
- organisational structure of the institution;
- length and intensity of the English course(s);
- cost of the book and its availability;
- resources in place, such as whiteboards, computers, or self-access facilities;
- support available to prepare new teachers for the use of textbooks;
- classroom conditions such as class size or seating arrangements.

Teacher factors include:

- proficiency in English;
- level of training and teaching experience;
- familiarity with different methodologies;
- attitudes towards use of textbooks;
- preferred teaching styles.

Learner factors include:

- learners' needs and aims;
- proficiency level;
- language learning experience;

- age range;
- interests;
- cultural background;
- language background;
- occupations;
- preferred learning styles.

As the factors above suggest, if a school decides to use a textbook there must be a good degree of fit between the book and the context in which it is going to be used. A brief review of the book should enable a decision to be made as to whether the book suits the needs of both the programme in which it could be used and the teachers and students in that programme.

Evaluating the book: Stage 1 – description

Evaluation is the judgement of how suitable something is for a particular purpose. Textbook evaluation can be divided into two phases: pre-use, and during or after use (Cunningsworth, 1995). Most textbook evaluation schemes distinguish two essential stages that are necessary at the pre-use phase: a description or analysis phase, and an interpretation or evaluation phase (Riazi, 2003).

In the first phase the contents of the book have to be carefully described in terms of the way the book is organised, the syllabus or scope and sequence plan of the book, and the types of texts and exercises it contains. Riazi (2003: 67) gives this explanation:

> Analysis: a detailed analysis of the materials. It is more or less neutral and provides the evaluator(s) with the information on categories of different elements presented in the materials.

This is distinguished from evaluation, which Riazi describes as follows (67):

> Evaluation: a professional interpretation of the information obtained in the analysis stage. The evaluator(s) may use their experience and expertise – reflecting their views and priorities based on a number of factors such as learner and teacher expectations, methodological preferences, the perceived needs of learners, syllabus requirements and personal preferences – and give weights or provide value judgement to the obtained information.

The analysis phase will involve identifying this kind of information:

- aims and objectives of the book;
- level of the book;

- skills addressed;
- topics covered;
- situations it is intended for;
- target learners;
- time required;
- components;
- number and length of units;
- organisation of units.

Information of this kind should be fairly easy to identify from the front and back matter of the book, from information provided by the publisher or book distributor, as well as by looking through the book and its table of contents. Lee (2003: 173) gives an example of this level of analysis in describing a book on academic writing:

The map of the coursebook as a whole

Focus	Description
1 Year of publication	1996
2 Title of book	First Steps in Academic Writing
3 Intended audience	High-beginning writing students of ESL
4 Type	Academic writing
	Not identified as main or 'core' course or supplementary
5 Design and layout	No colours. A4 size. 212 pages
6 Extent	(a) Components
	One book for students. No teacher book
	(b) Total estimated time
	Not mentioned
7 Distribution	(a) Materials
	* Visual materials (pictures & photographs)
	Yes
	* Guidance on use of the book
	No
	* Tests
	No
	(b) Access
	*Content list
	*Content name
	*Page number
	*Appendix
	*Index
8 Subdivision	6 units with 4 parts in each unit
	Part 1 (organisation); Part 2 (grammar and mechanics);
	Part 3 (sentence structure); Part 4 (writing process)

Evaluating the book: Stage 2 – evaluation

This stage of evaluation is more difficult since it involves subjective judgements and these often differ from one person to another. For this reason group evaluations are often useful. A number of checklists have been developed to assist at this stage of evaluation, such as Cunningsworth's (1995) that is organised under the categories of aims and approach, design and organisation, language content, skills, topics, methodology, teachers book, practical consideration. However, checklists such as these depend mainly on subjective judgements that cannot easily be answered and they generally need to be adapted to reflect the book under consideration. Criteria often need to be developed that reflect the context in which the book will be used and the kind of book being evaluated since factors of relevance in one situation may not necessarily apply in another. The following factors can be considered.

Pedagogical approach: what methodology does the book reflect and does it reflect an informed understanding of its subject matter? For example, if it is a reading book or reading series relevant questions will focus on what theory of reading the book is based on and on the kind of reading skills and strategies it addresses. If it is a speaking book it will be important to determine what theory of spoken interaction it reflects and what aspects of spoken interaction it addresses.

Methodology: the methodology of the book will determine the range of activity types and exercises employed throughout the book. Evaluation of these will focus on whether they are considered appropriate and adequate for developing the skills the book aims to teach.

Language content: the texts and linguistic input provided as the basis for learning and practising throughout the book can be reviewed in terms of their authenticity, accuracy, relevance to the students' needs, and difficulty level.

Other content: it will be important to review the relevance of the cultural content of the book, the suitability and appeal of the topics it includes, the values and assumptions the book communicates, as well as the way it represents gender and ethnic cultural diversity.

Teacher appeal: many factors can affect a teacher's impressions of a book, such as its design and layout, the clarity of organisation, how difficult it would be to teach, whether it is self-contained or would need to be supplemented by teacher-made materials, and whether it suits the teacher's teaching style. For example, does it depend on a teacher-fronted style of teaching or would it lend itself to pair and group-based learning? The teacher's opinion will also be influenced by the range of ancillaries provided, such as teacher book, tests, optional extra photocopiable activities, and web-based teacher support.

Learner appeal: factors of interest to learners will include how appealing its design is, including the photos and illustrations, the topics, the kinds of activities it includes, whether it has self-study components, and the relevance to their perceived needs of the language skills taught.

When a group evaluation process is used these issues, and others specific to the teaching context (e.g. the cost of the book), can be discussed and, if several books are being considered, a consensus can be reached on the book that most suits the teachers' needs.

Evaluating during and after use

In-use evaluation focuses on how well the book functions in the classroom. It depends on monitoring the use of the book and collecting information from both teachers and students. The information collected can serve the following purposes:

- to document effective ways of using a textbook;
- to provide feedback on how the book works in the classroom and how effectively it achieves it aims;
- to keep a record of adaptations that were made to the book;
- to assist other teachers in using the book.

This may involve regular consultation with teachers to address issues that arise as the book is being used and resolving problems that may occur. For example:

- Is there too much or too little material?
- Is it at the right level for students?
- What aspects of the book are proving least and most effective?
- What do teachers and students like most or least about the book?

Various approaches to monitoring the use of a book are possible:

- *Observation*: classroom visits to see how teachers use the book and to find out how the book influences the quality of teaching and learning that goes on in lessons.
- *Record of use*: documentation of what parts of the book were or were not used, and what adaptations or supplements were made to the book and why.
- *Feedback sessions*: group meetings in which teachers discuss their experience with the book.
- *Written reports*: the use of reflection sheets or other forms of written feedback (e.g. electronic) in which teachers make brief notes about what did and what did not work well, or make suggestions for using the book.
- *Reviews*: written reviews by a teacher, or group of teachers, on their experiences with the book and what they did or didn't like about it.

- *Students' reviews*: comments from students on their experience with the book.

Post-use evaluation provides information that will help decide if the book will continue to be used.

Adapting textbooks

As we noted above, in many situations textbooks form the basis of the curriculum in language programmes. Provided there is a good degree of fit between the textbook and the teaching context teachers use textbooks as the major source of input and direction to their teaching. This does not necessarily mean that the teacher plays a secondary role in the teaching process since teachers normally improvise around their teaching materials, moving back and forth between book-based and teacher-initiated input. Hence, even though a teacher may teach the same lesson from a textbook many times, each time it becomes a different lesson due to the improvisations the teacher initiates during teaching. These may result from on the spot decisions relating to timing, affective factors, and responses to learner difficulties. Experienced teachers use textbooks flexibly as a teaching resource (Savova, 2009).

Sometimes, however, adaptations may be required to reflect the needs of a specific teaching context. Various forms of adaptation are possible.

Adding material to address an examination requirement: sometimes supplementary material may need to be added to address the requirements of a specific institutional or other exam. For example, the reading component of an institutional text may make use of multiple-choice questions rather than the kinds of comprehension tasks found in a coursebook, so extra material to practise using multiple-choice questions may be needed.

Extending to provide additional practice: a book unit has a limited number of pages and at times the teacher may source other materials for the additional practise of grammar, vocabulary, or skills to supplement the book.

Localising: an activity in the book may be more effective if it is modified to reflect local issues and content, rather than using the content that is discussed in the coursebook.

Localisation also involves adapting or supplementing an activity to address the specific needs of a group of learners. For example, pronunciation problems might reflect interference from the students' first language that are not covered in the book. Additional activities can be added to address problems specific to the learners.

Modifying content: content may need to be changed because it does not suit the target learners, perhaps because of their age, gender, social background, occupation, religion, or cultural background.

Reorganising content: a teacher may decide to reorganise the syllabus of the book, and rearrange the units into what she or he considers a more suitable order. Or the teacher may decide not to follow the sequence of activities in the unit but to reorganise them for a particular reason.

Modifying tasks: exercises and activities may need to be changed to give them an additional focus (McAndrew, 2007). For example, a listening activity may focus only on listening for information, so it is adapted for students to listen a second or third time for a different purpose. An activity may be extended to provide opportunities for more personalised practice. Or some exercises within a sequence may be dropped.

While in many cases a book may work perfectly well without the need for much adaptation, in some cases different levels of adaptation may be needed. Through the process of adaptation the teacher personalises the text, making it a better teaching resource, and individualises it for a particular group of learners. Normally, this process takes place gradually as the teacher becomes more familiar with the book because the dimensions of the text that need adaptation may not be apparent until the book is tried out in the classroom.

Conclusion

Textbooks are an important resource for teachers and learners in language teaching and their role in a language course should be carefully planned for and monitored. Since they provide much of the input to their lessons, teachers should be involved in making decisions about the textbooks they will teach from. Teachers are sometimes overwhelmed with the large range of textbooks that are generally available for teaching every kind of English course. Teachers in training can benefit from learning how to analyse and review textbooks, to learn effective ways of using textbooks, and how to localise them for their specific teaching contexts.

Engagement priorities

1. What are the main advantages and disadvantages of using textbooks in language teaching? What can a school do to ensure that textbooks facilitate creative teaching rather than textbook dominated teaching?
2. What criteria do you use in choosing textbooks and other materials for your own teaching context? To what extent do you adapt published materials you use, and in what ways?
3. Examine a currently used, popular or successful textbook. In your opinion, what features of the book account for its success?

4. In view of the role of English as an international language, or lingua franca, to what extent do you think native-speaker usage should be reflected in textbooks? How can other users of English be represented in textbooks?
5. If you were asked to provide guidelines for a textbook writer creating your ideal ELT textbook, what would the guidelines contain?

References

Allwright, R. L. (1981). What do we want teaching materials for? *ELT Journal*, 36: 5–18.

Appel, J. (2011). Moments of practice: teachers' knowledge and interaction in the language classroom. In Huttner, Julia, Barbara Mehlmauer-Larcher, Susanne Reichl and Barbara Schiftner (eds), *Theory and Practice in EFL Teacher Education: Bridging the Gap*. Bristol: Multilingual Matters, pp. 38–54.

Brown, G. (1990). Cultural values: the interpretation of discourse. *ELT Journal*, 44(1): 11–17.

Byrd, P. (1995). *Material Writers Guide*. Boston: Heinle.

Carter, R. and McCarthy, M. (eds) (1988). *Vocabulary and Language Teaching*. London: Longman.

Chan, C. S. C. (2009). Thinking out of the textbook: toward authenticity and politeness awareness. In Savova, Lilia (ed.), *Using Textbooks Effectively*. Alexandria, VA: TESOL, pp. 9–20.

Cheng, X. (2002). *English Textbook Analysis and Design*. Beijing: Foreign Language Teaching and Research Press.

Crawford, J. (2002). The role of materials in the language classroom. In Jack C. Richards and Willy Renandya (eds), *Methodology in Language Teaching*. New York: Cambridge University Press, pp. 80–92.

Cunningsworth, A. (1994). *Evaluating and Selecting ESL Materials*. London: Heinemann.

Cunningsworth, A. (1995). *Choosing Your Coursebook*. Oxford: Heinemann.

Gray, J. (2010). *The Construction of English: Culture, Consumerism and Promotion in the ELT Global Coursebook*. London: Palgrave Macmillan.

Harwood, N. (ed.) (2010). *English Language Teaching Materials*. New York: Cambridge University Press.

Jones, C. and Waller, D. (2011). If only it were true: the problem with the four conditionals. *ELT Journal*, 65(1): 24–33.

Lee, Y. (2003). A package for an English paragraph: an evaluation of the coursebook used in two EFL writing courses. *English teaching*, 58(3): 165–188.

McAndrew, J. (2007). Responding to learners' language needs in an oral EFL class. In A. Burns and H. Joyce (eds), *Planning and Teaching Creatively within a Required Curriculum*. Alexandria, VA: TESOL.

McGrath, I. (2002). *Materials Evaluation and Design for Language Teaching*. Edinburgh: Edinburgh University Press.

Riazi, M. (2003). What do textbook evaluation schemes tell us? a study of the textbook evaluation schemes of the three decades. In Renandya, W. (ed.), *Methodology and Materials Design in Language Teaching*. Singapore: RELC.

Richards, J. C. (1993). Beyond the textbook: the role of commercial materials in language teaching. *RELC Journal*, 24(1): 1–14.

Richards, J. C. (1995). Easier said than done: an insider's account of a textbook project. In Hidalgo, A., Hall, D. and Jacobs, G. (eds), *Getting Started on Materials Writing*. Singapore: RELC, pp. 93–135.

Saslow, J. (no date). *Real Language – The Vitamin for the Student Studying English Outside the English-Speaking World*. Unpublished paper.

Savova, L. (ed.) (2009). *Using Textbooks Effectively*. Alexandria, VA: TESOL.

Tomlinson, B. (ed.) (2003). *Developing Materials for Language Teaching*. London: Continuum.

Waters, A. (2009). Ideology in applied linguistics for language teaching. *Applied Linguistics*, 30(1): 138–143.

An expanded version of this paper appears in *Key Issues in Language Teaching*: Jack C. Richards, Cambridge University Press (in press).

3
Global vs. Local: Does It Matter?

Mario López-Barrios and Elba Villanueva de Debat

Introduction

Teaching materials are used in specific teaching contexts (schools, universities, language schools, and so on), with specific learners (according to age and degree of L2 competence), and to meet specific needs (for example, to build a general communicative competence in L2, to train call centre staff in reading or speaking skills). This is why, when teachers use materials produced for international markets (so-called global coursebooks), they adapt them to fit their students' needs, to comply with curricular demands, to supplement any missing information, to provide extra practice, and so on. This is also true of locally produced materials. How do EFL teachers go about using global and locally produced coursebooks? Is there a significant difference between the way teachers implement global and local coursebooks? Do they supplement them with other materials? Do they skip some texts, activities, or other elements, and on what basis? These are questions we address in this chapter in order to find out about EFL teachers' practices when using both kinds of coursebook.

A typology of foreign language teaching coursebooks

Differentiation by target users, and specific teaching and learning contexts

The following typology is based on the contexts of use for which the coursebooks are designed. These include the characteristics of the intended learner groups, the location of the courses, and the institutional context in which the textbook is used. The characteristics of groups of learners can be regarded as homogeneous or heterogeneous in terms of relevant variables, among which are their L1, age group, and sociocultural background. Location refers to the actual country or region in which the coursebook is used. The term region allows for a greater degree of generalisation, for example, referring to the countries of Spanish-speaking Latin America. The institutional context is especially relevant in reference to specific school types for which the coursebook is intended. Apart from these contexts of use any explicit reference to particular exams that the coursebook may prepare for also constitutes a distinguishing feature in classifying coursebooks. The typology will be illustrated with reference to coursebooks that are or have been widely used in Argentina.

Different labels have always been applied to refer to types of coursebooks according to their context of use. The distinctions global and local are used by Tomlinson (1998b), and Gray (2002) adds the label glocal. Other labels include international, local, and glocal (Arnold and Rixon, 2008), imported, in-country, and regional (Dat, 2008), global, local, and adapted (Basabe, 2006), international, local, and localised (López Barrios, Villanueva de Debat and Tavella, 2008). In this chapter we will use the labels global and international interchangeably, plus the terms local and localised, as described in Table 3.1.

The international or global coursebook is defined by Tomlinson (1998a: x) as a 'coursebook which is not written for learners from a particular culture

Table 3.1   Contexts of use of three different types of coursebooks

Type	Definition	Target learners (L1, age group and sociocultural background)	Location of course	Institutional context	Target exams
Global	intended for use in any part of the world by learners of a specific foreign language level and age range	heterogeneous/ homogeneous	worldwide	schools (official curriculum), language schools, universities	Possible preparation for a target exam
Localised	a global coursebook adapted or localised to make it fit with the learners' background and a national curriculum	homogeneous	a specific country or region	schools (official curriculum)	Possible preparation for a target exam
Local	specifically produced for a country or region, sensitive to learners' background, draws on a national curriculum	homogeneous	a specific country or region	schools (official curriculum)	Possible preparation for a target exam

or country but which is intended for use by any class of learners in the specified level and age group anywhere in the world'. Gray (2002: 151–152) adds that international EFL coursebooks are typically 'produced in English-speaking countries'. A local coursebook is one 'specifically produced for a country or region and draw[s] on a national curriculum and on the learners' experiences by including references to local personalities, places, etc.' (López Barrios, Villanueva de Debat and Tavella, 2008: 300). A glocal coursebook is an adapted or localised version of a global coursebook that provides 'a better fit', in that it connects the students' world with 'the world of English' (Gray, 2002: 166). Tomlinson (2003a: 324) favours the localisation of global coursebooks, stressing the fact that for the materials to be successful they necessarily need to 'match the target learners and the environments they are learning in'. A coursebook type that is different from the classifications proposed by most of the authors mentioned above is Dat's 'regional coursebook', it is 'a unique category of materials, which are written by non-native speakers in one country but are exported to and become accepted in several other countries' (Dat, 2008: 268).

All these types of coursebook exist in Argentina and their relevance tends to change as a result of curricular innovations and economic conditions that favour or impede access to foreign books. International coursebooks are widely used, not only in private language schools that offer English courses to children, adolescents, and adults, but also in private primary and secondary schools. Examples of localised coursebooks are the series *For Teens* (Corradi and Rabinovich, 2004) and *Click into English*, (Casuscelli and Gandini, 2010), adapted from a Spanish and a Brazilian course respectively.

The less favourable aspect of publishing local and localised coursebooks relates to the lower profits they yield in commercial terms. This can be observed by comparing the number of international, local, and localised coursebooks produced by the main ELT publishers where a preference for the first type is clearly noticeable. Because local and localised coursebooks display characteristics that can have a positive impact on the educational contexts for which they are intended, notably schools, they can be agents of innovation. In this respect we share the view of Lopriore (2006), who claims that publishing houses contribute to a large extent to shaping teachers' preferences since they play a significant role in setting educational trends through the textbooks they publish. But this positive characteristic is affected by commercial reasons since, according to Tomlinson, 'local coursebooks don't generate as much profit as global coursebooks and, despite a recent trend of producing localised versions of coursebooks, the global coursebook is going to remain the resource used by the majority of learners of English in the world'. (Tomlinson, 2003b: 171). In sum, publishers' actions also exert an influence on the quality of teaching and learning a foreign language.

Theoretical underpinnings of local and localised coursebooks

As has been shown, the production of teaching materials with local contextual characteristics is not a new development. Many of the underlying
theoretical underpinnings only emerged towards the beginning of the 1980s,
coinciding with the rise of Critical Pedagogy as an educational theory and
of Communicative Language Teaching (CLT) as a foreign language teaching
approach.

Critical Pedagogy claims that power relations among the different actors
involved in the teaching and learning process should be amenable to questioning and, consequently, it opposes the transference of allegedly superior,
dominant methodologies. In the field of ELT, the opening up of the economies
of Eastern European, Far Eastern, and Latin American nations during the 1980s
and 1990s, coupled with the spread of globalisation, created new opportunities
for the large-scale introduction of English to these regions. The urge of the,
so-called, developing nations to join the global economy implied the need for
their citizens to acquire English, the medium of expression of globalisation
and progress criticised as linguistic imperialism by Phillipson (1992, in McKay,
2003). Thus, EFL became a coveted export commodity in the shape of teaching
materials and courses to train educators to implement CLT, the state-of-the-art,
centrally designed method that was thought to be an answer to the same needs
worldwide.

Regarding the export of foreign expertise, large-scale surveys of the teaching
and the training of EFL teachers in China in the late 1970s by a US commis-
sioned team (Cowan et al., 1979) and of a teacher training course run by a
Canadian team (Patrie and Daum, 1980) criticise the established EFL methodology that relies on memorisation, translation, and negligible oral use of
the target language. The Canadian specialists stress the impact of 'properly
designed teaching materials' (1980: 393) on ELT in developing countries. The
power attributed to teaching materials to effect a change in EFL, even if taught
through more 'traditional' teaching approaches, is questionable since teachers
adapt materials when planning classes and teaching, so it is not uncommon
for instructors to use teaching materials in ways very different from those
conceived by their authors. In our contemporary understanding the cases
described above are examples of unsuccessful attempts to impose change from
the top-down to solve, what is perceived as, a problem and we agree with
Widdowson's assertion that 'the local contexts of actual practice are to be seen
not as constraints to be overcome but conditions to be satisfied' (2004: 369).

In acknowledgement of the limited suitability of EFL coursebooks produced
for use in English-speaking countries or for an indeterminate target user,
context-specific teaching materials were produced. The ensuing, more flexible,
understanding and implementation of CLT paved the way for the development
of new coursebooks, many of them locally produced, and some of them as

localised versions of coursebooks produced for a similar setting, such as those mentioned above.

CLT went through a number of phases in its development, starting with the design of syllabuses that reflected the notion of communicative competence, the identification of learners' needs, and the design of activities compatible with the notion of CLT (Richards and Rodgers, 2001). A second point is one that is particularly relevant to the coursebook typology. Coupled to a further characteristic of CLT, namely the shift from a teacher-centred to a learner-centred approach, there emerged a recognition of the need to design teaching materials that are more sensitive of contextual characteristics, such as the local cultures of teaching and learning, time allotted to EFL, the availability of teaching resources, the learner's interests and needs, their L1, and the curricular demands of the local educational context. The search for more appropriate pedagogies that are sensitive to the local teaching and learning context is stressed by Kramsch and Sullivan (1996), they are also viewed by McKay (2003) in a critical light, who stresses the notion of diversity within particular contexts. The following section aims to capture what we consider the ideal characteristics context-sensitive foreign language teaching materials should display.

Distinctive features of local and localised materials

We identify four aspects that distinguish local and localised materials from international ones: contextualisation, linguistic contrasts, intercultural reflection, and facilitation of learning. The development of Critical Pedagogy and CLT mentioned above sparked applied linguists in some Western European countries, as well as in North America, to reflect on the need to produce context-sensitive teaching materials. The work of these applied linguists ran parallel at the end of the 1970s but developed along somewhat different lines, with German researchers Gerighausen and Seel (1983, in López Barrios, Dalla Villa, Jáimez and Villanueva de Debat, 2004) concentrating on the principles of regional-specific coursebooks. In characterising the distinguishing features we refer to both the presence of the category (as in conformity with the theoretical framework) and its absence (as in the distance between the theoretical category and the actual presence in the local and localised coursebooks). In the following sections we discuss each feature in turn.

Contextualisation

Contextualisation involves three aspects: personalisation, content topics included in the materials, and pedagogical fit. Personalisation implies primarily 'connecting coursebooks to the real world which the learners live in' (Tomlinson, 2003b: 171). One way of contextualising the coursebook is the inclusion of local references, such as familiar personalities, places, facts, and folklore among others. For example, Argentine local and localised coursebooks tend to include references to personalities from local showbiz, as well as from culture, science, and history who are familiar to learners.

Also, content subject matter covered by local and localised coursebooks should be sensitive to the sociocultural norms of the society where they are implemented. Today this is less of an issue in Argentina as there is a general tendency to discuss virtually any topic, albeit this may be less so in religious schools. Despite the current open attitude to controversial topics, local and localised coursebooks – which are almost exclusively used in schools – largely tend to avoid them. Banegas (2010) gives an example of how teachers deal with this absence in an action research project carried out in an Argentine secondary school. The syllabus content negotiated between teachers and learners included the addition of topics such as gay marriage and single parenting.

Pedagogical fit, the third aspect of contextualisation, refers to the degree of harmony between a coursebook with educational practices that suit the local teaching context and its conformity to a country's school curriculum. In our analysis of two localised coursebooks (López Barrios and Villanueva de Debat, 2006) we mention the agreement of these books with the foreign languages curriculum in effect at the time of publication. This is reflected in both the model syllabus to accompany *Dream Team* (*Planificaciones*), which is designed in accordance with the official curriculum and is offered to teachers as a planning aid, and in the Teacher's Book *New Let's Go for EGB!* (Mugglestone, Elsworth and Rose, 2000), where the authors state that the course was written to meet the curricular demands of Argentine lower secondary schools.

Linguistic contrasts

Linguistic contrasts focus on the opportunity to make learners reflect on the form, meaning, and use of the target language linguistic features by encouraging contrastivity. Despite the considerable amount of evidence reported in Second Language Acquisition scholarship regarding the positive impact of language awareness from a contrastive viewpoint, coursebooks do not respond, or only do so to a very restricted degree. A study carried out in Spain by Rodríguez Juárez and Oxbrow (2008) to find out the students' attitudes to the use of the L1 produced very interesting results. Even if the authors report a general positive attitude regarding the use of the L1 on the part of the learners, they found a less favourable opinion on their part in connexion with the value they attribute to cross-linguistic comparison. This may be due to a generalised belief that comparing the target language with the L1 may negatively affect the learning process.

As regards the distinction between international, local and localised coursebooks, the intended learners' L1 is an issue of interest. Courtillon (2003) contends that speakers of a language related to the target language – such as speakers of Romance and Germanic languages learning English – will profit from a coursebook that encourages learners to look for cross-linguistic similarities. Likewise, students whose L1 is more distant, for example in terms of morphological typology or writing systems as in Chinese, would need a coursebook that helps them explore these differences. The inclusion of such linguistic contrasts is feasible in local and localised coursebooks, but goes against the very notion of international coursebooks.

In local and localised coursebooks linguistic contrasts can take different forms. In *Explorer Starter* (García Cahuzac and Tiberio, 1999) learners are made to notice the English phonemes /i:/, /g/, /p/. Subsequently, learners look for words containing the sound in question and provide Spanish words with the similar sound. They then listen to the English words and reproduce them and do the same with the Spanish words, thus contrasting the selected sound and becoming aware of the differences. Comparing aspects of the grammar of English and Spanish is a feature of *In Focus 1* (Abbs, Freebairn and Barker, 2001). For example, after introducing and practising different forms of the plural of nouns, learners are asked how the plural is marked in Spanish nouns. Unfortunately, such examples are hardly found in more recent local and localised coursebooks.

Intercultural reflection

Intercultural reflection is defined as 'awareness of the relation between home and target cultures' (Council of Europe, 2001: 104). It presupposes a critical confrontation with facts about a foreign culture rather than the mere consumption of information related to the target culture (C2). However, an analysis of four coursebooks of this kind suggests that this is not a predominant practice in local and localised materials (López Barrios and Villanueva de Debat, 2007). In fact, the transmission of facts and practices of the C2, mainly restricted to the UK and usually treated in coursebooks in a special section under a label such as Culture Corner, is very frequent in the sample analysed. Opportunities to relate the C2 with the C1, when restricted to the mere 'what is it like in your country?', tend to emphasise unfavourable comparisons on the part of EFL learners in developing nations. The C2 is generally viewed by the learners as more elaborate, efficient, and desirable, thus dismissing the C1 as more backward, inefficient, and less favourable. For example, the photographs that show the homes of the, usually British or American, coursebook characters are generally considered by learners in developing countries to be those of wealthy families, the food consumed or the holiday plans discussed, usually in attractive foreign locations, can be interpreted as typical of any British or American person, thus inducing in learners a standardised, monochrome interpretation of the target culture, unless there is an intervention on the part of the materials to include a more balanced picture of different family backgrounds.

In brief, for intercultural reflection to develop, tasks should be included that make the learners go beyond mere surface impressions and engage them in activities whereby stereotypes are challenged and their world view is altered or defamiliarised. Furthermore, through intercultural contrast, local and localised coursebooks could make a significant contribution to the development of democratic citizenship by offering opportunities for learners to foster critical thinking, acknowledge and respect diversity and otherness, and take an active participation in different aspects of public life.

Facilitation of learning

By facilitation of learning we mean the inclusion of features that contribute to the learner's autonomy. In local and localised coursebooks, including the L1 when the learner's L2 competence is still very limited, could facilitate independent work. This, to date quite uncommon, feature can be found in *Click into English 1* (Casuscelli and Gandini, 2010), where instructions in the workbook section are given in Spanish. This coursebook also uses the L1 to contextualise dialogues, for example 'The Rovitti Family meets Karen and Ann Dillon at Ezeiza Airport' (6), or when questions with 'do they...?' are introduced, learners are asked in Spanish 'How does Ann ask if the vicuñas belong to the family of camels? How does she ask if they eat meat?' (56) for learners to notice the way questions are formed. A more common feature is the use of the L1 to clarify grammar rules, as in the Grammar View sections of *Click into English 1*. Lastly, *for teens 1* (Corradi and Rabinovich, 2004) opens up the coursebook with a two-page introduction in Spanish where the structure of the units is explained, the characters are introduced, and the main rubrics for activities and icons are clarified.

Overall, these four distinguishing characteristics of local and localised coursebooks are quality criteria that should be considered by materials developers when designing local or localised coursebooks, and by teachers when selecting coursebooks. Table 3.2 summarises these criteria.

Coursebook use by teachers: an Argentine perspective

The information presented in this section is based on data obtained from EFL teachers in the Argentine context through a survey, a follow-up open questionnaire and an interview. We received 30 responses from teachers working in different types of institutions in central Argentina. Our aim was to explore how teachers use and adapt textbooks in the belief that most of them adapt the materials used to the local context and their teaching style (Tomlinson, 2012: 151).

Table 3.2 Features of local and localised materials

Feature	Definition	Characteristics
Contextualisation	Connection of coursebook with learner's world and match with local pedagogical practices and curriculum	• inclusion of local references: places, personalities, etc. • context-sensitive subject matter • choice of controversial topics • harmony with local educational practices • conformity to school curriculum
Linguistic contrasts	Making learners reflect on form, meaning and use of the L2 linguistic features contrastively	Comparison with L1 of diverging L2 features at different levels: phonological, morphological, lexical, textual
Intercultural reflection	Awareness of the relation between home and target cultures	Learners go beyond mere surface impressions and engage in activities that challenge stereotypes and alter their world view
Facilitation of learning	Inclusion of features that contribute to the learner's autonomy	Inclusion of the L1 in rubrics and to contextualise, clarify or train learners

In many public educational institutions in Argentina, teachers are given the freedom to select textbooks. In private institutions procedures vary, but in most cases the heads make the choice, sometimes based on the opinions and consensus of the teachers. Sometimes choice is determined by factors that are outside educational concerns, such as availability or price, and that are resolved by 'the vicissitudes of a capitalist market, [where] decisions about the "bottom line" determine what books are published and for how long' (Apple, 2000: 184).

With the exception of primary schools, most educational institutions where English is taught as a foreign language in our context are represented by the informants who responded to the survey: public secondary schools (38 per cent), private secondary schools (29 per cent), language centres (29 per cent) and institutions of higher education (4 per cent). All of the participants are non-native teachers and most of them are qualified teachers who have received training in foreign language teaching.

The findings revealed that a high percentage of the teachers use an international book (74 per cent) and only a small percentage (26 per cent) use a local or localised coursebook. The responses also showed that all teachers adapt coursebooks and that most of them do so frequently (52 per cent) or very frequently (24 per cent).

Regarding the reasons for adapting the textbook, our survey included the following statement: *I adapt or supplement the coursebook for the following reasons (tick as many as necessary)* and a number of options to choose from. All teachers, regardless of whether they use an international or a local coursebook, answered this question. The results are presented in Table 3.3.

As Table 3.3 shows, the most frequent reason for adapting textbooks is the complexity of reading or listening texts. The second most frequent reason is to provide more reading or listening activities, and the third most frequent is that there are not enough language activities. For item b (complexity of reading or listening texts), we provided other options to explore why the texts are considered too complex. The responses indicate that most teachers believe complexity is mainly related to two issues: the relevance or familiarity of the topic to the learners (37 per cent and 15 per cent respectively), or the amount of unknown vocabulary or difficult grammar of the texts (30 per cent). Other reasons offered in the open item were that teachers adapt the coursebooks to expand on certain subtopics, to trigger conversation, or to integrate topics mainly regarding grammar and vocabulary. In addition, one teacher stated that she adapted the book to motivate the students.

We also asked participants to describe how they supplement the textbooks they use. Most teachers adapted or compiled from several textbooks (38 per cent) or designed their own activities (31). Contrary to what might be expected, downloading activities or texts from the Internet is not so common. Some of the teachers state that they also supplement the textbook with activities and/ or texts designed by colleagues who use the same coursebook, with simplified stories from other books, and also with audio books, films or TV series.

Table 3.3   Reasons for textbook adaptation

(a) the reading or listening texts contain outdated information	7%
(b) the reading or listening texts are too complex for my learners	24%
(c) to provide more reading or listening activities	23%
(d) the speaking or writing activities are too demanding for my learners	4%
(e) the speaking or writing activities are too simple for my learners	4%
(f) the topic of the speaking or writing activities is not interesting or motivating for my learners	12%
(g) the language activities are too mechanical and repetitive	9%
(h) there are not enough language activities	14%
(i) other	4%

The survey clearly shows that teachers supplement textbooks, but they also dealt with most of their contents. When asked how frequently they skipped activities, most of our informants – mainly those who use a localised book – answered that they only did so on few occasions; a smaller percentage said that they did so frequently, and a few of the teachers rarely or never leave out activities.

Among the features in the textbook that teachers tend to replace are mainly speaking and writing activities (33 per cent), followed by reading or listening texts and comprehension activities (19 per cent), which would be congruent with the fact that one of the reasons for adaptation is that texts are considered too complex for the students. In relation to this, teachers also marked the option *activities done as preparation for reading or listening activities* as one of the features they commonly replace, as well as vocabulary activities. To a much lesser degree they also include language practice and language reflection activities. When asked to justify why they skip activities, some respondents mentioned time constraints as the main reason.

Local use of coursebooks

In order to find out whether there is a significant difference between the way teachers implement global and local coursebooks, we asked seven teachers using a local book to answer an open-ended questionnaire and we interviewed two of them. The questions dealt mainly with the reasons for choosing a local book over an international one and the book's strengths and weaknesses.

The teachers' perceptions regarding the strengths of local and localised coursebooks are analysed in reference to the categories discussed above: (a) contextualisation, (b) linguistic contrasts, (c) intercultural reflection, and (d) facilitation of learning.

Regarding contextualisation, the teachers remarked that the topics of the texts included in the local books are more familiar to the learners. For instance, some books contain information about regional tourist landmarks or local personalities (such as a description of Montevideo or a fact file about hockey player Soledad García in *for teens*). However, some teachers mentioned that they would like more texts related to the local area and culture. One informant stressed that the books include situations that 'are useful and relevant for [the students'] lives and for their future', for example, the inclusion of topics that are significant to those students who usually start working right after their secondary education, such as applying for a job or how to prepare a CV. Teachers also value that local textbooks take into account aspects of the local educational system and the official curriculum. For example, lessons for a 40-minute class period with texts and activities that can be used with large and mixed ability groups are seen as important features that international books are not likely to consider. Other reasons for choosing a local book have to do with practical concerns that are also connected to the local context, such as its availability, an affordable price, or that textbook and workbook are published as a single unit.

The respondents made little direct reference to the other three categories: linguistic contrasts, intercultural reflection, and facilitation of learning. Despite this, the fact that they would like books to include more local themes might be in line with a desire to stimulate intercultural reflection as well as to motivate learners. Regarding facilitation of learning, teachers tend to adapt coursebooks by providing tasks and strategies not usually contained in the books that they believe will facilitate learning, for instance pre-, during and post-reading activities, or more guidance in communicative tasks. Even though no reference was made to the inclusion of linguistic contrasts (probably because virtually no book makes use of them), they did refer to the use of the students' L1 to facilitate learning. For example, one of the teachers said that she would also write instructions to tasks in the L1.

Informants also identified shortcomings in the coursebooks used. Some stressed that the local coursebook contained too many activities of the same type and that many of them focused exclusively on forms. In another case, the respondent complained about the lack of contextualisation and the negligible number of communicative activities. Another weakness mentioned by the teachers was the weight given to the macroskills such as listening or writing. Some think that there are too many written exercises, producing an unbalanced development of the four macroskills. Lastly, they remarked that the rubrics are often unclear or incomplete. In those cases, the teachers either changed or completed the rubrics or translated them into the L1.

Even when the teachers surveyed believe that the local coursebook is a better fit for the local context, they still see the need to adapt it by adding activities and texts and by modifying or translating instructions.

Global vs. local: does it matter?

Undeniably, regardless of the negative aspects perceived by the teachers and the need to make adaptations, virtually all teachers (93 per cent in our study) use a coursebook, which indicates that books still continue to represent the essence of the curriculum even when teachers and learners reconstruct and modify them (Hidalgo Dávila, 2009). Consequently, it is necessary to take into account that, as Apple states:

> texts are not simply 'delivery systems' of 'facts.' They are at once the results of political, economic, and cultural activities, battles, and compromises. They are conceived, designed, and authored by real people with real interests. They are published within the political and economic constraints of markets, resources, and power. (2000: 180)

An aspect valued in local or localised coursebooks by the teachers surveyed is the inclusion of references to the local culture and geography. However, critical analyses of localised textbooks used in Argentina have shown that these inclusions are negligible and therefore result in an unequal representation of the learners' and the target cultures (Basabe, 2009; López Barrios and Villanueva de Debat, 2006). Our study showed that teachers, regardless of whether they use global or local coursebooks, also adapt by adding texts that are more meaningful or familiar to the students in order to motivate them. A study with Colombian teachers indicated that they also supplement the coursebooks with texts that are more familiar to the students to motivate them (Hidalgo Dávila, 2009). In our study, the teachers who use a local book seem to have less of an urge to adapt the coursebook since it adjusts more appropriately to the local conditions, mainly to the local educational curricular demands, whereas the other areas (linguistic contrasts, intercultural reflection, facilitation of learning) do not seem to be an important concern. To understand the reasons for this, new studies should be carried out to find out about teachers' beliefs regarding the role of L1 use, about the development of intercultural competence, and to discover whether teaching at a specific type of school, or other contexts, reveals a difference in these two aspects. These are open questions for future research that may illuminate what is now a grey area.

To guide materials developers in the design of local or localised coursebooks, and teachers in the selection of a context-sensitive coursebook, in Table 3.4 we propose a set of questions based on the framework described in Table 3.2.

To conclude, we believe that changes also need to emerge from the bottom-up and that this will only be possible if the voices of teachers and learners – the coursebook users – are given the opportunity to be heard and considered. As one experienced teacher put it, 'I have been teaching for 24 years, and we have employed different kinds of books ... All of these books were good and when we adopted a new one, we always hoped that we would not have to prepare extra material, but sooner or later we realised something was missing.'

Engagement priorities

1. Critically analyse a coursebook you are currently using with the criteria proposed in this chapter. Use the questions in Table 3.4 to guide your analysis.

   How close is the coursebook to these features? What are ways of adapting the coursebook to suit a local context?
2. Research has shown that most teachers adapt the textbooks they use. This chapter has presented the most frequent reasons given by teachers in a specific geographical context. Do these reasons apply to you?

Table 3.4 Guiding questions in the design of local or localised coursebooks

To what extent is the book contextualised?	• Does it make use of the experiential world of the learners, their knowledge of the world? • Does it include topics, characters, places, information familiar to the students? • Does it propose pedagogical practices that suit the local needs?
To what extent does it promote intercultural reflection?	• Does it provide opportunities for learners to develop an awareness of the relation between their own culture and other cultures? • Does it offer learners opportunities to express their opinions when confronted with information about the target culture, rather than merely absorb the information uncritically? • Does it provide opportunities for learners to develop a critical and open attitude to other cultures?
To what extent does it make use of linguistic contrasts to raise students' awareness?	• Does it provide opportunities for learners to relate the features of the new language with their L1?
To what extent does it include elements that facilitate learning by the specific learners it was designed for?	• Does it offer ways to foster learner autonomy, for example with the inclusion of rubrics in L1, self-check tables, clear and explicit objectives, learner training (cognitive and metacognitive strategies), bilingual glossaries? • Does it provide guidance for the development of the macroskills, the study of vocabulary and grammar?

3. From the reading of this chapter and your personal experience, what do you think are the advantages of local or localised books over global ones? Can you think of other features of global coursebooks that do not fit in the framework we propose?

References

Abbs, B., Freebairn, I. and Barker, C. (2001). *In Focus 1*. Student's book + Workbook. Harlow: Pearson.

Apple, M. B. (2000). *Official Knowledge: Democratic Education in a Conservative Age*, 2nd Edition. London: Routledge, pp. 42–60.

Arnold, W. and Rixon, S. (2008). Materials for teaching English to young learners. In B. Tomlinson (ed.), pp. 38–58.

Banegas, D. L. (2010). Comment: teaching more than English in secondary education. *ELT Journal*, 65(1): 80–82.

Basabe, E. A. (2006). From de-anglicization to internationalisation: cultural representations of the UK and the USA in global, adapted and local ELT textbooks in Argentina. *Profile – Issues in Teachers' Professional Development*, 7: 59–75.

Basabe, E. A. (2009). Representaciones 'econoculturales' en la adaptación de libros de texto. El caso de *Go!* (1996) y sus versiones de Argentina (2000) y Chile (2003). *Educación, Lenguaje y Sociedad*, VI(6): 127–148.

Casuscelli, L. and Gandini, M. J. (2010). *Click into English 1*. Buenos Aires: Pearson Education; Tinta Fresca.

Corradi, L. and Rabinovich, A. (2004). *For Teens 1. Student's Book*. Buenos Aires: Pearson Education.

Council of Europe (2001). *Common European Framework of Reference for Languages: Learning, Teaching, Assessment*. Cambridge: CUP.

Courtillon, J. (2003). *Élaborer un cours de FLE*. Paris: Hachette.

Cowan, J. R., Light, R. R., Mathews, B. E. and Tucker, C. R. (1979). English teaching in China: a recent survey. *TESOL Quarterly*, 13: 465–478.

Dat, B. (2008). ELT materials used in Southeast Asia. In Tomlinson, B. (ed.), pp. 263–280.

Dream Team. Planificaciones. Available at http://fdslive.oup.com/www.oup.com/pdf/elt/catalogue/drm_tm_plnfccns_a.pdf [Accessed 2/9/12].

García Cahuzac, S. and Tiberio, S. C. (1999). *Explorer Starter. Student's Book*. Buenos Aires: Macmillan Heinemann.

Gray, J. (2002). The global coursebook in English Language Teaching. In Block, D. and Cameron, D. (eds), *Globalization and Language Teaching*. London: Routledge, pp. 151–167.

Hidalgo Dávila, H. A. (2009). Los libros de textos y su uso en el Departamento de Lenguas Modernas de la Universidad de Nariño durante el período 1966 a 1998. Una aproximación a la apropiación o adaptación de materiales. *Revista Historia de la Educación Colombiana (Rhec)*, 12(2): 47–76.

Kramsch, C. and Sullivan, P. (1996). Appropriate pedagogy. *ELT Journal*, 50(3): 199–212.

López Barrios, M. and Villanueva de Debat, E. (2006). Minding the needs of the Argentine learner: global textbooks and their adapted versions for the local context. *Folio*, 10(2): 14–16.

López Barrios, M. and Villanueva de Debat, E. (2007). Intercultural reflection in EFL coursebooks. *Cultural Awareness in ELT*. Córdoba: Comunic-arte, pp. 79–86.

López Barrios, M., Villanueva de Debat, E. and Tavella, G. (2008). Materials in use in Argentina and the Southern Cone. In Tomlinson, B. (ed.), pp. 300–316.

López Barrios, M., Dalla Villa, F, Jáimez, L. and Villanueva de Debat, E. (2004). Rasgos específicos de manuales de enseñanza de lenguas extranjeras para el contexto local. *Bitácora*, VI(11): 15–33.

Lopriore, L. (2006). À la recherche de la traduction perdue: la traduction dans la didactique des langues. *Éla. Études de linguistique appliquée*, 141: 85–94.

McKay, S. L. (2003). Toward an appropriate EIL pedagogy: re-examining common ELT assumptions. *International Journal of Applied Linguistics*, 13: 1–22.

Mugglestone, P., Elsworth, S. and Rose, J. (2000). *New Let's Go for EGB! Teacher's Resource Book: Book 1 and 2*. Harlow: Longman.

Patrie, J. and Daum, D. A. (1980). Comments on the role of foreign experts in developing nations: a summation of the findings of an exchange of ESL specialists with the People's Republic of China. *TESOL Quarterly*, 14: 391–394.

Richards, J.C. & Rodgers, T. (2001). *Approaches and Methods in Language Teaching,* 2nd Edition. Cambridge: Cambridge University Press.

Rodríguez Juárez, C. and Oxbrow, G. (2008). L1 in the EFL classroom: more a help than a hindrance? *Porta Linguarum* 9: 93–109.

Tomlinson, B. (1998a). Glossary of basic terms for materials development in language teaching. In Tomlinson, B. (ed.), pp. viii–xiv.

Tomlinson, B. (1998b). Comments on Part B. In Tomlinson, B. (ed.), pp. 146–148.

Tomlinson, B. (2003a). Comments on Part C. In Tomlinson, B. (ed.), pp. 324–352.

Tomlinson, B. (2003b). Humanising the coursebook. In Tomlinson, B. (ed.), pp. 162–173.

Tomlinson, B. (2012). Materials development for language learning and teaching. *Language Teaching,* 45(2): 143–179.

Tomlinson, B. (ed.) (1998). *Materials Development in Language Teaching.* Cambridge: Cambridge University Press.

Tomlinson, B. (ed.) (2003). *Developing Materials for Language Teaching.* London and New York: Continuum.

Tomlinson, B. (ed.) (2008). *English Language Learning Materials: A Critical Review.* London: Continuum.

Widdowson, H. G. (2004). A perspective on recent trends. In Howatt, A. (ed.), *A History of English Language Teaching,* 2nd Edition. Oxford: Oxford University Press, pp. 353–372.

4
Adapting Materials to Meet the Literacy Needs of Young Bahraini Learners

Sahar al Majthoob

Many educational systems in the world, including that in Bahrain, rely on globally produced materials to teach English. However, these materials are not developed for a specific context. Efforts were made to adapt global materials to meet the specific needs of the Bahraini context by making them appropriate for the traditions, beliefs, and values of their learners, teachers and culture.

This chapter will discuss the adaptations made to global materials prepared for children in the early grades, the rationale for those adaptations, and the issues in trying to adapt EFL materials for a world where the notion of English as a foreign language may no longer be appropriate. This chapter sheds light on literacy and how it is acquired, and it presents measures taken to support literacy through published materials.

The education context in Bahrain

As a first foreign language, English is taught in all public schools as a compulsory subject. Initially introduced in Grade 4 at primary level (nine to ten years old), it became compulsory in Grade 3 in 2001. This additional year was considered as a warm-up stage where children studied English for two hours weekly, unlike at higher grades where they had five hours study. However that was not enough, so, as in many countries worldwide, Bahrain decided to introduce English in Grade 1, starting in September 2004.

Several factors contributed to that decision. English plays an important role in Bahrain, whose cosmopolitan society has always been open to the world. English is a lingua franca in many situations in daily life. It is viewed as a means of attaining a better future when it comes to getting jobs, scholarships and education in general. Additional factors relate to parental influence, both out of concern for their children's future and driven by exam results, which were not always up to expectation. Private education had its share of the influence as the level of English in public schools was compared with that in private schools, where children started learning the language from pre-school. Additionally important were the expectations of the labour market and universities, who had expressed dissatisfaction at the level of English among high school graduates. On top of that came the boom in information technology and the increased use of computers and the Internet, which made the decision seem inevitable.

However, there were concerns about how to meet the needs of young Bahraini learners because of differences between Arabic, their mother tongue, and English. Young learners are challenged by the direction in which letters are formed and read, and by the limited sound–spelling correspondence of English. Because of these concerns, the Ministry of Education studied previous research on how children learn languages and carried out consultations with the support of the British Council before making the decision to start teaching English from Grade 1. Regional practices were also visited, especially in countries already teaching English from Grade 1, like Kuwait and the UAE.

Initially, teaching English in Grade 1 focused on the pre-literacy stage, concentrating on listening and speaking. The rationale for that step can be summarised in three points. First, they are the skills children acquire initially when learning their first language. Second, focusing on listening and speaking helps children acquire oral language and gives them confidence in learning the language and using it in a non-threatening way. Third, it helps students develop oral language and build a bank of vocabulary that will be beneficial when they start reading and writing.

However, follow-up meetings and feedback from teachers confirmed the need to pave the way to literacy. Therefore, initial adaptations were made to the prescribed textbook and children were introduced to the alphabet in the second semester of Grade 1, then a two-page spread with an alphabet poster was added for the year after. At this level, children worked on letter recognition, tracing, and some activity worksheets at a pre-writing level. Monitoring of the children's progress, especially after the first cohort reached Grade 3, revealed the need for other measures. It was also the time when our dilemma became very clear.

EFL or ESL, where do we fit?

EFL has traditionally been defined as English taught as a school subject with the purpose of communicating with native speakers (Al-Mutawa and Kailani, 1989). EFL can also be defined in terms of the relationship of the target language, English, with the context. In an EFL context the classroom (or school) is the only place that English is regularly encountered, since the learner's first language is the language of the school and the wider community. Graves (2008) has called this a 'target-language removed context', because the target language is removed from the context in which it is used.

On the other hand, in an ESL context English is the dominant language of the school and wider community, and is used extensively in everyday life. The target language, English, is embedded in the context (Graves, 2008; Graves and Lopriore, 2009). The learner lives in the target language community and the language is learnt for specific needs relating to that community (Harmer, 2007).

Bahrain has long been labelled as an EFL context, yet with a reality and expectations that are more proximate to ESL. English is widespread in the country; it is the language of business and finance, and is used on a daily basis in shops and restaurants. Films are in English and national TV has an English channel. Road signs, restaurants, shops, and many more have their signs in English. In other words, young learners are surrounded with environmental print, which means a child comes to the classroom with some background knowledge of English.

Although Bahrain has characteristics of an ESL context because English is widespread outside of the school context, within schools it exhibits characteristics of an EFL context. Table 4.1 illustrates some of the differences between how English is learnt in the two contexts.

The question in Bahrain is how to use the limited time in schools to prepare students to be able to participate in and take advantage of the widespread use of English outside the school. An additional issue is that learners in Grade 1 are simultaneously learning to be literate in their first language, Arabic, which uses a non-Roman alphabet. Therefore, the materials need to introduce learners to literacy in English, whereas most EFL materials for young learners do not provide a systematic approach to literacy.

Table 4.1 The contexts of EFL and ESL

	EFL in primary school	**ESL in primary school**
Age at onset of English instruction	Varies (but earlier is trend) (Grade 1 in Bahrain)	When student enters local school (or when started in home country)
Time spent studying or exposed to English	Varies (3–5 hours/week) (Five 45 min. classes/week in Bahrain)	The whole school day
Purpose for learning	As school subject; to learn other subject matter (CLIL)	To participate and succeed academically in all school subjects
Focus of lessons	Varies; English materials; other subject matter (CLIL)	Grade level curriculum (and may receive language-focused instruction)

Source: Graves (2011).

EFL materials for young learners

In Bahrain English is being taught from Grade 1 using internationally produced materials written for an EFL (TL removed) context without a particular learner in mind. The combined resources include a coursebook, workbook and a storytelling/shared reading programme. The materials immerse the learner in English through a thematic, whole language, top-down approach that involves lots of songs, chants, stories, and games.

This approach has helped children become confident during lessons conducted in English, albeit with some issues related to opportunities for real speaking that need addressing in teacher training. For example, units are built in a manner that immerses the learner in themes related to school, food, play time, and so on. They provide children with enough vocabulary and context clues to understand the theme, talk about it, and probably attempt to write about it, using age-related tasks. The different tasks done using the same vocabulary, and the whole language approach, help children to recognise these words and read them in isolation or in a familiar context.

However, this approach typical for EFL learners does not give children the same confidence in reading beyond these themes because they lack the necessary strategies to decode or read any unfamiliar text they encounter. Although EFL materials do provide opportunities for the teaching of literacy, they are not systematic or structured. What is needed, therefore, is a more systematic and structured approach that draws on practices from first language literacy. In order to describe such an approach, the next section explores what literacy is and how it is acquired.

What is literacy and how is it acquired?

At its simplest, literacy can be defined as the ability to read and write. In this context it refers to learning to read and write in English. However, a more important question is not what literacy is, but what it can do. According to Hudelson (1994) it is not just about constructing meaning from text; it goes beyond that to making the choice to read and write and having the desire to engage in these processes. Children's first encounters with literacy start with the print around them. This environmental print (Hudelson, 1994; Linse, 2005) helps children identify fast food chains, toy brands, restaurants, or road signs, for example.

The next contributor to literacy acquisition is reading stories. This happens at home for many families and at school as well. An adult reading a storybook to a child helps the child construct meaning from the adult's reading and the available picture cues. Initially, the child gains an overview of the story, such as what happened at the beginning or the end. Gradually, he or she will fill in the gaps with details. Finally, there will be a real attempt to focus on the print to decode words, to point while reading, before becoming a fluent reader. Younger children start with reading-like activities where they learn to handle books, turn pages, and pretend to read the text while applying directionality, as in left to right or top to bottom (Scott and Ytreberg, 1990).

Construction of meaning is at the heart of literacy (Graves, 2011; Hudelson, 1994). Common practices are shared reading, learning words in context, talking about pictures, predicting, and creating and sharing texts (Graves, 2011). Journal writing, or making a birthday card or alphabet book, are examples of creating and sharing text. Even a very simple text can give a clear example of a child's understanding of sound–letter correspondence. In the initial stages of journal writing a drawing with a few scribbles to label or semi-describe it can be enough.

Research suggests that the teaching of literacy be built around the five essential components involved in the process of learning to read (International Reading Association, 2002):

1. *Phonemic awareness*: this refers to the ability to recognise that words have individual sounds that work together. When children have phonemic awareness they are able, for example, to isolate the first sound in a word or a group of words that start with the same sound, like /k/ in cat and car. Having this skill helps children to read and spell because they are able to hear and identify sounds, as well as manipulate them in spoken language.

   When children manipulate phonemes or sounds, they delete, add, or sub-stitute them and hence they are able to spell better because they understand the predictable relation between sounds and letters.

   In a blended setting (EFL/ESL) where children need phonemic awareness and do not have the necessary lexicon knowledge, teaching materials and teachers need to carefully select lexis in themes that lend themselves to phonemic awareness. In a playtime theme children would learn that 'train' starts with /t/, and in a weather theme they would learn that deleting /t/ would leave 'rain'.

2. *Phonics*: in phonics, children learn the relationship between the written letters and their sounds (phonemes). Children gain knowledge of the alpha-betic principle, that is the understanding of the systematic relationship between the letters of written language and the sounds of spoken lan-guage. Eventually, this helps them to decode using the letter–sound rela-tionship and enhances their ability to read. Phonics instruction needs to be systematic and explicit if it is going to really boost a child's reading achievement. Linan-Thompson & Vaughn found that 'English language learners struggling with reading acquisition who receive explicit phonics instruction as part of comprehensive literacy instruction tend to develop

stronger foundational reading skills.' (2007: 33). According to Put Reading First (Adler, 2001) phonics instruction has a greater impact if started early.

One criticism of phonics teaching is that English spelling is irregular. English has 26 letters in its alphabet but 44 corresponding sounds, which creates a challenge for first language young learners, let alone second/ foreign language learners. However, without really knowing the rules that govern the difference between a soft 'g' and a hard 'g' or a soft and hard 'c' the learner would be confined to what he/she learns in a particular context and will not be able to decode properly outside it. When children are taught to read, the ultimate goal is to provide them with strategies to cope with the surrounding print beyond the frontiers of the classroom.

3. *Fluency*: this refers to the ability to read text accurately and quickly. The importance of fluency lies in the fact that fluent readers focus less on decoding and more on making connections between ideas in the text, at the same time connecting the text and their background knowledge. Fluent readers grasp meaning while recognising words (Antunez, 2002), whereas less fluent children pay more attention to decoding words in isolation, and are less occupied with the meaning of the words and how they contribute to the comprehension of the whole text (Adler, 2001).

4. *Vocabulary*: having limited vocabulary can impede effective communi-cation and text comprehension while reading. Being able to decode without constructing meaning is not really reading. Silverman (2007: 365) asserts that: 'Vocabulary knowledge is a key building block in children's early lit-eracy development.' She adds: 'It provides the foundation for learning to decode and comprehend text.'

Vocabulary needs to be taught explicitly and encountered in several tasks and contexts in order to be acquired (Fishkin, 2010). In a top-down context for example, teachers would decide what the essential vocabulary is for understanding the context of a story during a read aloud lesson and pre-teach it. This learning of vocabulary can be done directly through probes, realia, or visual aids. According to Silverman (2007), reading storybooks is an ideal way of introducing new vocabulary. While explicit instruction is important, children also learn indirectly through conversations with others, especially adults. Moreover, children are not always dependent on others to learn vocabulary; they do it also through reading on their own as autonomous learners.

It is important, however, that vocabulary instruction does not come at the expense of instruction in phonemic awareness, phonics, print knowledge, and word recognition. The balance between top-down and bottom-up approaches has to be maintained (Thornton et al., 2009).

5. *Comprehension*: people read for pleasure and for information. Uttering the sounds on a page becomes reading only when these sounds make words that

have meaning (Linse, 2005). Learners have to interact with the text before, during, and after reading to really comprehend it. This can be done through questioning using higher order thinking questions that promote thinking skills and strategies. Moreover, engaging in activities such as summarising, reflecting, or using graphic organisers, especially after reading, can contribute to comprehension.

Another factor that contributes to comprehension is oral vocabulary (which is related to the previous point). Deriving meaning from a text requires the use of background knowledge to process the encountered words. Having a wide range of oral vocabulary enhances comprehension. Cameron (2001) goes beyond that and states that knowing words orally is a condition for encountering them in writing. The rationale here is that if learners know it they will comprehend it.

Using L1 literacy strategies to teach L2 literacy

Children need explicit, structured and systematic instruction in reading to become readers, and teachers need to see that clearly in the materials they use. Unfortunately, this kind of teaching is lacking in EFL materials in general because the approach used assumes the acquisition of basic literacy. Few writers suggest using approaches and strategies in literacy with young EFL learners that are similar to those used with ESL or young native speakers. Young English language learners are no different from native speakers in many respects (Brown, 2000), but similarities, especially in needs and strategies, are not mentioned explicitly in the literature.

This issue is also related to beginning writing, not just reading. Native speakers and ESL learners are taught the basics of punctuation or print conventions at the earliest stages in a systematic way because it is important for writing and comprehension in reading as well as fluency (Linse, 2005). A child who is made aware of the full stop and the comma, for example, knows when and how long to pause while reading, which can improve his or her fluency.

Initial adaptation of EFL materials to provide literacy support for Bahraini learners

In order to address the needs of Bahraini learners, ministerial committees were set up to adapt the materials used in schools. Changes were driven by the results of classroom observations, teachers' views, and comments from parents. The committees included teachers, senior teachers, curriculum specialists, educational supervisors, and the publisher's resident teacher trainer who was, in addition to training, in charge of working out the adaptations and liaising with the editorial team to get them done. Each grade level had a separate committee, but they all shared some of the members from curriculum and educational supervision directorates in the Ministry, in addition to the teacher trainer. The members were selected carefully to make sure that informed adaptations were made. My role in the committees changed over time from being a member to leading the teams and doing the final revisions of the needed adaptations.

The initial phase focused mainly on screening the materials to guarantee cultural appropriateness and took place before the materials were used in the classroom. The second phase was concurrent with the actual implementation of the materials. Committees would suggest adaptations, or approve them based on classroom observations, meetings with teachers and senior teachers, feedback from teachers who used the materials, and members of the committee. The committee then submitted a table of the suggested adaptations that was sent to the publisher. It has to be noted that the editorial team was very cooperative, reflective in looking at the adaptations, and made suggestions that were found to be more effective in several cases. The process of adaptation continued to the year following, when the new activities were tested in class to verify their effectiveness. The third phase was done after using the series in the classrooms for Grades 1–3.

One set of measures was to modify the EFL materials to include more literacy work. Another was to prepare materials for developing handwriting. The handwriting materials were produced in two phases. The first was to practise letter formation and recognition for children in Grade 3. Later however, the need to start earlier resulted in the production of a patterns booklet for children to practise tracing the different shapes, lines and directionality which later help in letter formation and give children the basics for handwriting. Additional activities for class work, parental involvement, and homework were compiled in a CD that was given to all teachers to supplement the materials. The content of the CD included resources provided by the publisher, teacher-made activities, and worksheets prepared by curriculum specialists. The CD contained a wealth of other resources that made teachers of other subjects wish they were English teachers.

Including more literacy work in the EFL materials

Originally, there was a recurrent section called *Find, draw, and write* that focused on identifying an object or character, drawing it, and labelling the drawing using the given words, as shown in Figure 4.1. It was changed after discussions within the Ministry and collaboration with the publisher to create a section called *Think about English*, to include strategies related to literacy. For example, the activity in Figure 4.2 helps students learn print convention strategies by recognising the use of a capital letter at the beginning of the sentences and the use of a full stop at the end. It presents a good start to learning the mechanics of writing.

Find, draw, and write.

Fgiure 4.1   Find, draw, and write activity from Happy House 2 Bahrain edition

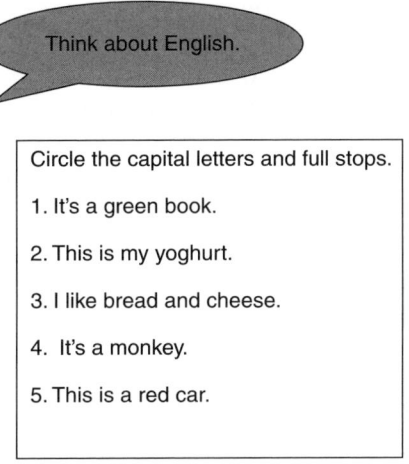

Figure 4.2   Think about English activity from Happy House 2 Bahrain edition

In another *Think about English* activity students are asked to circle the sentences in a paragraph. This helps students recognise sentence boundaries and that paragraphs are made up of sentences. Every sentence makes a whole unit of meaning, with a beginning marked by a capital letter and an end marked by a full stop. At a higher level, one of the *Think about English* activities asks students to circle the adjectives in a list of sentences such as, 'She's got long black hair.' This type of activity focuses on strategies related to identifying parts of speech, in this case for children to identify adjectives as words that describe nouns. This is a typical activity in first and second language learners' materials which is useful for foreign language learners too. At this age children are engaged in many activities where they have to describe or talk about personal things or pictures in a story. It helps them to engage in speaking activities like show and tell.

Handwriting framework: an initial stage towards the literacy strategy

Another issue was the teaching of handwriting – how and when to start. Based on feedback from the field (teachers, supervisors, trainers, principals, and parents), classroom observations, and reports (Graves, 2010), in addition to reports on the national examinations, handwriting was identified as an area that needed development. Children's handwriting was illegible and they needed more practice. Modern EFL materials basically let the child practise writing in a minimal way that does not really improve their skills. The *English Syllabus for Basic Education* that guides educational decisions in Bahrain did not have a clear policy, especially for students in Grades 1–3, and so teaching materials again dictated the amount of attention given to handwriting. The solution was to write a handwriting framework that specifies expectations for primary students starting with pre-writing activities in Grade 1.

Writing the framework was not easy due to the shortage of literature on handwriting for EFL young learners. Most of the literature found was written for first language young learners so, considering the stages of development young learners go through when learning the alphabet, the framework adopted similar stages and strategies as those for first language learners. A structured schedule was prepared and accompanying materials were written to fill in the gaps at the initial stages of handwriting. The framework starts with pattern practice to help children acquire the basic movements needed to form letters, and aims to ensure a uniform and principled approach to the development of basic handwriting skills in Grade 1. Since the framework targets children who do not use the Roman alphabet, it emphasises the need for more time to develop the basic patterns that will eventually lead to automatic hand movements when forming letters. This is important in developing the children's ability to communicate as thoughts, ideas, and feelings are expressed more easily if the learner does not have to worry about letter formation.

The next step: a literacy framework

Adapting the materials helped to fulfil the needs of the learners. Along with the other resources, they made the teachers' task easier. Yet, and despite the cooperation of the publisher, adaptations were limited to a certain percentage as they were confined to the number of pages in the original edition of the book. Other supportive resources, which were not part of the original programme, came at different intervals because the need for them was not identified initially. That situation affected the cohesion of the programme and caused inconsistencies in classroom practices. Those two issues therefore needed to be addressed.

The proposed solution lies in producing a literacy framework. Such frameworks are a common practice in the US and the UK. Nevertheless, importing a framework that has been written for a different context would not be appropriate. The Bahraini model will be a framework written locally with a particular learner in mind: one who is learning to be literate in his/her first language; uses a non-Roman alphabet; reads right to left; and is viewed as an EFL or TL removed context learner while in reality he or she is exposed to the language in a manner that corresponds with an ESL context. This framework is based on a premise that children, regardless of whether they are learning to read English as their mother tongue or as an additional language, learn to read it the same way. They need to learn letter shapes, sounds, initial sounds, final sounds, and to use the same decoding strategies. The literacy framework will combine top-down and bottom-up approaches to reading. It will focus on reading strategies and include an extensive reading programme, which, although common in the ESL context, is not a very common practice within the EFL context.

A top-down approach focuses on topics and themes and uses stories, while a bottom-up approach focuses on contextualised phonics. The two approaches are equally important and complement each other (Jannuzi, 2010). While the top-down approach requires the application of background knowledge for comprehension, it assumes that learners have already mastered decoding, which is important for reading and fluency (Purewal, 2008). Given the limited vocabulary of the language learner, the top-down approach can be scaffolded with different strategies to pre-teach vocabulary. The use of the bottom-up approach, on the other hand, will help learners decode the symbols on a page but does not necessarily lead to understanding. According to Moats (1999: 18), 'A child cannot understand what he [sic] cannot decode, but what he decodes is meaningless unless he can understand it.'

The framework will focus on reading readiness and reading skills with an emphasis on reading strategies. The aim of reading and writing will be described specifically and systematically. The framework will be the reference upon which the materials are selected and should also be reflected in the materials in order to provide the right support for teachers. Many teachers attempt to apply strategies that support the teaching of reading, nevertheless, without the framework, materials dictate what teachers do and how they do it. The ultimate goal is to have a consistent, structured, and systematic approach.

The framework will also address extensive reading as a means to improve learners' reading skills and contribute to literacy. Most EFL materials lack age-related extended readings that really help children become readers. On the other hand, native and second language learners generally work with literature-based materials in addition to accompanying reading programmes, which include fiction and non-fiction books. This is a major difference in approach and has a great impact on acquiring reading strategies. Moreover, systematic exposure to reading does not only create a good reader but also a good writer.

Children need to experience reading starting with storytelling and picture books, shared reading, and guided reading, until they become independent readers who can ultimately handle chapter books. Strategies like reading aloud, predicting from the book cover before reading, pointing to illustrations during reading, checking for comprehension upon completion need to begin as early as Grade 1, even before children learn to read.

The objective here is to establish a bond between the child and the book, and develop an enjoyment of reading and literature while developing literacy skills. As Moats (1999: 11) puts it, 'the teacher must instruct most students systematically and explicitly to decipher words in print, all the while keeping in mind the ultimate purpose of reading, which is to learn, enjoy, and understand'.

The importance of teacher training

No matter how strong the materials or how clear the framework, their successful use in the classroom depends upon how well teachers understand the principles and rationale that underpin them. Lack of proper training is a universal issue, both in ESL and EFL contexts. In the US teachers do not always have the proper training to teach English language learners, especially in mainstream classes (Moats, 1999), while in EFL contexts teachers of English language learners enter classrooms with a varied language proficiency or a lack of training in language teaching (Fishkin, 2010). Teachers of young learners also need special preparation since understanding how children learn is crucial before embarking on language related activities, whether in an EFL or an ESL setting.

Before English was introduced in Grade 1 in Bahrain, teachers, supervisors, and curriculum specialists went through intensive training that laid the ground for teaching young learners. This gave teachers a good start in coping with the demands of lowering the age of teaching English. The course aimed to:

- deepen and strengthen the understanding of key issues surrounding the teaching of English to young learners in Grades 1–3, and to explore these issues in relation to practise in the classroom;
- address concerns related to this age group;
- investigate and share best practice;
- deal mainly with pre-literacy activities that children need to learn English.

The proposed literacy framework will require new training programmes to support teachers. The absence of a structured training programme that deals with phonics and opportunities to raise phonemic awareness, for example, could mean an unfair delay in literacy acquisition for children. Although teachers are capable of handling literacy strategies that support learners' autonomy, a hit and miss approach leaves teachers the sole judges of how to handle literacy. To guarantee a fair start for all children, in-service teachers need intensive training on the five pillars of teaching reading described earlier: phonemic awareness, phonics, fluency, vocabulary, and comprehension (Nat'l Reading Panel Report, 2002). There should also be a focus on meaning and comprehension of text through common practices like shared reading, learning words in context, talking about pictures, predicting, and creating and sharing texts

Training also needs to tackle how children learn their first language and how that affects second language acquisition. Having strong literacy skills in the native language leads to transferring these skills into English (Linse, 2005; McKay, 2006). Understanding the relationship between how one learns first and second language literacy can lead to more cooperation between teachers of both languages in local contexts and can have positive effects on the strategies of teaching one language or another.

The next generation of EFL materials

This chapter has described the process of developing materials for the Bahraini situation. However, the situation in Bahrain is not unique. The relationship between education, society, and language in many countries has contributed to, and been affected by, the changing role of English in the world today (Tomita, 2009). Bahrain is not the only country that has lowered the age of introducing English, and these changes have created a new set of needs and priorities. Although English is widely used outside the classroom in many countries, the context is different to that of immigrant English language learners in, for example, Canada or the US. Therefore the context of English language learning in countries like Bahrain lies in between ESL and EFL.

The growing population of speakers of English and the lowering of the age children start learning it in many countries has created a learner with different needs. English has become a global language (Tomita, 2009) and that has created a global learner who cannot be categorised as an EFL or ESL learner. Young learners worldwide share the same characteristics and need similar approaches to help them learn to read and write in English, and traditional EFL materials are no longer sufficient to provide learners with the strategies they need to unlock symbols on pages. Blending the two approaches, top-down and bottom-up, has to be reflected in the new generation of materials. Changing the approach has to be met with an increase in the time spent reading. Finally, the success of any shift in education relies on the teachers' preparation that goes with it.

Engagement priorities

1. The debate used to be about how young to start English language instruction. Now that more and more countries are choosing to start at a younger age, the question is no longer 'How young?' but 'How can we make learning another language better for young learners?' How would you answer this question?
2. The number of countries with a similar context to Bahrain is growing. From a materials development perspective, what are the lessons learnt from the Bahraini story?
3. How explicit should the focus on literacy be in EFL/ESL materials?
4. Learners' needs are at the heart of any educational system and programme. What kind of research into the characteristics and needs of young learners is needed to help us determine whether new materials, methods, and techniques are needed? How much research is required before these needs will be addressed? How can the international materials market address these needs?

References

Adler, C. R. (ed.) (2001). *Put Reading First: The Research Building Blocks for Teaching Children to Read*. Washington, D.C.: National Institute for Literacy and U.S. Department of Education.

Al-Mutawa, N. and Kailani, T. (1989). *Methods of Teaching English to Arab Students*. UK: Longman Group.

Antunez, B. (2002). Implementing reading first with English Language Learners. *Directions in Language and Education*, (Online Journal), 15 Spring. Available at http://www.ncela.gwu.edu/files/rcd/BE024311/15.pdf [Accessed 16/3/12].

Areglado, N. and Dill, M. (1997). *Let's Write: A Practical Guide to Teaching Writing in the Early Grades*. New York: Scholastic.

Asworth, M., and Wakefield, H. (2004). Teaching the world's children ESL for ages three to seven. *English Teaching Forum*, 43(1): 2–7.

Blevins, W. (1998). *Phonics from A to Z*. New York: Scholastic Professional Books.

Brown, H. D. (2000). *Principles of Language Learning and Teaching*. New York: Pearson.

Cameron, L. (2001). *Teaching Languages to Young Learners*. Cambridge: Cambridge University Press.

Cullinan, B. E. (1992). *Read to Me: Raising Kids Who Love to Read*. New York: Time Life Inc.

Graves, K. (2011). *EFL+ESL=A literacy strategy for Bahrain*, 45th TESOL convention, New Orleans, with Sahar al Majthoob.

Graves, K. (2010). A literacy strategy for English Basic Education in the Kingdom of Bahrain. Report prepared for the Directorate of Curriculum, Kingdom of Bahrain. Unpublished report.

Graves, K. and Lopriore, L. (2009). Challenges and opportunities in designing a new curriculum for school-age learners. In Graves, K. and Lopriore, L. (eds), *Developing a New Curriculum for School Age Learners*. Alexandria VA USA: TESOL.

Graves, K. (2008). The language curriculum: A social contextual perspective. *Language Teaching*, 41, 149–183. Available at http://www.scottsclasses.com/uploads/6/9/0/3/6903668/the_language_curriculum_-_a_social_contextual_perspective.pdf (Accessed 17/3/2012)

Hudelson, S. (1994). Literacy development of second language children. In Genesee, F. (ed.), *Educating Second Language Children: The Whole Child, the Whole Curriculum, the Whole Community*. New York: Cambridge University Press.

Fishkin, O. (2010). Effective primary literacy strategies for English Language Learners. *Illinois Reading Council Journal*, 38(4), 14–19.

Harmer, J. (2007). *How to Teach English*. England: Pearson Education Limited.

International Reading Association. (2002). Summary of the (US) national reading panel report: Teaching children to read. Washington, DC: US Government Printing Office.

Jannuzi, C. (2010). *Key Concepts in EFL Literacy: Phonics vs. Whole Language*. Available at ELT in Japan http://eltinjapan.com [Accessed 16/3/2012].

Linan-Thompson, S. and Vaughn, S. (2007). *Research-Based Methods of Reading Instruction for English Language Learners, Grades K-4*. Alexandria. VA: Association for Supervision and Curriculum Development.

Linse, C. (2005). *Practical English Language Teaching: Young Learners*. New York: McGraw-Hill.

Lapitskaya, L. and Linse, C. (2009). Teaching reading to EFL students in Belarus. In Graves, K. and Lopriore, L. (eds), *Developing a New Curriculum for School Age Learners*. Alexandria VA USA: TESOL Inc.

Maidment, S. and Roberts, L. (2006). *Happy House International Edition*. Oxford: Oxford University Press.

Maidment, S. and Roberts, L. (2008). *Happy House Bahrain Edition*. Oxford: Oxford University Press.

McKay, P. (2006). *Assessing Young Language Learners*. Cambridge: Cambridge University Press.

Moats, L. C. (1999). *Teaching Reading is Rocket Science: What Expert Teachers of Reading Should Know and Be Able To Do*. Washington, DC: American Federation of Teachers.

Purewal, S. (2008). Synthetic Phonics and the Literacy Development of Second Language Young Learners; A Literature Review of Literacy Ideologies, Policies, and Research; The University of Leeds. Available at https://www.jiscmail.ac.uk/cgi-bin/filearea.cgi?LMGT1=ESOL-RESEARCH&f=/L2literacy [Accessed 12/3/2012].

Scott, W. and Ytreberg, L. (1990). *Teaching English to Children*. New York: Longman.

Silverman, R. D. (2007). Vocabulary development of English-Language and English-only learners in Kindergarten. *The Elementary School Journal,* 107: 365–383. Available at www.uww.edu\conteduc\camps\otherevents\Docs\Papers\Silverman%202007.pdf [Accessed 01/10/2012].

Thornton, B., Touba, N. A., Bakr, A. and Iannuzzi, S. (2009). A new way for a new age: developing a standards based curriculum for young learners in Egypt. In Graves, K. and Lopriore, L. (eds), *Developing a New Curriculum for School Age Learners*. Alexandria VA USA: TESOL Inc.

Tomita, Y. (2009). The introduction of English for communication in a Japanese Elementary School: 'Having an English Shower'. In Graves, K. and Lopriore, L. (eds), *Developing a New Curriculum for School Age Learners*. Alexandria VA USA: TESOL Inc.

5
Cultural Representations in Algerian English Textbooks

Hayat Messekher

Introduction

Culture, whether taught explicitly or implicitly, permeates many aspects of foreign language teaching. Teachers, then, need to be cognizant of how to approach culture and how to teach it in the language classroom. In Algeria, where exposure to the English language is rare, teachers rely heavily on textbooks as the source of both language and culture for their teaching. This underscores Riazi's (2003: 52) argument that 'textbooks play a very crucial role in the realm of language teaching and learning and are considered the next important factor in the second/foreign language classroom after the teacher'.

How culture is represented in textbooks plays an important role in how it is taught. This chapter reports on a study that looked at the cultural representations in the English textbooks used for public middle schools in Algeria, and the reactions of practising teachers to local and global cultural representations. The chapter begins by looking at the way culture has been framed in ELT textbooks in general and what is meant by culture and cultural representations in textbooks. It then introduces the Algerian context by looking at the place of ELT in Algeria and the quality of teacher education in relation to the mandated textbooks. This is followed by a discussion of the cultural representations in four Algerian textbooks and implications for the teaching of culture in today's globalised world.

Which culture is represented in English textbooks?

The way culture is conceived of, and hence represented, in textbooks is a crucial matter. Cortazzi and Jin (1999) describe three patterns of culture representation in English textbooks. These are: (1) the source culture, representing the learner's own culture; (2) the target culture, where the foreign language is used as the first language; and (3) international target cultures, which are the different cultures that do not represent the source or the target culture, which can be English-speaking or non-English-speaking countries. Kramsch (1993) has argued that one important issue with how culture is represented in textbooks, regardless of whether it is the source, target, or the international culture(s), is that they only represent one or very few cultures for one language. In other words, textbooks have a simplistic approach to the representation of a culture; for example, they do not include various sub-cultures related to the English language within American culture (African-American, Hispanic-American). Similarly, Gray (2010) has been very critical of the 'essentialism' prevalent in English textbooks whereby the target culture is reduced to a set of generalised characteristics.

It has been reported that in some English as a Foreign Language (EFL) contexts English textbooks produced locally represent the source or local culture (Gray, 2000). Cortazzi and Jin (1999) point to Venezuelan English textbooks that feature national heroes and cities, and Turkish textbooks displaying Turkish culture, including Turkish food and history. Additionally, Gray (2000) gives the example of Saudi Arabia and China producing materials with almost no reference to English-speaking cultures. However, culture is not always represented in terms of the source/local culture vs. the target culture(s). In South Asia some English textbooks feature international cultural contexts with characters from all over the world using English as an international language (Cortazzi, 2000). Hence, when considering how culture is represented in English textbooks, one has to bear in mind that there is a lot of variation as to which culture is represented, whether it is local, target, international, or a combination.

Language and culture: two sides of the same coin

Although language and culture are often treated as separate, they are inextricably linked. One cannot expect language to exist in a vacuum without being embedded in a given culture, but at the same time one cannot imagine a culture without an accompanying language that mediates it. It is noticeable that, when talking about languages, we often say things like, 'in Arabic we say so and so; in French we do so and so'. Arguably then, when we use language referring to ways of speaking, behaving, and thinking, we are in fact referring to culture, or as Kramsch (1996: 3) eloquently argues:

> [O]ne of the major ways in which culture manifests itself is through language. Material culture is constantly *mediated, interpreted and recorded – among other things – through language*. It is because of that mediatory role of language that culture becomes the concern of the language teacher. Culture in the final analysis is always *linguistically mediated membership into a discourse community, that is both real and imagined*. Language plays a crucial role

not only in the construction of culture, but in the emergence of cultural change. [italics in original]

Indeed, sociocultural behaviours are part of a given culture and they manifest themselves through language. To take a simple example, we greet differently in different cultures, using different formulas that are context-dependent, so any language learner needs to learn how to use the language in a culturally appropriate manner. In EFL educational settings, this can only be achieved if instruction includes a culture teaching component that might be explicit or implicit. EFL teachers need to raise their learners' awareness and draw their attention to the language structures (both spoken and written) that are culturally bound. They may also give similar or counter examples from the learner's L1 and local culture.

Moreover, as Kramsch (1996) argues, changes in language bring about cultural changes, and vice versa. Changes in language, namely vocabulary, such as that related to gender or race, mirror changes in the sociocultural reality of individuals and nations. The dynamic and changing nature of language and culture, then, can make it challenging for a teacher and for a textbook writer to represent current culture. Any cultural representation depicted in a textbook is going to be situated in time and may make little or no sense to students who receive those cultural representations years later.

When learning a language, we learn a new cultural frame of reference. Alpetkin (2002: 57) argues that 'learning a foreign language becomes a kind of enculturation, where one acquires new cultural frames of reference and a new world view, reflecting those of the target language culture and its speakers'. In EFL instruction learners are likely to be exposed to new values that they may pick up. Such values might constitute a new cultural frame of reference. However, in my experience, learners of a foreign language may not acquire a new cultural frame of reference but might just develop awareness and an understanding of the existence of such a frame of reference.

The relationship between language and culture is further complicated because one cannot assume that for a given language there is one accompanying culture. In the case of English for example, the accompanying culture can be the culture of any of the Inner Circle Countries, e.g. British, American, or Australian. It can also be the culture of one of the Outer Circle Countries, e.g. India or Singapore, where English is an official language. Conceiving of the target culture in ELT as monolithic is particularly problematic or 'unrealistic because [this] fails to reflect the lingua franca status of English' (Alpetkin, 2002: 57).

When learning English, since there is not one but many cultures, even within the same country, that can be associated with English, acquiring a new cultural frame of reference becomes problematic. This gives rise to the questions: when learning English, what culture do we learn? What is the new cultural frame of reference being acquired? These questions suggest that, rather than focusing on specific cultures, teaching should raise students' awareness of the role culture plays in communication. It should not impose different frames of reference, but prepare students for understanding that there are different worldviews and to be able to communicate their own culture in order to develop cross-cultural understanding. Being a global citizen means being able to communicate across cultures.

Culture representations

In order to understand what and how culture is represented in Algerian textbooks of English, it is first necessary to define what culture is. To this end, I have drawn primarily on two analyses of culture as the basis for defining cultural representations in the English textbooks used in Algerian schools, Watson's four categories (2010) of which I used the first two, and Yuen's four P's (2011).

Drawing on the definition by Bousquet and Pessin (2003: 41) that culture represents 'cultural objects produced and distributed by practitioners [that include] all of the styles of doing, thinking, and feeling that distinguish a particular group, its conscious or semi-conscious shared beliefs', Watson (2010: 478) proposes four categories of culture: big C culture, small c culture, commodity culture, and hybridised culture. He defines them as follows:

1. big C culture, which includes the canon of great artistic and intellectual works along with the institutions that produce and preserve them;
2. small c culture, the anthropological definition which encompasses a social collectivity's shared values, behaviours, entertainments, and artefacts;
3. commodity culture, which not only consists of the products of the culture industry but also commodifies the products of big C and small c culture;
4. hybridised culture, which has emerged as a result of post-colonialism and globalisation and which enfolds big C, small c, and commodity culture.

Big C culture can include, for example, the Seven Wonders of the World, or world renowned paintings like the *Mona Lisa* or *The Last Supper* by Leonardo da Vinci. Small c culture represents how, where, when, and what people from a specific community do. These include verbal and non-verbal communication styles, such as ways of greeting, thanking, and so on. Commodity culture can be seen through how a product of big C culture, such as Harry Potter, has become a commodity that is traded like any other manufactured goods. Finally, hybridised culture includes examples of any form of big C, small c, or commodity culture that has been appropriated and given local meanings and values such as a Barbie doll turning into a Fulla doll, and Palestinian youths using hip hop as a tool in their struggle and resistance. I have used Watson's interpretations of big C culture and small c culture as a basis for analysing cultural representations in the Algerian textbooks. Watson's commodity and hybridised cultures are very difficult to use when analysing textbooks because their interrelation and abstraction makes them challenging to delineate.

For practical purposes, I have also adopted Yuen's (2011) analytical tool of the four Ps. These are: (1) products, (2) practices, (3) perspectives, and (4) persons. Products are the products of literature, fine arts, and the sciences, along with historical figures, and social, political and economic institutions. These overlap with Watson's 'Big C' culture. For example, Charles Dickens's *Oliver Twist* as a cultural product overlaps with literature as an example of big C culture. Practices are the way of life and patterns of behaviour. These overlap with the behaviours, entertainments and artefacts of Watson's small c culture. For example, sports and games as practices overlap with entertainment. Perspectives refer to 'subjective culture' and include inspirations (equality), myths (horoscopes), and worldviews (Yuen, 2011: 6). Perspectives representing worldviews in a given culture can give value to some things that may or may not be similarly or equally valued by other cultures, such as privacy and personal space. Persons are well-known icons or individuals as stressed by Moran (2001). Persons are at the centre of recognised cultural productions that range across music, television, journalism, and the Internet. Such 'celebrity culture', according to Friedman (1999: 5), is one that the average person usually embraces and which becomes part of the 'aspirational content...in the ELT industry [that is believed] to be inherently motivating for language learners' (Gray, 2012: 87). Indeed, persons, or 'celebrity culture', is important for analysing textbooks because celebrities are used frequently throughout the four analysed textbooks as they raise learners' interest and make the books appear current.

The relationship between the four Ps is not mutually exclusive. For instance, while one item, such as Charles Dickens, might be categorised as belonging to the Products category or big C culture, it might also be categorised as belonging to the Persons category.

By cultural representations, then, I mean any mention (text or image) in the textbooks of any of the categories represented in the framework depicted in Figure 5.1 that is related to Britain, Western countries (i.e. the rest of Europe), the United States, Algeria, Arab-Islamic countries, Africa, Asia, and Latin America.

The Algerian context

Continuous reforms

The Algerian educational system has been subjected on several occasions to many reforms (Miliani, 2000), on different levels that have ranged from minor

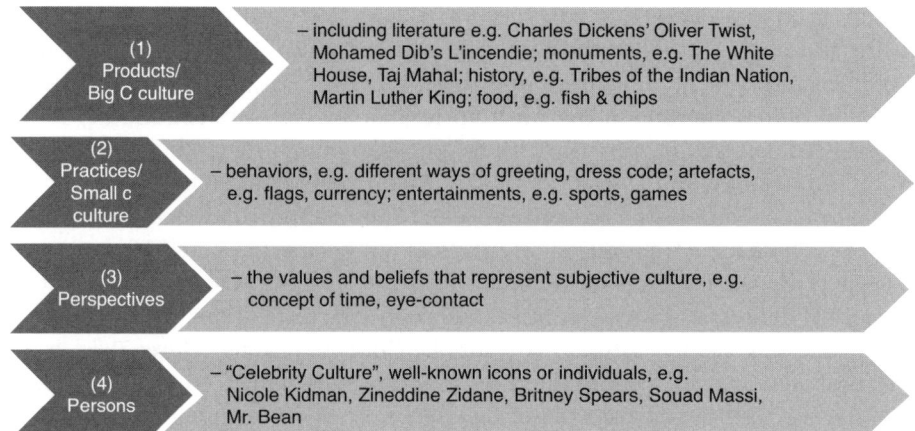

Figure 5.1   A framework for cultural representations in textbooks

to major revisions of textbooks, curricula, assessment, and teaching methods. The reforms are often motivated by political considerations.

In the 1990s Algeria experienced sociopolitical unrest due to the rise of Islamist Fundamentalism. The Black Decade, as it has been called, had serious ramifications on societal and educational realms. Education was at the heart of political changes and reforms because it was blamed for developing a certain ideology in the youth. One field that noticed many reforms was ELT. As in many developing countries, the Algerian government has made ELT a priority to keep up with regional and global advancements, to make up for the delay caused by the Black Decade, and to be active agents in globalisation (Tsui and Tollefson, 2007). This necessitates mastering English as a requisite for technological and economic advancement.

However, the preparation of English teachers has been problematic because one Ministry, the Ministry of Higher Education and Scientific Research, is responsible for educating them, and another, the Ministry of National Education, is responsible for employing them, with little connection between the two. As a result, although student teachers receive a lot of training through courses on language-based skills, educational psychology, English teaching methodology, school legislation, and so on, in practice the training they receive does not equip them to fully understand and face the classroom realities they will have to deal with. They continue to complain, as one teacher interviewed for this study put it, that they 'were not prepared enough especially to use the English textbooks that are discovered fully once facing pupils in the classroom when it is somehow too late'.

The continual reforms have also caused problems for teachers. In the early 2000s, the Ministry of National Education, which oversees primary and secondary education, started massive reforms that looked at the textbooks, curricula, teaching methods, and in-service teacher training. However, nothing has been done for pre-service teacher training because that is the responsibility of the Ministry of Higher Education and Scientific Research. This explains in part why novice English teachers are constantly confronted with the challenge of adapting to the new demands of the ELT field without being fully prepared, and their considerable reliance on the mandated textbooks, which continue to serve as a vehicle for cultural content and are the main source of information for many students in EFL contexts like Algeria.

Feedback from practising English teachers is not solicited prior to undertaking reforms and this has a negative influence on teaching and learning practices, which can clearly be seen in views about the newly designed textbooks that are often described as boring and not aesthetically appealing to students.

Cultural representations in Algerian textbooks

A two-stage study was conducted in order to understand how culture is represented in Algerian textbooks. The first stage was a content analysis of the four English textbooks used in public middle schools in Algeria. In the second stage eleven practising English teachers from eleven different schools were interviewed, including both novice and veteran teachers. The study was guided by the following questions: (1) How is culture represented in Algerian textbooks? and (2) What are teachers' perceptions of how culture is represented?

Although many EFL countries from what Kachru (1986) called Inner Circle Countries (ICC) use textbooks designed by experts for students using English as their second or foreign language (Gray, 2010), Algeria is one of those countries that has promoted the local design and production of English textbooks. The textbooks analysed in this chapter are written by Algerian experts solicited by the Ministry for students in Grades 6–9 in middle schools, aged between 12 and 15 years. Each textbook is divided into files that are the equivalent of traditional teaching units. There is a section for explicit culture teaching named *Learn about Culture* in Textbooks 1 and 2, and *Snapshots of Culture* in Textbook 3. Culture does not have an independent section in Textbook 4 because the cultural component is integrated into different aspects of the language learning components.

The study's initial focus was on the explicit teaching of culture in the *Learn about Culture* and *Snapshots of Culture* sections. However, after interviewing the teachers, I went back and added other cultural representations that were not part of these two sections because the participant teachers referred to them as part of the teaching of culture. For example, in Table 5.1 below, the last item comes from the *Listen and Speak* section. The cultural representations in Textbook 4 were analysed throughout the whole book right from the beginning.

Table 5.1   Examples of culture in the textbooks

Book	Topic	Section	Page	Type of culture	Cultural representation	Country
Year 1	File 1: Hello!	Learn about Culture	32	Big C culture Product	TV show 'What, Where quiz show'	US
				Big C culture Product	Pictures of monuments	US–2, Algeria, England–2, France, India
			34	Persons	Pictures of the British Royal Family	England–7
			34	Small c culture Artefact	Money bills	Algeria, Morocco, Japan, US, UK, Germany (Euro/Europe)
			35	Small c culture Artefact	Flags	England, Kenya, Canada, Lebanon
			38	Big C culture Product	Pictures of monuments and *Oxford English Dictionary*	UK–4
			38	Small c culture Artefact	Flag, currency, map	UK–3
			39	Small c culture Artefact	Travel brochures, leaflet	UK–2
	File 3:	Listen and Speak	71	Perspective	Valuing time (Sue's agenda), and exercising sports	UK

The cultural representations were coded according to the four Ps of: (1) Products/big C culture: including books, foods, laws, music, games, history, geography, artistic and intellectual works, and institutions such as arts, literature, drama, and dance; (2) Practices, which are the equivalent of small c culture: including patterns of interaction, behaviours, entertainment, and artefacts; (3) Perspectives: including meanings, attitudes, values, and ideas; and (4) Persons: or the 'celebrity culture' representing famous people and icons. They were also coded according to the country representing each 'P'. These were categorised into: British, US, local Algerian, Western, Arab/Islamic, Asian, Latin American, and African cultures.

For example, in Table 5.1, in the *Learn about Culture* section of the first unit (file) of Textbook 1, there were three instances of big C culture – TV show, pictures of monuments and the *Oxford English Dictionary*. There were images of, or references to, monuments from the US, Algeria, England, France and India. There was also an image of the *Oxford English Dictionary*. There was one instance of Persons – seven pictures of the British Royal Family. There were four instances of small c culture in the form of artefacts from nine different countries; the artefacts were grouped according to tasks they were associated with. There was one instance of perspectives from the UK, Sue's diary, which showed both how time and sports are valued.

Overall, culture appeared to be a solid teaching component in the textbooks for the first, second, and third years. Furthermore, as in Textbook 4, it was pervasive throughout the units, not just in the sections devoted to culture.

Cultures represented

An analysis of the cultural representations found in the textbooks shows a global cultural perspective taught as part of ELT, as shown in Table 5.2. The cultural representations not only encompassed the target culture (British and US), and the local Algerian culture, but also encompassed different cultural aspects of English-speaking and non-English-speaking countries.

Table 5.2 shows how many times a cultural representation related to a given culture appeared in each textbook. When looking across the four textbooks, the US comes first, followed by the UK and Algeria, which are almost equally represented. Although Africa, including Anglophone Africa, and the Arab-Islamic, Asian, and Latin American cultures are under-represented, this should not be taken as a criticism. The mere fact that such cultural variety is represented is in itself significant. What is worth noting though is that British culture is massively represented in Textbook 1 and later overtaken by US representations in Textbooks 2, 3, and 4. Local Algerian culture is represented in all four textbooks and is anchored to a certain extent in representations of big C, small c, and 'celebrity' cultures. Overall, although the cultural representations are dominated by Inner Circle English-speaking countries, local and regional cultures are also represented to varying degrees.

Table 5.2 Regional representations of culture in Textbooks 1–4

	UK	USA	Algeria	Arab-Islamic	Western	Africa	Asia	Latin America
Textbook 1	29	15	22	6	22	2	3	5
Textbook 2	10	18	16	1	13	3	3	1
Textbook 3	12	22	10	7	15	1	4	2
Textbook 4	17	30	17	7	6	3	10	0
Total	68	85	65	21	56	9	20	8

How culture was represented

Big C culture, depicted through different forms of products, made up the majority of cultural representations in the textbooks. These included iconic historical monuments, such as the Statue of Liberty, Big Ben, Maqam Echahid, and also travel to some of these places that reappear in different files throughout the four textbooks. Books representing great literary works, such as Charles Dickens's Oliver Twist and Mohamed Dib[1]'s *L'Incendie*, were another form of big C culture. Games and foods, such as McDonald's products, fish and chips, local (Tamina[2]) and different ethnic foods were also represented (see Figure 5.2).

Products of mass media entertainment, such as Hollywood movies and television programmes, including Harry Potter, Cat Woman, Spiderman, and 'The Battle of Algiers[3]' were another common form of representation.

Most of the time, big C cultural representations revolved around mentioning the product or picture of the product with some basic information to practise language structures. For example, a picture of Big Ben followed by a *Where is it?* section. Is Big Ben in {Leeds? Manchester? London?} Answer: It's in London. There were also many instances, such as the *Learn about Culture* section in file 1, Textbook 1, that asked students to recognise cultural artefacts with the purpose of learning cultural information.

Likewise, small c culture representations of practices included mainly artefacts such as flags, currency, travel brochures, and leaflets; religious and popular celebrations and customs, such as Eid El Fitr[4] for Muslims, Christmas, and Halloween; aspects of daily life, including conversation about pets in the US, dress codes in Algeria throughout history; and sports, such as soccer and baseball. These representations were not as inclusive as those of products and they were limited in scope – mainly Algeria, the US or UK, and very few other countries. Similar to the representations of products/big C culture, they are not treated in depth. For example, in the activity about Eid El Fitr, Christmas and Halloween, students are asked to look at pictures representing each festival and say 'What they have'. The example given is 'In Algeria, for Eid El Fitr, children have new clothes and have money'. There was no information given about Christmas or Halloween, their history or the role they play in the culture.

Representations of perspectives were more difficult to find. Coding something as a perspective was a more subjective process of deciding that the item represented a perspective or worldview. For example, as shown in Table 5.1, although Sue's timetable could be considered an artefact, it was coded as a perspective because one teacher referred to it as a representation of how time and exercising are valued in British culture in a way that are not common or valued in Algerian culture.

'Celebrity culture' representations included famous sportspersons, singers, actors, inventors, and scientists, as well as the British Royal Family. They were not limited to international celebrities; they also included locally and regionally famous people, such as Assia Djebbar, El Anka, Rouiched, and Souad

READ AND CONSIDER

▶ **Before you read**

① **Suppose you have all the ingredients in the recipe below. Ask your partner which cake among the following s/he can make.**

Tcharek

Pancakes

Doughnuts

Tamina

Example
You: We have flour, eggs, sugar ...Well, I suppose we can make *Tamina*, can't we?
Your partner: I'm afraid/sorry, we can't. We haven't got any honey.

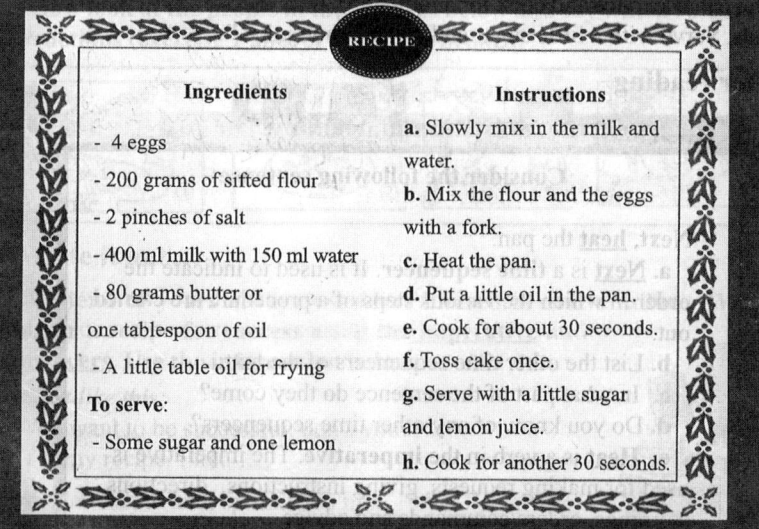

Ingredients	Instructions
- 4 eggs	a. Slowly mix in the milk and water.
- 200 grams of sifted flour	b. Mix the flour and the eggs with a fork.
- 2 pinches of salt	c. Heat the pan.
- 400 ml milk with 150 ml water	d. Put a little oil in the pan.
- 80 grams butter or one tablespoon of oil	e. Cook for about 30 seconds.
- A little table oil for frying	f. Toss cake once.
To serve:	g. Serve with a little sugar and lemon juice.
- Some sugar and one lemon	h. Cook for another 30 seconds.

② **The instructions in the recipe above are not in the right order. Re-order them to get coherent instructions. Ignore the list of ingredients.**

Numbers	1	2	3	4	5	6	7	8
Letters	b							

21

Figure 5.2   Textbook sample 1: local foods

Massi. Most celebrities were American, closely followed by Algerian, then British, and Western; African, Latin American, Asian, and Arab-Islamic celebrities were barely represented. As with other types of cultural representations, the activities around celebrities focused mainly on information. For example, one activity (Figure 5.3) provided the date/place of birth, nationality and nicknames of Souad Massi, Rowan Atkinson, and Youssou N'Dour. Students were asked to, 'Be one of these stars and introduce yourself to the class.'

As discussed earlier, there is often no clear-cut distinction between the different categories of culture. The British Royal Family, for example, can represent big C culture (history), perspectives (values) and persons. The blurring of categories can make it problematic for teachers because it is not always clear what the items are meant to represent or what should be done with them.

One important advantage of the textbooks being locally produced is the large number of representations of local culture. Yet, while Algerian culture features prominently, there is still a big emphasis on Western culture.

Teachers' perspectives on representations of culture

In the second stage of this study, 11 Algerian practising teachers of English who were using the textbooks analysed were interviewed about what they thought of them, whether the textbooks contained much culture-related information, the type of culture-related information they contained, and what the teachers thought of, and how they felt about, the culture-related information they identified. The eleven participants were eight novice English teachers with 1–2 years teaching experience and three veteran English teachers with 10–20 years of teaching experience.

The novice teachers were more willing to be critical of the textbooks and discussed the need to supplement what was in them, particularly with regard to culture. For example, one teacher, Nadia (all names are pseudonyms) described developing materials to supplement a *Learn about Culture* section about the different types of sports practised, whose layout she thought was neither attractive nor motivating. She went to an internet outlet, made a search about typical sports in the US, UK and other countries, printed the pictures and brought them to class. She used some of the pictures to emphasise the popularity of football, even in the US, where it is called soccer. She reported:

> I sometimes develop some teaching materials to use in my classroom and I share them with my colleagues who make fun of me for losing my time, energy, and money preparing extra materials instead of sticking to the textbook. It's really annoying that they would stick to the textbook blindly.

Practise

Be one of these stars and introduce yourself to the class.

Name : **Souad**
Surname : **Massi**
Date of birth : 23/08/1972
Place of birth : Bab El Oued
Nationality : Algerian
Nickname : The "Tracy
Chapman" of the Maghreb

Name : **Rowan Sebastian**
Surname : **Atkinson**
Date of birth : 24/12/1955
Place of birth : London
Nationality : English
Nickname : "Mr Bean"

Name : **Youssou**
Surname : **N'Dour**
Date of birth : 1959 (presumed)
Place of birth : Dakar
Nationality : Senegalese
Nickname : Ø

  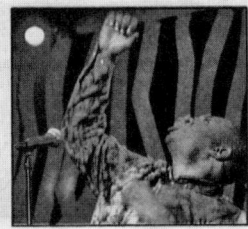

Go forward

1. Look at the photo and read the title.
   Who is the article about ?
2. Who sent the letter to the fan club ?

Fan Club

Who is Britney Spears?

Hello, I'm a fan of Britney Spears and I want to know more about her career and her projects. Thanks.

Wang, 14, London

Britney Spears
FAN CLUB

Dear Wang,

Britney Spears was born on December 2nd 1981 in Kentwood, Louisiana (USA). At the age of 8, she auditionned for "The Mickey Mouse Club" in Atlanta. She was too young for this programme, so a producer gave her an introduction to a New York agent. She joined the "Dance off-Broadway Centre" and she spent three summers at the "Professional Performing Arts School" to learn dancing and comedy. She acted in many films as a child actor. At the age of 11, she returned to the "Mickey Club" and stayed there for two years. At the beginning of 1998, she completed her first single and an album of the same title "Baby One More Time". In autumn 1998, she toured the USA to promote her songs. In 1999, "Baby One More Time" was first in the "Top Ten". It was also a hit in the UK and Europe. In January 2000 "Born to Make You Happy" topped the UK charts.

3. Look these words up in a dictionary and write their definitions in your exercise-book :
   to audition / an introduction / to join / to tour / to promote / a hit
4. Now, translate them into a language you know (Arabic, Tamazight, French).

13

Figure 5.3 Textbook sample 2: locally and regionally famous people

Nadia, like the other novice teachers, questioned much of the quality of the cultural representations in the textbooks. For her, they did not serve a clear teaching purpose. The students were not always enthusiastic during the culture teaching section because, according to some of the teachers, it was not clear to students how such cultural information could inform their language use. One of the participants, for example, reported that when she first taught her students about holidays, they argued that they were learning the English language and should not be learning about Christmas because it is a Christian holiday. The next time she taught that section, she provided some background information on how different religions have different holidays and why it is important to know about these holidays.

With respect to the sources of culture represented, most of the teachers reported their satisfaction with the inclusion of Algeria in the teaching of culture. They posited that this will enable students to talk about their culture using English and this may, in turn, promote intercultural communication in the long run. However, one teacher was very critical as to the selected Algerian cultural representations. For her, these were included only when they converged with Western culture and they were not authentic nor faithful to the local culture. For instance, her argument was that Souad Massi, an Algerian singer who has been called the Algerian Tracy Chapman, is not representative of Algerian female singers (see Figure 5.3). For her, Souad Massi made it into the English textbook because she converges with Western cultural norms.

In summary, cultural knowledge is omnipresent in the Algerian textbooks, while cultural awareness and how it informs language use and communication is missing. The representations of culture did not show how language structures (both spoken and written) are culturally bound or how to use the language in a culturally appropriate manner. They did not raise students' awareness and understanding of the existence of different worldviews or frames of reference. There was no provision for any intercultural communication teaching or even activities to raise students' awareness of the role culture plays in communication when one uses an additional language. Teachers had trouble teaching about culture because they were unable to see its usefulness for communication. The burden of linking language to culture fell on the teachers, some of whom were prepared to do so and some of whom were not.

Implications

The analysis of cultural representations in Algerian textbooks and the teachers' perspectives suggest that culture is an important component of language learning materials, but it is also highly problematic. The following points should be borne in mind when responding to the challenges this represents:

- In order to be effective, cultural representations and the tasks associated with them need to serve clearly defined learning objectives to determine what is culturally valued, appropriate, and expected. For example, when and how to pay and respond to a compliment is culture specific. If compliments are included in the textbook, they should serve the objective of learning about a cultural aspect (complimenting) and how it is linguistically realised (developing linguistic competence) in the target culture. This can be achieved by using activities in which students are invited to formulate and respond to compliments, and discuss whether a given compliment can be realised in their own culture, and if so, how. By doing so, students will learn how complimenting is culturally determined, how to use compliments appropriately, and what is expected from them according to the norms of the target culture.
- Materials should judiciously incorporate different aspects of the students' local culture in order to help them communicate about their own culture as well. This will enable them to use their local cultural perspectives to think about, critique, and appreciate the target culture in different ways.
- Cultural representations should highlight the changing and dynamic aspect of culture, and include different representations of sub-cultures in order not to be essentialist or foster stereotypes. For example, if a unit deals with family, it could depict current representations of American or British families (target culture) along with an Algerian family. This could be followed by activities in which students can learn linguistic elements, such as the comparative and adjectives, but could also include another activity inviting students to discuss family representations from different sub-cultures or social classes in the target culture so as to avoid essentialist representations. Similarly, if a family representation across time is used, it will depict the inherent dynamic and changing aspect of culture. A discussion of representations from both the target and local cultures would enable students to use their cultural perspective to discuss, compare, and make sense of them.
- No matter what cultural representations are used in textbooks, their effectiveness depends on how they are taught. Teachers should be cognizant of the overall aims of teaching culture and help develop students' cross-cultural competence, which in turn can contribute to developing cultural awareness and respect for cultural diversity. The case of the Algerian teacher who met resistance from her students for just mentioning Christmas is a good example. If that same teacher had been prepared to relate religious and popular celebrations to learning about what is culturally valued in the local and target cultures, the inclusion of Christmas in the textbook would have made more sense to her students.

- Teachers should also be aware of the cultural representations in the textbook they use. These may be explicit, such as products, practices, and persons, or implicit, such as perspectives. They should be careful not to offend students, impose meanings and, by extension, a whole frame of reference on their students. Teachers should allow for the interaction between teachers, students, and cultural representations in the text to be a process that may result in different interpretations.
- For teachers to be able to use materials to teach culture effectively, they need good teacher preparation programmes to ready them for the language classroom. Such preparation should be aimed at helping them define students' needs, set objectives for culture teaching and to know what content will help attain those objectives. With clear objectives it will be easier for them to adapt cultural representations in the textbooks, or to choose or develop substitute materials to teach culture.

When using textbooks to teach culture it is also important to:

1. Understand the purpose of teaching culture in the language classroom by clearly defining the learning objectives to be achieved.
2. Incorporate different aspects of the learners' local culture to help them better conceive of the aspects of the target culture being taught about.
3. Highlight the dynamic nature of language and culture and how they influence each other.
4. Understand the key role teachers play in the teaching of culture that should work towards developing cross-cultural competence, cultural awareness, and respect for cultural diversity.
5. Expose a new frame of reference to the learners, but not necessarily impose it.

Engagement priorities

1. A number of frameworks have been proposed to analyse culture in textbooks. Take a textbook you use or are familiar with and analyse it in terms of which local, source, and international cultures are represented. Then analyse it in terms of the four Ps: products, practices, perspectives and persons. Which predominate? Why do you think this is so? What do you learn about your textbook from this activity?
2. Choose three different representations of culture in a textbook. What purpose do the representations serve? Do they promote cultural awareness? Do they point out sociolinguistic features of the language? Are they used as information about the culture, or as a basis for a grammar point?

3. What role do you think culture should play in language teaching? If you were to prepare a course on teaching culture, what would you include in it?

Notes

1. Renowned Algerian author who wrote in French advocating for Algeria's fight for independence.
2. Tamina: a traditional Algerian dessert prepared when babies are born and to celebrate Prophet Mahomet's (PBUH) birthday.
3. A historic movie on Algeria's War for Independence.
4. A Muslim festivity marking the end of the Islamic holy month of fasting called Ramadan, celebrated by a prayer, breaking the fast, and visiting relatives among other things.

References

Alpetkin, C. (2002). Towards intercultural communicative competence in ELT. *ELT Journal,* 56(1): 57–64.

Bousquet, G., and Pessin, A. (2003). Culture and identity in postwar France. In Hewitt, N. (ed.), *The Cambridge Companion to Modern French Culture*. Cambridge: Cambridge University Press, pp. 41–60.

Cortazzi, M. (2000). Languages, cultures, and cultures of learning in the global classroom. In Kam, H. W. and Ward, C. (eds), *Language in the Global Context: Implications for the Language Classroom*. SEAMEO Regional Language Centre.

Cortazzi, M. and Jin, L. (1999). Cultural mirrors: materials and methods in the EFL classroom. In Hinkel, E. (ed.), *Culture in Second Language Teaching and Learning*. Cambridge: Cambridge University Press, pp. 196–219.

Friedman, L. (1999). *The Horizontal Society.* New Haven: Yale University Press.

Gray, J. (2000). The ELT coursebook as cultural artefact: how teachers censor and adapt. *ELT Journal,* 54(3): 174–183.

Gray, J. (2010). *The Construction of English: Culture, Consumerism and Promotion in the ELT Coursebook*. Basingstoke: Palgrave Macmillan.

Gray, J. (2012). The marketisation of language teacher education and neoliberalism: characteristics. In Block, D., Gray, J. and Holborow, M. (eds), *Neoliberalism and Applied Linguistics*. New York: Routledge, pp. 85–102.

Kachru, B. (1986). *The Other Tongue: English across Cultures*. Oxford: Pergamon.

Kramsch, C. (1993). *Context and Culture in Language Teaching*. Oxford: Oxford University Press.

Kramsch, C. (1996). The Cultural Component of Language Teaching. *Zeitschrift für Interkulturellen Fremdsprachenunterricht* [Online], 1(2): 1–13. Available at http://www.spz.tu-darmstadt.de/projekt_Ejournal/jg_01_2/beitrag/kramsch2.htm [Accessed 01/10/2012.]

Miliani, M. (2000). Teaching English in a multilingual context: the Algerian case. *Mediterranean Journal of Educational Studies,* 6(1): 13–29.

Moran, P. (2001). *Teaching Culture: Perspectives in Practice*. Boston, MA: Heinle & Heinle.

Riazi, A. M. (2003). What do textbook evaluation schemes tell us? a study of the textbook evaluation schemes of three decades. In Renandya, W. A. (ed.), *Methodology and Materials Design in Language Teaching*. Singapore: SEAMEO Regional Centre, pp. 52–68.

Tsui, A. B. M. and Tollefson, J. W. (2007). Language policy and the construction of national cultural identity. In Tsui, A. and Tollefson, J. (eds), *Language Policy, Culture, and Identity in Asian Contexts*. Mahwah, NJ: Lawrence Erlbaum, pp. 1–21.

Watson, J. (2010). Culture and the future of French studies. *Contemporary French and Francophone Studies,* 14(5): 477–484.

Yuen, K-M. (2011). The representation of foreign cultures in English textbooks. *ELT Journal*, 65(4): 458–466.

Part II
Materials in the Classroom

6

Coping with New Teaching Approaches and Materials: An East-European EFL Teacher's Interpretation of Communicative Teaching Activities

Kristjan Seferaj

Overview

Reforms in language teaching, implemented in many countries around the world, have focused on introducing Communicative Language Teaching (CLT) and various attempts have been made to change the traditional way non-native (NNS) English as a Foreign Language (EFL) teachers teach. As a result, educators in several countries are officially required to use communicative textbooks in their classes and to incorporate student-centred approaches in their teaching, even though many of them do not have adequate knowledge and expertise of CLT (Savignon 2010).

At present, little evidence is available on how experienced teachers use textbooks and teachers' books, and even less is known about the connections between teacher cognition, teaching resources, and classroom practices when textbook instructions concerning operations in the classroom do not match teachers' views about how languages are learnt/taught. Unfortunately, this is the case for thousands of EFL teachers in many countries that are seeking to improve and westernise their educational systems.

This chapter will focus on the difficulties faced by EFL teachers in using CLT teaching resources and the effect of communicative materials on teacher behaviours. These issues will be addressed and illustrated through the analysis of how one Albanian state schoolteacher interprets communicative activities in her context. In addition, a number of practical implications for educational authorities and EFL teachers who find themselves in a similar situation will be suggested.

The Albanian context

During the communist period (1945–1990), education systems in all East European communist countries mirrored the Soviet educational model (Webber and Liikanen, 2001, mentioned in Dyrmishi, 2005: 38). From the early 1990s, when these countries abandoned communism in favour of capitalism, the new East European governments have been implementing reforms to purge schools and textbooks of the Soviet influence and to westernise the education system.

In Albania, among other reforms, attempts are being made to develop new national curricula and change the philosophical orientation of teachers and students. The reforms have been carefully planned with the involvement of foreign experts. However, the Albanian Ministry of Education (MASH) is now being faced with the need to work with the public to gain acceptance of these reforms. Among several financial, organisational, and opposition challenges the authorities admit that 'the change of philosophical orientation is a particular problem, notably with some teachers' (Qano, 2005: 24).

L2 learning in Albania

Nowadays, English is the dominant foreign language learnt in state schools and private tuition classes, although Italian, French, and German can also be studied as L2. Albanian pupils start learning a foreign language at Grade III, when they are eight years old, and attend three forty-five minute classes weekly until the end of compulsory schooling (at 15-years old). Students who continue their education study two foreign languages and attend four L2 classes every week, two of which are in English, in both high school and university courses. Thus, most Albanian students take two to three EFL classes weekly for a 10–12 year period under the current national education system.

Since communism was overthrown in 1992, Albanian governments have continuously emphasised the importance of English as the lingua franca. Indeed, the Anglophone Albania policy that seeks to motivate students to be conversant in English was launched in 2008 (see www.mash.gov/anglophonealbania.al for more details). In 2012, the government re-emphasised the importance of the English language by officially requiring MA/PhD candidates to present proof of English language proficiency before degrees could be issued by Albanian post-secondary education institutions (decree 14/2012). MASH has recently proposed adding a foreign language to the two obligatory Albanian exams (language/literature and mathematics) that complete secondary education in Albania and authorities are currently holding public meetings to discuss the proposal.

L2 teaching in the country

In the way other subjects were taught in Eastern European countries during the communist period, Albanian teachers of foreign languages adopted a teacher-centred approach in their everyday teaching practice, relying heavily on rote learning (Dyrmishi, 2005). Because the traditional approach considers language learning 'as little more than memorising rules and facts in order to understand and manipulate the morphology and syntax of the foreign language' (Richards and Rodgers, 2001: 5), EFL classes during the years 1945–1992 mainly focused on grammar, and the only L2 speaking activity that took place in the class was translation drills from L1 to L2 or vice versa (Dyrmishi, 2005: 42).

The majority of today's Albanian teachers are likely to have formulated their very first ideas about English and ELT when they were L2 students. The above-mentioned rote learning image of L2 teaching and learning will have been further consolidated during their university studies. Indeed, the BA in ELT and Translation offered at four Albanian state universities during the communist era included several modules that took an in-depth deductive look at different components of both Albanian and English language and literature (Dyrmishi, 2005). The seminars were conceptualised as the transmission of knowledge from the lecturer to the students and classes were mainly conducted in Albanian.

Recently, Albanian democratic governments have recognised the importance of learning and using English as an international language and have taken many initiatives to encourage EFL teachers to change the way they teach, such as the review of syllabi and textbooks to accommodate new teaching ideologies, piloting new learner-centred approaches throughout the country, and the decision taken in 2008 (decree 186) to compensate maths and L2 teachers at a higher level than teachers of other subjects. Additionally, several agreements have been signed by MASH and its international partners to provide professional development opportunities for Albanian EFL teachers. For example, British Council Albania trained a number of local EFL teachers to act as teacher development coordinators through a National Team of Trainers Programme (for more details see http://www.britishcouncil.org/it/albania-newsletter-march-2008.htm).

Reforms and CLT

Underlying the above-mentioned institutional initiatives, there is the perception that the post-communist system of education is neither efficient nor appropriate for the new democratic epoch. Richards and Rodgers (2001) mention a number of scholars who have criticised the traditional method of teaching, the authoritative role of the teachers, and the formal class interactions typically used during the communist period. They have recommended the use of Western teaching approaches in L2 classes, arguing for a shift of emphasis to communication aims.

The much referred to communicative teaching method of CLT is an approach to second language teaching that first appeared in Europe in the late 1970s as a reaction to traditional teaching methodologies. This approach emphasises the use of communicative activities in L2 teaching, often attempting an imitation of real-life situations in L2 classes. In addition, CLT classrooms may involve cooperative learning activities such as group or pair work (Savignon, 2010).

East European EFL practitioners might find it difficult to implement this approach in their classes for a variety of reasons. To begin with, as Nunan (1992, in Husbands et al., 2003) notes, it can be challenging to use CLT in big classes – in Albania there are sometimes more than 40 students in a class. The lack of proficiency in English of NNS EFL teachers can also be a barrier (Harmer, 2007). Additionally, there is an uncertainty as to what the specific features of CLT are because communicative language teaching continues to adopt any technique that aims to improve the learners' ability to communicate in English (ibid., 2007: 70). Therefore, many EFL teachers who are new to CLT can find it difficult to make an informed choice about what and how to teach communicatively in their classes. To make things easier, Wesche and Skehan (2002: 208) identify the following as the main qualities of communicative classrooms:

1. Activities that require frequent interaction among learners or with other interlocutors to exchange information and solve problems.
2. Use of authentic (non-pedagogic) texts and communication activities linked to real world contexts, often emphasising links across written and spoken modes and channels.
3. Approaches that are learner-centred in that they take into account learners' backgrounds, language needs and goals, and generally allow learners some creativity and role in instructional decisions.

These characteristics at the heart of CLT methodology are essentially Western concepts that represent a particular ideology, very often different to that of many EFL teachers around the world. Indeed, collective learning is a very common pattern in the ESL classes in the US (Donato, 1994, in Savignon, 2010) and other developed English-speaking countries. In contrast, the traditional teacher-fronted pattern of classroom interaction still seems to be dominant in many EFL classes worldwide (Fishman and Garcia, 2011). Likewise, the real world context in many ELT materials is representative of the Western social, cultural, political, and historical environment in which English is used as L1 for everyday communication. Unfortunately, a great number of non-native EFL teachers who have studied English as L2 through books possess little knowledge of this context and, thus, are not in the position to link communicative activities to the real world context. Lastly, as Harmer (2007) points out, learner-centred approaches often do not meet the learning expectation of non-Western students and teachers who are used to teacher-centred learning/teaching practices.

This is the case for many Albanian EFL students and teachers. The former seem to have developed their cultural and educational background from the influence of their early rote learning experiences, their parents' expectations, and the perception of uncertainty that comes from the ongoing efforts of Albanian authorities to overhaul the communist era's pedagogical philosophy (Dyrmishi, 2005). The latter, who have neither studied CLT theory during their university programme, nor attended any CLT teacher training practice courses, are likely to have their L2 teaching/learning beliefs rooted in the transmission model of learning they were exposed to as learners.

To try to minimise the impact on their practice of teachers' knowledge and beliefs resulting from their L2 learning, Albanian authorities introduced a number of top-down policy directives. These include a communicative syllabus introduced in 2006, and the requirement to develop a new student-centred, daily lesson plan with details of students' learning goals, minimal and maximal learning objectives, lesson procedures, lesson descriptions, and means of evaluation. In addition, Albanian EFL teachers are officially required to use coursebooks and other teaching materials in their classes that provide learners with some communicative functional input. By so doing, it is hoped that 'the more an ESL teacher uses communicative resources in the class, the more communicative his/her approach becomes' (Qano, 2005: 24).

Given the great emphasis placed on textbooks in the Albanian context, the following section provides an overview of communicative materials and relates the discussion to a specific textbook used by the teacher whose practices are reported on in this chapter.

CLT and communicative teaching resources/textbooks

Richards (2006) claims that the textbook can play a significant part in the professional lives of EFL instructors. However, the extent to which communicative teaching materials can foster communicative learning and teaching is dependent not only on the extent to which a textbook embodies communicative characteristics, but also on other factors discussed above. Clarke (1989) discusses the features of the first generation of CLT materials 'that are still relevant to language teaching today' (Richards, 2006: 14), and claims that the majority of commercial EFL/ESL textbooks have been careful to reflect on:

- text authenticity – as opposed to artificially constructed texts. It is believed that the use of authentic teaching materials exposes students to real world knowledge and, thus, provides cultural information about the target language and prepares learners to participate in real world language events by developing strategies for dealing with its complexity.
- realism – Richards (2006: 14) notes that real communication occurs 'when a speaker engages in meaningful interaction to get information he/she doesn't possess, produces language that might not be predictable, seeks to link language to context and maintains comprehensible and ongoing communication'. Mirroring these features, the majority of commercial textbooks

contain real world language activities that put learners in a position where they have to use their linguistic and communicative resources in order to obtain purposeful information.

- context – establishing a coherent context in materials means 'a learner uses the information obtained from one activity in order to perform another and this relationship between tasks simulates the kind of "accountability" required of the real world language user' (Johnson and Johnson, 1981, in Clarke, 1989: 77). Attempts to integrate activities or to create activity sequences in published textbooks reflect this principle.
- a focus on the learner – as in a learner's response to teaching materials irrespective of their intrinsic nature. Most commercial textbooks contain visual clues, colourful pictures, authentic texts, interesting topics, and a wide selection of materials to enable learners' appropriate responses to materials.

In Albania, since 2006, EFL teachers have been given freedom to choose from a list of different coursebooks approved by the authorities. The majority of these textbooks are published by British publishers and virtually all of them claim to be communicative in their aims. Nonetheless, the degree to which CLT principles are translated into actual teaching materials seems not to be the main selection criteria in Albania. Instead, as the participating teacher in this project, Miss Landa, points out, 'the not so favourable economic situation of many Albanian families has led to heightened sensitivity to cost as criteria in textbook selection'. As a result, the cheapest textbooks are the most widely used around the country.

Coping with CLT and communicative materials: classroom practices

In order to better understand how EFL teachers respond to the changes and challenges outlined above, a case study of a teacher's delivery practices was carried out. The participating teacher, Miss Landa, was awarded a BA in ELT and Translation from the University of Tirana in 1985 and has been teaching English to secondary school students since then. She has also worked as a free-lance teacher, offering afternoon classes in her own house, for more than eight years. She teaches English to Grade IX students (aged 14). There are thirty-six students in her class and, like in any other Albanian EFL class, there are some intermediate students who have attended private English courses for years and other low-level students who need to improve all four skills.

Qualitative and quantitative methods were employed to explore and understand how communicatively the participant used communicative teaching materials. Firstly, the way the teacher used the textbook was documented by observing her teaching four EFL classes in her normal classes. Secondly, a questionnaire, informal interviews and discussions with the teacher, and lesson plans were also used to explore the factors that informed the teaching behaviours of the participant and to determine how particular teaching behaviours related to the teaching guidelines provided by the textbook/teacher's book. To achieve this, the researcher recorded four EFL classes and walked the teacher through the lesson by stopping the video at important events and asking the participant why she behaved in that way.

Miss Landa's textbook

Miss Landa has used several English coursebooks, such as *English for You*, *Headway* and *Opportunities* during her teaching career. Since 2010 she has been using the *Access* coursebook series, a four level, multilayer course prepared by Evans and O'Sullivan (2000) and published by Express Publishing Ltd. *Access 3* contains eleven modules, each divided into six main components: Grammar, Vocabulary, Reading and Listening, Speaking and Functions, Writing, Culture/Curricular. There are five units in every module, each unit focuses on a particular theme and all the texts and activities within a unit are related to that theme.

The Reading and Listening section follows a topic-based approach and covers topics which seem to appeal to teenagers, such as celebrities, vampires, cool sports, travel, and so on. The textbook includes some authentic texts (including news reports, teen magazine articles, emails and internet blogs) in addition to a number of doctored passages. Likewise, an attempt is made to represent speech with all its accents at a nearly normal speaking rate, but the scripted recordings lack some key features of everyday speech, such as repetition, hesitation, and unplanned interruptions. Listening and Reading passages are often followed either by traditional comprehension checking questions, such as True/False statements, Wh questions, and fill in the blank sentences, or by more communicative exercises, like the one shown below:

> Exercise 2: Read the text again. In which of
> these places can you see the following?
> Tell your partner.
>
> **bluebells   field mice   golden eagles**
>   **swans   puffins   deer   geese**

Figure 6.1   Speaking exercise illustration
Source: From *Access 3* Student-book, p. 85.

The coursebook features a strong morphological emphasis (as in, determiners, prepositions, singular/plural markings, and so on), it proceeds from apparently simple structures to more complicated ones, and presents new grammatical structures or rules inductively to the students in a real language context.

The Speaking and Functions section adheres to a situational syllabus, as there are a number of tasks that link the development of language skills with the context in which to use the language by inviting learners to imagine something that inspires them for creative writing/speaking. *Access 3* targets a wide range of communicative tasks designed with 'the information gap' as the central principle and emphasises pair/group work. The syllabus also devotes some time to the development of writing skills (for instance, paragraphing, writing a thesis statement with supporting sentences and linkers) through the use of several portfolio tasks, as exemplified below:

Writing (a letter of invitation)
7 Portfolio: Use your dialogue from Ex.6 to write a letter to invite your friend who lives in another city to your party.
Follow the plan below (50 –80 words)

Dear ...,

Part 1   opening remarks, reason for writing
Part 2   details about the party (food, theme, clothes etc.)
Part 3   closing remarks

Best wishes,

Figure 6.2   Writing exercise illustration
Source: From *Access 3* Student-book, p. 94.

Insights into how communicatively the teacher used the communicative teaching materials

Initially, an observation scheme was used to obtain an overview of classroom patterns in three main quantifiable categories: Activity, Content, and Class Dynamic. For all the activities, the principal focus was marked, for example, a listen for pleasure song was classified as a listening in isolation activity. Where there was more than one equal focus, the activity was coded Combinations. To exemplify the point, a listen and fill in the gap exercise was classified as Combinations since it targets listening and writing skills. The start and finish times of activities were rounded to the nearest minute.

The observations indicate that Miss Landa's classes are mainly organised around whole class activities and her students are primarily engaged in teacher-led textbook activities. Miss Landa engaged her students in individual work for almost one third of the total class time.

A considerable amount of class time was also spent in activities that pushed the students to process language more deeply, such as speaking and writing in isolation. Oral activities coded as speaking in isolation involved reading aloud and oral grammar/pronunciation drills, and written activities coded as writing in isolation involved written grammar gap filling/drills. Teacher's explanations of grammar rules, correction of grammar/pronunciation errors, and pronunciation drills, coded in the categories System and Pronunciation respectively, accounted for 10 per cent of the total class time. Activities like greeting students, giving instructions, keeping records of class attendance and discipline related issues (coded in the category Other) occupied 11 per cent of the class content. Lastly, students spent about one-third of their class time (33 per cent) in activities that integrated and developed real-life receptive and productive skills.

A primary focus on form comprised 39 per cent of the content of the observed classes. Likewise, the students spent a quarter of their class time engaged in meaning-based activities (like listening/reading comprehension activities). Participation in activities that foster genuine language use occupied 13 per cent of class time and, in most cases, students' participation depended on Miss Landa's management of classroom communication. Indeed, the majority of oral interactions in the observed classes developed through a teacher question/student answer type of exchange, following the typical IRF (Initiation, Response, Follow-up) pattern of classroom discourse (Sinclair and Coulthard, 1975, in Fishman and Garcia, 2011). Integration with equal emphasis on meaning/use, form/use, and form/meaning comprised 23 per cent of the content in the observed classes.

Miss Landa engaged in a number of teaching practices that can be associated with communicative uses of teaching materials. She consistently used pre-listening and reading activities to prepare students for what they were going to listen to or read about. In addition, she taught receptive and productive skills in combination with each other, explicitly asked students to pay attention to the content of the text, and engaged her students in comprehension-based exercises. In one of her classes, the teacher also asked students to listen to the tape and read the transcript at the same time, 'to develop a sense of English rhythm, intonation and stress because they are not very exposed to native (L2) speaking', as she put it. Moreover, Miss Landa used L2 as the primary means of communication and asked students to communicate authentic information in English.

Insights into how the teacher interpreted communicative teaching activities

When asked about her approach, Miss Landa replied that she uses mainly English in her classes because she rarely speaks English outside and she does not want 'to lose it'. 'On top of it, it's good for them (students)', she added.

As regards the importance of activating student knowledge, Miss Landa believes that 'much depends on the difficulty of the text; students understand the reading/listening when its content and form are familiar to them and guessing does not necessary help them'. In her view, pre-reading exercises can be a hindrance, particularly for low-level students who read at the limits of their linguistic abilities and their comprehension of the text is likely to be influenced by other students' guessing. She used the example of the class just observed to illustrate her point[1]:

> As you saw this morning, Gladjol [one of the students] was misdirected by his friend's wrong guess, who thought that the woman in the picture, you know, because she was wearing a suit and carrying a briefcase, she looked more like a banker. I did not correct the student's guess because I did not want to give them the right answer. However, Gladjol's comprehension was pretty much influenced by this answer, because he circled banker as the right answer in the listening comprehension exercise.

In spite of her belief regarding the importance of pre-reading/listening activities, Miss Landa still made sure students completed the warm-up exercises because, in her view, it is important to stick to the textbook:

> It shows students that they have to take learning seriously; they cannot neglect any part of the material. You know, I have realised that when you [the teacher] skip an exercise or any other part of the book, students will do the same and they will particularly skip homework exercises.

Likewise, Miss Landa followed the textbook steps for teaching language as a whole, although she is not sure whether L2 students can 'get' the L2 by just integrating language skills and focusing on L2 speaking. She personally believes that if students do not work on discrete language items they will either 'not say the right word or not use the right form in a certain situation'. That's why she often supplements the textbook with extra materials. Indeed, in one of her classes, she explained the grammar item by writing extra rules on how to use possessive pronouns on the blackboard and, in another class, she revised the grammar by asking each student to read a sentence completion exercise and explain why he/she used the simple present or present continuous in that sentence. The teacher used a similar traditional approach to do two free speaking activities ('Use the prompts to make true sentences about yourself' and 'While you were abroad on holidays, you witnessed a car accident. Tell your friend: Where and when the accident took place, who was involved, and so on'). Instead of getting students to pair with the person beside them, the teacher asked them to write down their answers. She explained her decision:

> they do need some prep time. Most of them have neither been abroad nor witnessed any accident. That's why, if I don't give them some time to think about what to say and what form to use, for sure they will repeat the same scenario they read in the reading passage.

No supplementary vocabulary exercises were used in the classes observed and, when asked, the teacher said that 'the textbook does a good vocabulary presentation/revision job, so there is no need for any extra exercise'. However, she pointed out that 'from time to time I recycle vocabulary items by asking students to form a sentence with previously seen words'.

Miss Landa did not follow textbook directions when it came to teaching/ practising speaking. Indeed, instead of engaging students in pair/group work fluency speaking activities, she focused on students' accuracy through controlled teacher/student exchanges. The rationale behind this adaptation of the textbook activity is that:

> classroom learning should be provided by the one who has the knowledge and understanding of the subject. Obviously, students come to school, and parents send their offspring to school, to be instructed by someone who has the skills and ability to teach, not by a pair who lack an understanding of English. For sure, a teacher cannot monitor thirty students speaking simultaneously. Then, if I pair up Eva (an upper intermediate student) and Adi (a beginner student) for example, OK, Eva is able to correct some of Adi's mistakes, but who will monitor Eva's speaking?

This strong position clearly reflects Miss Landa's teaching belief that 'it is very important for students to participate in whole class, teacher-directed instruction' (Item No. 8 – Questionnaire). On the subject of pair work, she added the following in one of our informal discussions:

> We [teachers of English] keep hearing 'pair work, pair work'. However, any experienced teacher knows that this idea, along with other initiatives that successive governments have tried to foist on secondary schools, simply does not work. Indeed, our students do not come here [the school] to study only English. They study mathematics, geography, history, Albanian language, and so on – they never do any pair work or things like that in other geography/mathematics classes. Are they expected to be taught by each other just in one subject, English? That's unrealistic and I am not surprised, because these ideas originate from either politicians or educational theorists who are largely ignorant of classroom practice.

Miss Landa also feels that she would like to do more drills and additional grammar and translation exercises because:

> At the end of their study, students take a national exam which is designed to assess their knowledge of grammar. So, teaching and practising grammar is a must do thing.

However, environmental factors also seem to affect what Miss Landa does in her classes. Indeed, she feels that the whole issue of not teaching enough grammar is a 'matter of time and money' and elaborates as follows:

> It is mainly lack of time and resources. Lack of time because the textbook provides so many activities and I simply do not have much time to do other activities. And it is a lack of resources because writing grammar exercises on the blackboard is very time consuming and handing out photocopies to students is out of the question because I would have to use my own money to photocopy handouts as there is no photocopier on the school premises.

Overall, it can be concluded that Miss Landa, dictated to by the textbook in her choice of activities, exhibited a number of CLT features in her teaching, such as using non-pedagogic texts and real world tasks, focusing more on meaning than on system, activating her learners' schemata before listening/reading activities, and relating different exercises and tasks with each other with a emphasis on the links across different modes and channels. However, she carried out a number of adaptations to make her students consciously learn/ reinforce items of language in isolation and implemented most activities in a traditional, teacher-led way.

Implications

As Miss Landa integrated some communicative teaching behaviours into her teaching, it can be argued that the use of communicative resources can contribute to the development of a communicative approach to the teaching of foreign languages. This is in line with previous findings (Hutchinson and Torres, 1994) that have suggested that contemporary textbooks can be seen as agents of change, in that they provide classroom materials, as well as 'a level of structure that appears to be necessary for teachers to fully understand and routinize changes' (Hutchinson and Torres, 1994: 323).

Yet, Miss Landa's experience suggests that it is certainly not enough to just give a teacher a textbook to change his/her behaviour. Indeed, the participant did not always stick to the methodological procedures clearly described in the textbooks, as in the case of replacing pair/group interaction with teacher/ student(s) interaction, or changing the focus of some activities from fluency to accuracy. Borg (2011) suggests that certain types of communicative teaching behaviours can only be acquired if teachers' cognitions are acknowledged and discussed, not merely challenged. Borg (2011) notes that many teachers find it difficult to put their thoughts into words because they have never been asked to articulate their beliefs in a direct way. Therefore, using indirect strategies, such as using a lesson plan as the basis for exploring a teacher's beliefs, can help teachers to acknowledge the difference between what they actually do in their classes (contextualised concepts) and what they believe they do in their classes (abstract concepts).

However, the crucial question here is not how to motivate EFL teachers to acquire certain communicative behaviours, but rather how to motivate EFL teachers in countries such as Albania to use CLT in an appropriate way, in accordance with the context they work in. Miss Landa gives very good reasons why she does not use CLT in all its forms. For example, she questions the effectiveness of teaching mainly speaking in her classes because:

> The English Matura Exam [the national exam that students take when they finish the high school] is designed to assess students' knowledge of grammar and reading and does not involve any speaking section.

Urging her to incorporate into her teaching pair/group interactions and other communicative behaviours that do not necessarily fit with the local context would mean treating teachers as implementing agents who should strictly apply a set of theoretical principles in their classes. Hence, we need to ask what changes are really desirable. Is it teacher training by foreign specialists in developing countries that is really desirable?

It is certainly the responsibility of local educational experts to develop educational reforms that best suit the teaching/learning reality in a country. Allowing EFL teachers to have their own say in educational reform-related decision-making processes might give authorities a clearer view as to why they want EFL teachers to use a communicative approach, and how possible this aim is within the teaching/learning context of the country. In addition, local experts have to take a more active role in developing teacher training policies. Currently, teacher training services in many developing countries is inevitably provided by foreign specialists. However, Holliday (1994, in Harmer, 2007) notes that BANA (Britain, Australasia, North America) specialists and materials might not take into account local teaching realities and, thus, their efficacy is questionable. It is for this reason that local experts, who fully understand the linguistic, educational, and cultural needs of local EFL teachers, should be in charge of preparing teacher training materials and delivering teacher training courses for local EFL teachers.

An alternative response to the issue of desirable changes would be to motivate EFL practitioners to develop locally appropriate communicative pedagogies rather than impose models of communicative teaching. Husbands et al. (2003) argue that the teachers' awareness of their students' needs and the influence that a teacher's colleagues can have on his/her own teaching are two potential external factors that might considerably impact the teaching approach of EFL teachers. It follows that authorities should encourage: on-site discussions;

exchanges among colleagues about effective teaching experiences; and teacher observation practices where teachers feel free to express their own points of view, discuss their beliefs, and accept, reject, and discuss new ideas. Previous research (Wiścicka, 2006) in this area suggests that an on-site supportive atmosphere can contribute considerably to the professional development of novice teachers. In addition, devising a scheme to evaluate the teaching approach of EFL teachers through communicative tests periodically given to students might motivate EFL practitioners to accommodate more teaching of communicative behaviors in their delivery. Indeed, because EFL teachers would like their students to do well in national exams, they would be willing to incorporate more communicative activities in their teaching.

Engagement priorities

While a considerable number of developing countries are spending large sums of money to mirror Western-style educational systems, stakeholders involved in this process should ask a number of hard questions, among others:

1. Is it right to ask experienced EFL teachers in developing countries to follow a CLT model that doesn't necessarily fit their teaching context, or should authorities emphasise the central role of the teacher to learning, as many post-method pedagogy experts recommend?
2. The post-method pedagogy (see Kumaravadivelu, 2003) encourages EFL practitioners to develop their own teaching methods based on their learning/ teaching experiences, their pedagogic knowledge, their own beliefs, and their students' needs. This might be the case in many Western countries where ESL/L2 teachers' beliefs and previous learning experiences are rooted in communicative learning approaches. However, EFL teachers in many developing countries possess a limited knowledge of CLT practices. Hence the question: is it possible for inexperienced EFL practitioners to develop their own communicative teaching styles based on their own GT learning/ teaching experiences?
3. Sticking with the content and methodological procedures clearly described in a textbook might help teachers to approach their teaching more communicatively. Is there anything else EFL practitioners in developing countries can do to use communicative teaching resources more effectively?

Note

1. Albanian was the main interview language and the extracts are translated by the author.

References

Borg, S. (2011). Doing action research in English language teaching. A guide for practitioners. *ELT Journal*, 65(4): 485–487.

Clarke, D. (1989). Communicative theory and its influence on materials production. *Language Teaching*, 25(1): 73–86.

Donato, R. (1994). Collective scaffolding in second language learning. In Lantolf, P. J. and Appel, G. (ed.), *Vygotskian Approaches to Second Language Research*. New York: Ablex Publishing Corporation, pp. 33–56.

Dyrmishi, A. (2005). Permbledhie esses mbi Metodat e mesimdhenies se gjuhes angleze ne Shqiperi. *Shtepia Botuese Fitimi*, Vlore (AL).

Evans, V. and O'Sullivan, N. (2000). *Access 3 – Student's Book*. Newbury: Express Publishing.

Fishman, J. and Garcia, O. (2011). *Handbook of Language and Ethnic Identity: The Success-Failure Continuum in Language and Ethnic Identity Efforts* (Volume II). New York: Oxford University Press.

Harmer, J. (2007). *The Practice of English Language Teaching*, 4th Edition. London: Longman.

Husbands, C., Kitson, A. and Pendry, A. (2003). *Understanding History Teaching: Teaching and Learning About the Past in Secondary Schools*. Oxford: Oxford University Press.

Hutchinson, T. and Torres E. (1994). The textbook as agent of change. *ELT Journal*, 48(4): 315–328.

Johnson, D. W. and Johnson, R. (1981). Student-student interaction: the neglected variable in Education. *Educational Research*, 10(1): 5–10.

Kumaravadivelu, B. (2003). *Beyond Methods: Macro-Strategies for Language Teaching*. New Haven, CT: Yale University Press.

Qano, K. (2005). Raportmbimbarevartjen e reformaveinstitutcionale neShqiperi. *GazetaMesuesi*, 6: 22–24.

Savignon, S. J. (2010). Communicative language teaching. In Berns, M. (ed.), *Concise Encyclopedia of Applied Linguistics*. Oxford: Elsevier Ltd, pp. 254–260.

Sinclair, J. and Coulthard, R. M. (1975). *Towards an Analysis of Discourse: The English Used by Teachers and Pupils*. Oxford: Oxford University Press.

Richards, J. C. (2006). *Communicative Language Teaching Today*. Available at: http//www.cambridge.org/other…/Richards-Communicative-Language.pdf [accessed 28/7/2012].

Richards, J. C. and Rodgers, T. S. (2001). *Approaches and Methods in Language Teaching*, 2nd Edition. Cambridge: Cambridge University Press.

Webber, S. and Liikanen, I. (2001). *Education and Civic Culture in Post-Communist Countries*. New York: Plagrave.

Wesche, M. and Skehan, P. (2002). Communicative, task-based and content-based instruction. In Kaplan, R. (ed.), *The Oxford Handbook of Applied Linguistics*. Oxford: Oxford University Press, pp. 207–228.

Wiścicka, E. (2006). *Teacher Development: Novice Teacher Training and Development Some Reflections*. Warsaw Scientific Publisher: Piotrkowski.

7
Materials Adaptation in Ghana: Teachers' Attitudes and Practices

Esther G. Bosompem

Introduction

Adapting teaching materials is about effecting changes to make them suitable for learners and their needs. Indeed, textbooks are not merely artefacts, and teachers have a fundamental role to play as 'mediators' (McGrath, 2002: 20) between the books and learners. This implies that teachers will almost inevitably adapt the materials they use in class. While a number of writers have focused on reasons why teachers need to adapt and how this might be achieved (see, for example, Cunningsworth, 1995; Maley, 1998; McDonough and Shaw, 2003), little attention has been paid to how teachers actually adapt materials, their underlying rationale and, above all, their attitudes towards adaptation.

Against this backdrop, the present chapter examines the adaptation of ELT materials by a group of Ghanaian teachers. By uncovering the practices of this group of teachers, this chapter will shed some light on what teachers actually do in their use of materials and why. The chapter will conclude with some recommendations for how teachers can become more aware of their practices and thereby exert greater control over their use of materials, particularly in contexts where there are few opportunities for teacher training and development. There are also implications for teacher who can promote creativity and positive attitudes towards adaptation and for materials writers, who need to develop ways of encouraging the adaptation of their materials through, for example, built-in flexibility.

The Ghanaian context

Like many countries in Africa and elsewhere, Ghana is a multilingual setting in which English is the official language and the medium of instruction in schools (Opoku-Amankwa, Brew-Hammond and Elsbend Kofigah, 2011: 305). All textbooks, apart from those for the teaching and learning of local languages, are written in English. Therefore, the effectiveness of English language teaching, learning, and use determines whether the country's education will succeed or fail (Akagre, 2006). Moreover, globalisation means that competence in both spoken and written English is seen as very necessary in Ghana.

In the Ghanaian education system, the textbook is considered the principal teaching and learning material (Opoku-Amankwa, 2010: 159) for both children and adults. For many children, the textbook is their first encounter with written texts (ibid.: 160). Besides, since Ghana is a context in which students have limited opportunities to encounter authentic spoken or written materials, the textbook assumes a pivotal role in English language education. Despite the central role of textbooks in this setting, how teachers use them is generally taken for granted (ibid.). Yet, this is not necessarily straightforward. In my experience, while some teachers adapt materials with confidence, others do so with guilt and uncertainty, feeling that the authority of the textbook or of the government syllabus should not be challenged. Still others practise adaptation without even being aware of what they are doing. Finally, some Ghanaian teachers, particularly in rural areas, have actually rejected textbooks prescribed by school authorities because 'the books were not aligned with the children's reading ability' (Moulton, 1997: 6) and 'the teachers did not have the skills to adapt the books to the children's skill levels' (ibid.). The teachers reverted to writing on the chalkboard since that was the medium of reading and writing familiar to them.

Given the situation outlined above, this chapter seeks to find answers to the following questions:

1. Are teachers aware of what the adaptation of ELT materials entails?
2. Do they adapt materials? Why?
3. What approaches do they employ? Why?
4. What are their opinions on adaptation, and their attitude towards it?

Teacher autonomy vis-à-vis textbook selection

According to Meddings and Thornbury (2009: 86):

> Most teachers – perhaps 99% – work in contexts where the use of a coursebook is mandated. A few lucky ones may actually have a say in which coursebook to use, but most don't.

This observation reflects the general practice in most Ghanaian language schools, especially government institutions like the one under investigation. Although the classroom teacher is the direct user of the books, selection usually goes beyond them to involve the Ministry of Education, institutional and departmental heads, and even fellow teachers (McGrath, 2002; McDonough and Shaw, 2003).

As a result, teachers who claim books are 'imposed on them from above' (Meddings and Thornbury, 2009: 86), sometimes become dissatisfied and frustrated. They may hesitate to use the textbook or, in a worst-case scenario, they may simply abandon the book completely (Moulton, 1997). In the words of Opoku-Amankwa (2010: 161), 'teachers may be reluctant to use textbooks because their interests and experiences, and those of their students, are not reflected in the content'. However, regardless of whether they choose their own textbooks, teachers generally need to make changes and modifications for the books to work for their students (McGrath, 2002). Yet many teachers may have no training in materials analysis and adaptation, and can only rely on their experience or intuition. Considering such responsibility, it is worth knowing how teachers generally perceive textbooks and how such views affect how they use them in the classroom.

How and why ELT materials are adapted

The importance of ELT materials adaptation and the variety of approaches involved are widely recognised in the literature (see Maley, 1998; McDonough and Shaw, 2003; Edge and Garton, 2009). As McDonough and Shaw (2003: 76) state, the general purpose of adaptation

> is to maximize the appropriacy of teaching materials in context, by changing some of the internal characteristics of a coursebook to suit our particular circumstances better.

Since no material can meet the needs of every single teacher or learner in any given context (Edge and Garton, 2009), adaptation is almost inevitable in ELT. Previous writers have identified a number of ways in which teachers can adapt materials, and these are outlined below.

Addition

In this approach, teachers retain what the textbook contains and add materials from other sources to it. This method has sub-types such as extemporisation, supplementation, exploitation and extension.

Extemporisation: This type of addition is instinctive and is the one most widely employed by teachers. It entails a teacher's natural reaction to situations that come up during lessons. Examples include paraphrasing, referring to preceding lessons, and providing explanations, illustrations and examples. It is mostly done orally (McGrath, 2002: 64–65) before, during, or after the use of textbooks for lead-ins, elicitation, and to help students comprehend lessons effectively.

Supplementation: This entails the addition of exercises, activities, and texts to those in the textbook. These can be from other published materials or materials improvised by the teacher. This approach is generally used by teachers for variety, stimulation, active student participation, and to make up for inadequacies in the textbook in terms of addressing particular needs of learners (Maley, 1998).

Extension: This is the addition of extra items of the same kind as are already in the textbook. For instance, when tasks or exercises in the book are not enough for learners' practice and comprehension, the teacher supplies extra activities that have the same learning objective. The difference between supplementation and extension is that while the former involves materials that are structurally different from those available, the latter deals with items that are structurally akin to existing ones (McGrath, 2002: 65).

Exploitation: This kind of addition refers to teachers making the most of materials by exploring means of increasing their original use as suggested by the textbook. Parallel to extemporisation, exploitation can be employed before, during, and after the use of a textbook in class for lead-ins, examples, and practice respectively. In this approach a teacher uses portions of the material, such as the text, topic, or pictures to generate or stimulate more language use, vocabulary, personalisation, localisation, etc. (McGrath, 2002: 65).

Modification

This is another form of adaptation where teachers alter the form, use, or order of different features of materials (McDonough and Shaw, 2003: 81–82). They usually do this by changing activities and linguistic content in order to exploit their communicative elements, rendering them more intriguing and relevant to learners and their context. In terms of form modification, this may be 'rewriting' (Maley, 1998: 281) an activity or text; 'restructuring' (Maley, 1998: 281) the way an activity is implemented or 'reordering' (McDonough and Shaw, 2003: 81–82) by changing the sequence in which tasks, activities and exercises appear in a book.

Replacement

Replacement concerns the substitution of some portions of the book deemed unsuitable for learners, the learning context, or learning objectives (Maley, 1998: 281). For instance, a teacher can replace closed questions following a comprehension text with open-ended ones for original and interesting answers from students. Another reason for replacement may be to avoid content that is culturally inappropriate for the students in that particular learning context (Gray, 2000).

Deletion

Finally, 'deletion' (McDonough and Shaw, 2003: 81–82), or 'omission' (Maley, 1998: 281), is another form of adaptation. In this case, all or some material is rejected by teachers for various reasons, including disparity with learners' proficiency level, with teaching and learning styles, as well as the teacher's inability to adapt materials, or a need to avoid culturally inappropriate materials.

Investigating adaptation

In order to gain an insight into how teachers adapt materials, their rationale and their attitudes towards the practice, questionnaires were completed by 12 teachers at a Ghanaian government-run tertiary institution, and an additional four were interviewed about the type of materials they used and the extent of adaptations made. The interview questions also covered areas such as teachers' reasons for adapting materials, factors that influence their decisions or their attitudes, their sources of supplementary materials, how they deal with socio-culturally sensitive contents, challenges faced when adapting materials, the benefits derived from adaptation, and their suggestions on how novice teachers can use books better, or how they can be helped to do so.

English classes at the institution are divided into four levels: Beginner I, Beginner II, Intermediate and Advanced. The Beginner I classes are for learners with a very low level of proficiency, who can hardly understand or communicate in English. Students in the Beginner II, Intermediate and Advanced classes have various needs, including communication, preparation for specific examinations and higher education. Students are from countries like Burkina Faso, Togo, Mali, Equatorial Guinea, Nigeria, Ivory Coast, Burundi, Sierra Leone, Benin, Portugal, Niger and Ghana.

Table 7.1 Participating teachers

Level	Questionnaire	Experience	Interview	Experience
Beginner I	Ama	1 year to 3 years	Abena	2 years
	Charles	3 years to less than 6 years		
	Dede	3 years to less than 6 years		
Beginner II	Efua	3 years to less than 6 years	Kwasi	5 years
	Ben	3 years to less than 6 years	Peter	3 years
Intermediate	Getty	6 years to 10 years	Kofi	7 years
	Irene	More than 10 years		
	Kwame	6 months to less than 1 year		
	Lamptey	6 months to less than 1 year		
Advanced	Fiifi	6 years to 10 years		
	Henry	More than 10 years		
	John	More than 10 years		

Formal teacher training is not a compulsory requirement, but having a university degree and appreciable language proficiency is necessary for teachers at this institution. Thus, the teachers all have at least a first degree. Teachers of lower-level classes are mostly university graduates who are posted to the school for a one-year national service, whereas advanced classes are taught by experienced teachers.

Selection of textbooks

Teachers of the beginner and intermediate classes use African-authored books, while those of the advanced classes use both local and global books. Only teachers of the Advanced level (Fiifi, Henry, and John) get to choose their own textbooks. Significantly, they attribute their autonomy in textbook selection to experience. Regardless of who selects the textbooks, school authorities expect all teachers to make the books they use work for their students at all costs. This leads to dissatisfaction due to wide disparities between book content, learner proficiency level and learning objectives. Thus, some of the teachers expressed the desire to be involved in the selection and even the writing of textbooks to be used for their students. As Efua puts it, textbooks 'should be generated in consultation with the language teachers to avail their practical experience in the classroom'. Although teachers' involvement in textbook writing and selection is a legitimate suggestion, it is not easily accepted in educational settings like the one under investigation.

Teachers' views on textbooks

The teachers both identified benefits and expressed reservations about the use of coursebooks. Firstly, they underscored the facilitating, supportive and guiding roles of textbooks as identified by McGrath (2006). In the questionnaires, for example, when asked to comment on the use of textbooks, teachers responded that they are 'very helpful' (Dede), 'absolutely necessary for a good lesson' (Getty), 'help the teacher to teach effectively' (John) and 'makes teaching less difficult' (Kwame). These assertions echo Ur's (1996: 184) observation that coursebooks provide 'helpful support and guidance'. Such support can be linguistic, methodological, cultural or contextual (Hutchinson and Torres, 1994; McGrath, 2002).

Another benefit mentioned is the evaluative role of textbooks. According to Irene, 'well written textbooks can provide means of assessing students' progress'. This highlights their role in helping teachers to evaluate and account for their work with learners (McGrath, 2002; Hutchinson and Torres, 1994). In addition, the teachers pointed to the time-saving role of coursebooks because, as Abena puts it, 'it is tedious and time consuming for me to prepare new sets of materials for each lesson I teach'.

Although the teachers generally support the use of textbooks, some also make mention of their disadvantages. For instance, Ama claims that 'sometimes, textbooks and other materials are too restrictive'. Kofi observes that 'at times, textbooks do not allow me to teach what I want to teach fully'. These reservations reflect the fact that books may leave little room for teachers to make 'curriculum decisions' (Littlejohn, 1992: 83) while using them. The books may lack the flexibility to accommodate a variety of teaching and learning strategies, a characteristic of a good course book (Cunningsworth, 1995). At the same time:

> Materials will always be constraining in one way or another, so that teachers will always need to exercise their professional judgement ('or sense of plausibility') about when and how a particular piece of material is best implemented in any particular case. (Maley, 1998: 287)

When asked to show a 'restrictive' book, Kofi provided a book with a set structure and sequence meant to prepare students for particular external exams. In fact, such a structure does not mean the book prohibits or inhibits adaptation. Rather, Kofi's misgivings about such constraints could also point to a lack of experience or confidence to adapt the books when necessary.

Attitudes towards and influences on the practice of adaptation

The questionnaire responses show that the teachers generally have a positive perception of adaptation. Responses from all 12 teachers to the question 'What is your general opinion about the practice of changing (some) contents of English language teaching materials/textbook(s)?' showed a positive attitude. One teacher stated, 'I believe every teacher knows the level of his students and for this reason, whenever it is necessary, additions and subtraction [sic] can be made.' Nine teachers endorsed adaptation as a legitimate teaching practice that needs no authorisation and nine encouraged teachers to do it with confidence. Above all, ten of them attested to the inevitability of adaptation due to the diversity of teaching situations.

However, while the teachers showed a generally positive attitude to adaptation, their accounts of their own practices sometimes presented a different picture. For example, three teachers, Irene, Lamptey, and Henry said they never intentionally made changes to the content of their textbooks. However, Henry said he would 'leave the contents as they are but look for addition elsewhere to supplement'. This may imply that he is not aware that supplementation is a form of adaptation.

One reason presented for eschewing adaptation of textbooks is the adequacy of content to meet learners' needs. For Irene, with 'content well structured' and 'adequate' there is no need for her to adapt her book. For Lamptey, 'the textbook has enough passages and all the necessary components' so adaptation is not necessary.

There may be hesitation in adapting the textbook because of the absence of a formal directive by the school authorities. For instance, although Peter went through the school's mentoring scheme by understudying a teacher for some time and observed the usefulness of making changes to the contents of the textbook when necessary, he felt reluctant because he claimed he had not been authorised by anyone to do so. Thus, although by giving examples, explanations and illustrations in class, he intuitively practised extemporisation and modification, he felt the practice of adaptation was reserved for experienced teachers. When asked to suggest means of helping teachers overcome their reluctance to adapt, he recommended a sensitisation programme to educate novice and newly employed teachers on how to use and adapt materials. He also proposed that such teachers should be specifically made aware that adaptation is a legitimate and integral part of language teaching and so does not need any authorisation.

Probing further into factors that influence participants' practice of adaptation, experience seems to be a key factor. For example, Kwasi mentioned that due to his five years of teaching beginner and intermediate students, adapting materials comes to him with so much ease that it has become an integral part of his teaching practice. Kofi gives credit to his seven years of experience in teaching intermediate and advanced levels. Thus experience may help teachers anticipate how students 'will cope with and respond to certain types of published material' (McGrath, 2002: 4).

Abena pointed out that, in her experience, although novice teachers are made to 'understudy experienced teachers', they are not 'coached on how to use materials'. She felt reluctant to adapt textbooks given to her by the school authorities because she was not confident about the outcome of her adaptations and feared they might negatively affect the lessons and her students. When asked how she overcame her reluctance, she said she approached a senior colleague who took her through 'a few days of grooming on how to make changes when necessary'. She added that after a few weeks of practice she became 'master over the book', 'improved with more practice', and gained confidence.

Kofi's experience echoed Abena's. He not only feared making changes at the initial stages of his teaching career, but 'also felt guilty challenging the authority of the book writers and that of the leaders who gave me the books for my lessons'. However, continuous practice with adaptation boosted his confidence. His creative nature made adaptation a skill he became proud of and something he later helped novice teachers he came into contact with to practise.

At the end of the interviews it emerged that Kofi, Kwasi, Peter, and Abena had all been practising adaptation without even realising it. For instance, they practised extemporisation as a spontaneous reaction to classroom situations (McGrath, 2002) in the form of illustrations, explanations, and examples they gave in class to help students understand lessons better. The experiences of teachers at the initial stages of their teaching career also tie in with Richards' (1993: 47) assertion that non-native speakers of English who are not experienced in teaching 'may tend to follow the textbook very closely... and to be relatively reluctant to discard sections of the book and replace them with other materials'.

Reasons for adaptation

The teachers identified a variety of reasons for adapting materials. These include deficiencies in textbooks, the needs of the learners, evaluation, variety, and stimulation.

Deficiencies in textbooks

In this study, the teachers' reasons for adaptation reiterate its gap-filling role (Block, 1991), particularly with regard to being up-to-date and meeting the needs of particular learners in particular contexts. Teachers said that they make changes in order to 'make up some ground the textbook couldn't cover' (Dede), 'to make room for other topics not treated', or to streamline those that are not 'well treated' (Getty). They want 'to make the topic more understandable' to students (Kwame), or to 'meet the exact needs of my students' (Ama).

Block's (1991: 214) concept of 'timeliness' of materials showcasing current happenings in the world also resonated with the views of the teachers. For John, 'making changes from time to time is good to meet changing situations and should therefore be encouraged'. Abena mentions the importance of using up-to-date materials to teach 'since the world is fast changing and information has become more powerful than weapons'. In Kofi's opinion there is the need for the use of materials containing 'trends and current affairs because the world has become a global village'.

Learner needs

One significant aspect considered by the teachers is their recognition that they are the 'mediators' (McGrath, 2002: 20) between the coursebooks and their learners. The chief reason attributed to this vital role is the teachers' proximity to students, which affords them the opportunity of knowing particular learners, their level of proficiency, and their specific needs (Jolly and Bolitho, 1998: 111). For instance, Peter said, 'I am the best person who know [sic] my students, so I know how I can make changes to meet their needs.' For Efua adaptation is 'very necessary because students have different language needs and can only be identified by the teachers in class'. For Ama, it is 'necessary since the writers [sic] knowledge about learners may differ from the learners I come into contact with'. Surprisingly, even Irene, who earlier denied adapting her textbook, admits that adaptation 'is the mark of a good teacher who has the interest of his/her students at heart'.

As teachers do their best to make textbooks work for their students, one important consideration they make is the proficiency level of the learners (McDonough and Shaw, 2003: 75). When materials are above a learner's level, they lose motivation and discouragement sets in (Humphries, 2011). On the other hand, when materials are below a learner's level, they get bored due to lack of challenge. Charles and Getty, respectively, mention that 'the level of the students' and 'the standard of the learners' are the basis for adapting textbooks. Efua specifically identifies vocabulary 'beyond their levels' as a reason for adaptation. Peter describes a section of the textbook for his Intermediate class as irrelevant because it does not contain much on 'the past perfect tense it is supposed to illustrate in context' and 'the exercises too are not challenging enough for my students'. For these reasons, he maintains the topic and replaces the exercises and illustrations with materials from another book.

Stimulation, variety, and exploration

Teachers also adapt materials for the sake of stimulation, variety, exploration, and active student participation. Teachers in this study said they make changes to 'spice the lesson with varieties' (Fifii), to make 'the lesson interesting' (Kwame), to make 'teaching and learning fun and easier' (Ama), and 'to enrich students' awareness and experience' (John). Furthermore, for Efua the multicultural setting of the school propels adaptation, possibly because the Ghanaian-authored book she uses mostly contains local illustrations and examples. The teachers personalise, localise and improvise to achieve their aims (McGrath, 2002: 74).

All these reasons boil down to the vital role played by the teacher who observes the students in various contexts and manipulates the materials to facilitate and enrich their language learning through adaptation.

Learner assessment

Learner assessment was also given as a reason for adapting textbooks. One reason Ben adapts is 'to find out whether the students really understand the topic'. For Dede, the reason is 'to find out if students could identify similar exercises in other books'. Similarly, Fiifi indicates he makes adaptations 'to ascertain if students can work outside the course book'.

Creativity and method exploration

Teachers also explore techniques for adaptation in a quest for creativity. For instance, Fiifi practises adaptation 'to see how creative I can be without the book'. Charles makes adaptations because his 'teaching styles' are different from those found in the textbook. Thus, apart from efforts to meet learners' needs, teachers can use adaptation as a means of trying out their own skills and ability. This is a commendable step towards professional development since the outcome of adaptation can help a teacher improve decisions and actions regarding the use of teaching materials in general.

Thus far in this chapter, we have looked at teachers' attitudes to textbooks and adaptation and the reasons they give for their practice. In the next section, we will consider what teachers say they actually do when adapting materials.

How teachers make adaptations

The questionnaire presented the teachers with a number of situations in which they may need to adapt their materials and asked them to complete the sentences with what they do. The situations concerned topic, language content, exercises, language skills, activities, and student engagement. The responses show that the approaches mainly identified by respondents are addition, modification, replacement and deletion (McDonough and Shaw, 2003). For example, the first sentence to be completed was, *When topics are not likely to stimulate students' interest and participation*; Charles says he would 'skip or swap the topic', implying rejection or replacement, and Efua replaces such topics with related interesting ones. Both Dede and Ben employ addition, Dede through explanation and Ben with examples from other sources. Henry, however, opts for rejection. In his words, 'I don't teach it, I leave it out.'

Regarding *contents that do not generate language learning and language use*, Charles and Efua replace the contents with suitable ones, while Henry and Dede reject them. In dealing with *contents that do not exploit students' experience, prior knowledge and creativity*, Charles says he gives 'detailed explanations to bring them on board', while Henry creates and integrates engaging contents. Getty and Ama make modifications to exploit students' experience and creativity. Dede, however, rejects such contents. Efua uses the familiar as a starting point 'to lead them to the unknown', as suggested by Meddings and Thornbury (2009: 87).

Interestingly, when asked to indicate how they handle *materials with socio-culturally or ideologically sensitive contents,* more than half of the questionnaire respondents (Ama, Ben, Charles, Irene, John, Kwame and Lamptey) did not give any response at all. Considering that they all use books produced by Ghanaians and Nigerians, it could be that the content is culturally appropriate. On the other hand, Efua states that she groups the students in accordance with similar cultural settings to 'discuss what pertains to their cultures'. Dede reports using 'experiences and happenings in other places rather than those of my students'. Fiifi modifies such contents, Getty avoids them and Henry leaves 'those parts out'. When interviewed, Kofi explained that due to the multiplicity of learners' backgrounds in the institution, issues of ethnicity and religion are very sensitive. Thus, he usually resorts to rejection. When asked how learners can learn about other cultures he said he preferred directing learners to conduct individual research than to 'risk stepping on people's toes'.

Other questions focused on grammar items and exercises that are not challenging, exercises that are too difficult for students, unbalanced concentration on the four language skills, as well as unsuitable and unavailable activities to accompany lessons. It is worth noting that, as suggested by McDonough and Shaw (2003: 80), when it comes to addition, it is not obligatory to bring it in at the end. It can be done in the form of a warm-up or a lead-in activity 'to prepare the ground for practice' (ibid.), as done by Efua who creates 'the right atmosphere to stimulate the targetted [sic] teaching/learning activities' when none is suggested by her textbook.

Overall, the teachers' answers show the whole range of possible responses that reflect *addition, modification, replacement* and *rejection*. According to information gathered from the interviews, the differences in approach can be attributed to a teacher's personality, personal beliefs, experience, professional competence, and available facilities. Although teachers react differently to the same situation, they all ultimately aim to meet the diverse needs of specific learners in a specific context (McDonough and Shaw, 2003: 75). Thus, not only do participants demonstrate an awareness of the possibilities, they are also able to articulate the reasons underlying their choice of one approach over another. This would seem to show that, while some teachers at least may not consciously be aware of their practices in adaptation, when they are asked to reflect on those practices they are able to give a clear rationale for what they do.

Implications

The study suggests the following:

- No textbook can perfectly meet the needs of any given group of students. Thus, not only is it acceptable to adapt a textbook but vital to do so in order to meet the particular needs of students in a particular context.
- A textbook is not a sacred object, but a raw material for teaching and learning. As such, teachers need to understand how to use their textbooks and feel free to make necessary changes.

- Teachers, especially novices, may be afraid to adapt their textbook because they don't know whether it is permissible to do so, and/ or because they don't want to be seen as questioning the authority of the book.
- Teachers don't necessarily know how to adapt a textbook, they need to learn how to do so.
- There are a variety of reasons for and a variety of ways to adapt a textbook. Teachers need to learn what they are.
- Adaptation not only benefits learners, but also benefits teachers by allowing them to stretch their capabilities.

Educational institutions, teacher educators and materials writers all have roles to play in helping teachers learn how to use, adapt and develop materials effectively.

Educational Institutions

The concerns raised by teachers in this study underline the importance of educational institutions becoming more aware of how teachers use ELT materials. Newly employed teachers need to be sensitised to what is possible and feasible in a particular institution. Teachers may not be aware that they are free to adapt materials, and thus avoid adaptation due to their perception that it is not authorised. One reason institutions may not make newly employed and novice teachers aware of what is possible is the assumption that adaptation is an integral part of language teaching, so no teacher needs a formal mandate before practising it. This reflects McDonough and Shaw's (2003: 75) assertion that issues on adaptation are 'frequently overlooked, perhaps because it is so much a part of our everyday professional practice that we are unaware of its implications'.

However, from the teachers' comments in this study, taking such sensitisation for granted can affect teachers' confidence to adapt materials, and thus deprive learners of the best input. Accordingly, measures can include orientation programmes where teachers can be briefed on the nature of their teaching contexts and the particular ways of doing things in the institution, including the extent to which autonomy in materials use is possible. Further, the role and importance of adaptation, where this is possible, needs to be mentioned explicitly so that new teachers can adapt materials with certainty and confidence.

New teachers need support in the use of materials, especially those who have not undergone formal training. However, even trained teachers may not be prepared in materials development and adaptation, though it is a skill that is expected to be the core of language teaching (McGrath, 2002; McDonough and Shaw, 2003). To address these issues, institutions can assign mentors to novice teachers for guidance and support on the use of materials, which also involves adaptation. With such measures, teachers can gain the necessary confidence to make decisions that will benefit them and their students.

Considering the changing trends in language teaching, it is also advisable to provide refresher courses for upgrading teachers' knowledge and skills to help them keep up with developments in the field (Canniveng and Martinez, 2003: 482). In developing countries like Ghana, in-service training for teachers is rare (Opoku-Amakwa, 2010). Even when there are opportunities for teacher development, focus on materials use is virtually absent. On the one hand, this results in the deification of textbooks, since some teachers may lack the competence or confidence to make adaptations. On the other hand, the absence of such training may result in the rejection of materials that could be profitable for English language teaching and learning in Ghana and countries with similar conditions. Without such preparation, the lack of monitoring of how teachers use materials can also have telling effects on learners.

To equip teachers with skills in materials use and production, institutions can organise regular seminars and workshops with the help of experts in materials development or senior teachers. Moreover, institutions can subscribe to different sources of online ELT materials to help teachers access literature on materials use and general ELT practices. Although they may appear challenging to achieve, these are feasible ventures with great benefits.

Teacher educators

There is a general concern about the absence or lack of emphasis on materials development in teacher training programmes (Canniveng and Martinez, 2003: 482). For example, Kofi, one of the only two TESOL trained teachers in this study, reported the lack of a materials development module in his UK MA course. In Africa, although there are various pre-service training programmes for English language teachers, most of them lack the essential ingredient of materials development. This is true of Ghana, where even one of the most renowned training colleges in Ghana has no provision for materials use and development in its syllabus.

The lack of training in materials use and development affects teachers' attitudes towards adaptation. In line with Milambiling's (2001: 3) proposal for 'context-sensitive' teacher training for non-native teachers, teacher training in materials use and development with the local context taken into account is recommended. With the right competence, teachers will be empowered to graduate from unquestioningly accepting any material they come across, to making appropriate decisions and choices (Jolly and Bolitho, 1998), which include adaptation. In addition, given that adaptation may involve teacher-produced materials, teachers must be trained to prepare materials that can expose learners to more tailored input in situations where materials in textbooks may have been inappropriately presented (Gray, 2000), cannot address learners' needs, or are absent.

Materials writers

Due to the diversity of teaching and learning contexts, textbooks will always be constraining to an extent. Nevertheless, writers of textbooks and other materials can help make adaptation less challenging for teachers by incorporating more flexibility, which Cunningsworth (1995) presents as a criterion for book evaluation and selection. Writers are encouraged to make the books easily accommodate teacher input as well as various teaching and learning styles (McGrath, 2002: 159). Such materials will make materials adaptation easier and reduce the uncertainty and anxiety that make teachers hesitant to practise it.

Conclusion

This chapter has delved into an area of ELT that has not received much attention: what teachers think of and actually do with the materials they use. Teachers are generally aware of the existence of adaptation, though some may not know what it entails. Consciously or unconsciously, all of them adapt materials, using various approaches. Careful selection of materials to suit a particular learning context can minimise the volume of adaptation that teachers need to make. Teachers should be involved in materials selection and development to suit local contexts since they are close to the learners.

Although this chapter has focused on one particular context, Ghana, the issues that have emerged are relevant across a wide variety of countries and contexts. Whatever type of materials are used by teachers, wherever they are, teachers are mediators and are therefore responsible for making the materials work for learners in the best way possible. Since this reflects the essence of adaptation, the subject must not be taken for granted. Rather, it must be addressed explicitly to raise teacher awareness, increase confidence, and help develop positive attitudes towards adaptation. Thus, to make the most of the textbook, teachers need to have the necessary knowledge, skills, and support to adapt materials and make language teaching and learning a fruitful venture.

Engagement priorities

1. In what ways does your experience with textbook selection and adaptation resemble that of the teachers in the study described in the chapter? In what ways is it different? Why do you think this is so?

2. Do you think teachers should be able to develop their own materials? What would you include in a course on materials development and adaptation?
3. Examine an existing textbook. How is it amenable to adaptation, for example in terms of learning styles, topics, or task types? What are ways in which it could be more flexible and amenable to adaptation?

References

Akagre, J. (2006). *Effective Teaching and Learning of English in Ghana*. Available at http://www.ghananewsagency.org/details/Features/Effective-Teaching-and-Learning-of-English-in-Ghana/?ci=10&ai=1853 [Accessed 20/8/2011].

Block, D. (1991). Some thoughts on DIY materials design. *ELT Journal*, 45(3): 211–216.

Canniveng, C. and Martinez, M. (2003). Materials development and teacher training. In Tomlinson, B. (ed.), *Developing Materials for Language Teaching*. London: Continuum, pp. 479–487.

Cunningsworth, A. (1995). *Choosing your Coursebook*. Oxford: Heinemann.

Edge, J. and Garton, S. (2009). *From Experience to Knowledge in ELT*. Oxford: Oxford University Press.

Gray, J. (2000). The ELT coursebook as cultural artefact: how teachers censor and adapt. *ELT Journal*, 54(3): 274–281.

Humphries, S. C. (2011). *Exploring the Impact of the Introduction of New EFL Textbooks on Teachers' Practices and Attitudes at a Technical College in Japan*. Sydney: Macquarie University (Unpublished doctoral dissertation).

Hutchinson, T. and Torres, E. (1994). The textbook as agent of change. *ELT Journal*, 48(4): 315–28.

Jolly, D. and Bolitho, R. (1998). A framework for materials writing. In Tomlinson, B. (ed.), *Materials Development in Language Teaching*. Cambridge: Cambridge University Press, pp. 90–115.

Littlejohn, A. L. (1992). *Why are ELT Materials the Way They Are?* PhD Thesis: Lancaster University. Available at http://www.andrewlittlejohn.net [Accessed 10/8/2011].

Maley, A. (1998). Squaring the circle – reconciling materials as constraints with materials as empowerment. In Tomlinson, B. (ed.), *Materials Development in Language Teaching*. Cambridge: Cambridge University Press, pp. 279–294.

McDonough, J. and Shaw, C. (2003). *Materials and Methods in ELT: a Teacher's Guide*, 2nd Edition. Malden, MA: Blackwell Publishing.

McGrath, I. (2002). *Materials Evaluation and Design for Language Teaching*. Edinburgh: Edinburgh University Press.

McGrath, I. (2006). Teachers' and learners' images for coursebooks. *ELT Journal*, 60(2): 171–180.

Meddings, L. and Thornbury, S. (2009). *Teaching Unplugged: Dogme in English Language Teaching*. Peaslake: Delta Publishing.

Milambiling, J. (2001). More than talk: a proposal for TESOL teacher education. *TESOL Journal*, 10(4): 3–4.

Moulton, J. (1997). How do teachers use textbooks? a review of the research literature. *Academy for Educational Development*. Washington DC: SD Publication Series: Technical Paper No. 74, 1–29.

Opoku-Amankwa, K. (2010). What happens to textbooks in the classroom? Pupils' access to literacy in an urban primary school in Ghana. *Pedagogy, Culture & Society*, 18(2): 159–172.

Opoku-Amankwa, K., Brew-Hammond, A. and Elsbend Kogigah, F. (2011). What is in a textbook? Investigating the language and literacy learning principles of the 'Gateway to English' Textbook Series. *Pedagogy, Culture & Society*, 19(2): 291–310.

Richards, J. C. (1993). Beyond the textbook: the role of commercial materials in language teaching. *Perspectives*, 5(1): 43–53.

Ur, P. (1996). *A Course in Language Teaching: Practice and Theory*. Cambridge: Cambridge University Press.

8
Multilevel Materials for Multilevel Learners

Apiwan Nuangpolmak

Overview

The presence of learner diversity is inevitable in any language classroom. Not only do our learners differ in their ages, interests, learning styles, goals, and motivation, but their levels of proficiency may also vary. In everyday teaching, practitioners are constantly faced with the problems of finding the right materials for all their learners. The situation may be worse if there is a required material, such as a coursebook, involved since, on many occasions, language teachers are left to cope with a mismatch between the assigned coursebook and the actual proficiency levels of the learners.

This chapter describes the design and implementation of multilevel writing tasks created by the author and used in a mixed ability, tertiary English class. These materials were utilised as a supplement to the main coursebook in order to accommodate learners of different proficiencies. A multilevel task can be described simply as a material that offers learners the choice of working at different levels. This multilevel task approach also encourages learners to monitor and reflect on their performance so that they can select the level at which they prefer to work, based on self-evaluation.

Teaching context

Currently in Thailand, English is mandated as a compulsory foreign language. Having a good command of English is essential for career advancement since English is commonly used by Thais as a medium for international communication in various domains, such as diplomacy, business, academia, and tourism. The push for the establishment of the ASEAN (Association of South East Asian Nations) community by 2015, a regional economic integration similar to that of the European Union, also necessitates the knowledge of English as a tool for cooperation, networking, and sharing information.

The importance of English in both academic and professional domains has led to many educational reforms in Thailand over the years. Since 1996 English has been mandated as a compulsory subject in primary (P. 1–6) and secondary (M. 1–6) curricula. Students at tertiary level are also required to complete at least six credits of English courses as a condition for graduation (Wongsothorn et al., 2002). Despite the mandatory status of English, each school and university still maintains its administrative freedom with regard to teaching materials, methods, assessment, and time allocation for English classes (Foley, 2005). Furthermore, the pressure from school achievement tests and university entrance examinations has led many learners, especially those with higher economic status, to seek extra tuition in private language schools (Prapphal, 2008). The lack of uniformity in English syllabi and the unequal access to English learning have resulted in various levels of proficiency among school graduates.

Through my teaching context at Chulalongkorn University Language Institute (CULI) in Bangkok, Thailand, I have dealt with students from various disciplines and of different English proficiency. Despite their differing levels of English, these students are required to take the same compulsory English course called *Experiential English* (EXP ENG), which is the course that forms the basis for discussion in this chapter.

EXP ENG is a foundation English course which aims to enable students to communicate effectively about topics of interest in daily life using the four skills. It is also specified in the syllabus that the course should promote the active participation of the students in the learning process and develop autonomous learning behaviours. Students who enrol in EXP ENG are required to purchase a commercial English coursebook at upper intermediate level for the class. CULI's academic affairs department still produce some supplementary exercises, mostly grammar and vocabulary review, to be used in conjunction with the coursebook, and they allow instructors to supply supplementary materials, if needed.

There were three main issues with the EXP ENG classes. First, there was a mismatch between the coursebook level and the actual proficiency of some students. A number of students were clearly below upper intermediate level; some could even be considered high level beginners. On the other hand, there would be a few advanced students in each class who possessed an exceptional level of English. Since the whole class were assigned the same material some students would have to struggle in order to get it done, while others would finish it very quickly and perhaps think that it was not challenging enough. Second, there were certain shortcomings of the coursebook in that it did not fully address the needs of the students. Since most secondary English curricula in Thailand placed a heavy emphasis on receptive rather than productive skills, especially reading, the students commencing tertiary education were usually proficient readers, but not competent writers. The content of the commercial coursebook did not provide sufficient support for this skill. Last but not least, there was also a tension between policy and real practice. The course syllabus specified that EXP ENG promoted autonomous learning. However, there was no specification of how to achieve this goal in the teacher's coursebook manual. Furthermore, due to syllabus constraints, there was no time to spare for learner training activities, which could have been employed to foster autonomous behaviours. Consequently, the policy which was mandated by the institute was not fully implemented in practice.

In order to address these issues the idea of a multilevel task was born with the proposition to develop materials that could offer flexibility in terms of task levels, while maintaining the same learning objectives. This set of materials would focus specifically on developing the writing proficiency students were lacking. Additionally, it would develop a practical procedure to foster autonomous learning. However, this procedure had to be incorporated into the existing syllabus and implemented within the classroom hours. As a result, three levels of the same set of writing tasks were designed and incorporated into the established EXP ENG syllabus to offer the students a choice. The students themselves chose at which task level they would like to perform. By encouraging the students to decide for themselves, it was anticipated that they would undergo the process of monitoring, evaluating, and reflecting on their previous performance in order to make informed choices. It is believed that skills such as self-monitoring, reflection, and making decisions about learning are the fundamental foundation for the development of learner autonomy (Holec, 1981).

Theoretical framework

McGrath (2002: 80) claims that 'the needs of a specific class of learners can never be perfectly met by a single coursebook'. Consequently, many teachers decide to supplement the main coursebook with other materials. There are two main reasons for the use of supplementary materials. The first is the teacher's recognition that the coursebook does not fully address the syllabus objectives neither does it prepare learners for the required examination. The second reason is the teacher's obligation to provide optimal learning opportunities for their learners. Therefore, additional materials are given to learners so as to enhance exposure and/or practice of the target language.

Affective considerations may also influence classroom teachers to adapt some parts of the required coursebook. McDonough and Shaw (2003: 77) emphasise teachers' needs to 'personalise', 'individualise' and 'localise' coursebook materials in order to achieve greater appropriateness in their teaching environments. To increase relevance in relation to learners' needs and interests, teachers sometimes adapt the materials to provide personalised content. Teachers also adapt the activities in the coursebook to address learner diversity and individuality in terms of proficiency and learning styles. Lastly, it is common for teachers in EFL contexts to adapt the content of commercial coursebooks to fit in with local settings and local demands for language use.

Furthermore, materials adaptation is considered when classroom teachers wish to conduct learner training in a specific area. Islam and Mares (2003) propose enhancing learner autonomy as one of the reasons for materials adaptation. They posit that materials should be adapted to offer activities in which learners are encouraged to discover independently rules about the target language. Also, materials should be adapted in a way that can assist learners in developing skills useful to independent learning.

Linked to the notion of materials adaptation is the idea of flexible learning materials. Hemingway (1986) asserts that it is possible to turn any material designed for teaching a homogeneous class into a potential learning activity for a mixed ability class, as long as such materials are open to interpretation. According to McKay and Tom (1999), one way to address mixed ability class issues is by manipulating one of the three main components in any learning activity – materials, task and performance level – to create various versions of the same activity in order to accommodate learners of different proficiency levels and interests.

In task-based language teaching, pedagogical tasks (such as classroom tasks which aim to bridge the gap between the learners' current ability and the real world task demands) are also purposely graded into a continuum of difficulty levels and presented to learners in sequences, each one with 'increasingly accurate approximation' to the target task (Long and Crookes, 1993: 40). These sequences of tasks are graded in order to accommodate the learner's growing proficiency (Skehan, 1998), as well as to maintain an ideal that tasks should appear challenging but attainable to learners (Prabhu, 1987). Appropriate levels of task difficulty can therefore enhance a learner's motivation since they realise that their efforts are exerted towards achievable goals (Dörnyei, 2001).

A discourse oriented, or genre based, approach in writing instruction promotes the use of a learning/teaching cycle which offers a number of activities in sequential stages (see for example, Feez, 1998; Thai, 2009). Through these stages, it is anticipated that learners will gradually gain independent control of their texts. Since the discourse oriented approach advocates explicit instruction of text structure – as it is believed that genre knowledge 'develops with repeated experiences' (Hyland, 2004: 55) – model texts and language samples are commonly used to elicit analysis and discussion, and to support the learner's comprehension and construction of texts, especially at the early stages of learning a new genre. This support is usually withdrawn, in a gradual manner, in the later stages of the learning cycle when learners have gained the knowledge and skills necessary to construct the text independently (Feez, 1998).

The conceptual framework for the design of multilevel writing tasks which will be described in this chapter was largely influenced by the notions of scaffolding (Vygotsky, 1978) and flexible learning materials. To specify, a multilevel task approach offers choices for learners so that they are able to work at their own level. Weaker learners may choose to work at a less challenging level than their more proficienct peers. Working at an appropriate level, each learner has an equal chance of succeeding at the task. Essentially, the multilevel writing tasks become a scaffold to assist learners in their production of texts and at the same time provide a practical solution for mixed ability class management.

Designing writing tasks

A series of ten writing tasks, each task with three different levels, were designed to be used as supplementary writing materials. Since it was proposed that each set of multilevel writing tasks be incorporated into the existing syllabus, ideas for the tasks mostly derived from the activities specified in the coursebook. Some writing tasks were developed in extension to, or in lieu of, existing activities, which were focused on different skills. At the same time, to promote meaningful communication through the use of tasks, each of the tasks contained some relevance to the students' academic and real world contexts. Accordingly, some of the writing tasks aimed to replicate real-life tasks (like writing a postcard) whereas others resembled academic assignments (such as writing a report). With these different genres to cover, it was important to be certain that the students understood the relationship between language forms, features, and functions. Hence, the tasks were designed in such a way that they raised the student's awareness of the textual structures specific to each genre.

To illustrate, a writing task called *Information Report* (see Figure 8.1) was developed to replace a pair work oral communicative activity in the coursebook that required learners to share ideas on the development of a technological invention and its impact on society.

Instead of having the students discuss the issue orally, it was assigned as a writing task so that the students could still address all the questions raised in the coursebook, namely (1) which technological invention has made the biggest impact in this century, (2) why such technology was invented, and (3) how such technology has changed people's lives. Additionally, the students got a chance to practise the past tense and passive voice, which were the focus of the unit of study. Therefore, this writing task was designed to ensure that the students were exposed to the content and language points specified in the coursebook. Furthermore, the context of writing was created to add a communicative purpose to the task. Usually, when assigned to write a report, the

Name _____ I.D. _____

Unit 2: Technology Task 1: Information Report (A)

Which invention has made the biggest impact on people's lives?

Write a short report (about 150 words) about the chosen technology including reason(s) why it was invented and how it affected our lives.

- ➢ You can begin your writing by giving a short description of the chosen invention.
- ➢ Then you may write about the purpose of invention and its impact on society.
- ➢ When writing about the history of the invention, remember to use Past Tense to indicate finished actions *e.g. Mr. X invented machine Y during the first World War.* However, you may use Present Perfect to talk about the impact as it is continued to the present *e.g. This invention has changed the way people travel.*
- ➢ You may use Passive Voice to emphasize more on the action rather than the actor *e.g. Machine Y was invented fifty years ago.* It is also useful when the actor is unknown.
- ➢ To complete the report, you need to include factual information from other sources. Do not copy words directly from the source. Use some of paraphrasing techniques you've learned in class to retell the information.

CHULALONGKORN UNIVERSITY SCIENCE FAIR

Invention of the Century

_____
_____
_____
_____
_____
_____
_____
_____
_____
_____
_____
_____
_____
_____
_____
_____
_____
_____

Figure 8.1 'Information report'

students would expect the teacher to be their sole audience. However, this task was linked to the situation where the student's report would be showcased at the university science fair. This context of a public audience encouraged the students to express their thoughts more meaningfully.

Grading task levels

The most distinct characteristic of the multilevel writing tasks is the three tasks levels offered. The decision to have three task levels was originally based on the common assumption that there are three broad groups of learners in a mixed ability class: beginner, intermediate and advanced (McKay and Tom, 1999). However, the levels were named according to stages of writing development – controlled writing, guided writing, and free writing (McDonough and Shaw, 2003) – in order to avoid labelling the learner's ability. Accordingly, the terms Supported Writing, Guided Writing and Free Writing were coined for task levels A, B and C respectively. This way, the name of the task levels implied both the task characteristics and the relationship between the task and the writer.

To assign different levels to the writing tasks, criteria were developed drawing on a literature review in the areas of task difficulty and task sequences (see Prabhu, 1987; Brindley, 1987; Long and Crookes, 1993; Skehan, 1996; Nunan, 2004; Duran and Ramaut, 2006). The criteria were concerned with the following factors:

The steps involved in completing the task

The first aspect concerned in grading the three levels was the number of steps the students were required to take in order to successfully complete the tasks. These steps were in relation to both cognitive skills involved in the writing process, such as brainstorming, planning, outlining, revising (Skehan, 1996; Ellis, 2005), and the schematic structures involved in the production of a certain text type (Wing Jan, 2009).

To reduce the steps in Level A (Supported Writing) so that the degree of task difficulty appeared the lowest among the three levels, partial texts were provided in some tasks (see Figure 8.2). For example, in an essay task, the students who chose the tasksheet in Level A would be given a partially written text in the writing space. All they had to do was to complete the partial text and add more content to the body of the essay. Providing parts of the text made Level A tasks appear more manageable compared to tasks in Level B (Guided Writing) and C (Free Writing) where the students were required to produce the whole text by themselves (Figures 8.3 and 8.4 show Levels B and C for this task, respectively).

Name _____ I.D. _____

Unit 4: Make an Impact Task 3: Essay (A)

'Watching television is bad for children'
To what extent do you agree or disagree with this statement?

Write an essay (about 180 words) on this topic. Use specific reasons and examples to support your opinion.

➢ First, you need to decide whether you agree or disagree with the statement above.
➢ If you agree, find reasons and examples from sources that talk about *bad things* that can happen when children watch television. However, if you disagree with the statement, find other reasons and examples which show *good things* children get from watching television.
➢ You may use the guided writing to begin and end your essay. Make sure you explicitly express your opinion on the issue e.g. *'I absolutely agree that watching television is bad for children.'* OR *'Most people believe that watching television is bad for children but I strongly disagree.'*
➢ Keep your writing logical and coherent – use some of the connectors such as *in addition, furthermore* to group similar ideas and *however, on the other hand* to show contrast of ideas.
➢ End with a conclusion that summarizes the key points that support your opinion.

Television is a big influence in the lives of most of us. People, young and old, spend hours every week watching television program. _____

_____

I think watching television is _____ for children because of these reasons. First of all, _____

_____

_____

_____

_____

_____

_____

In conclusion, I believe watching television is _____ for children because

_____

_____

Figure 8.2 Partial text in 'Essay' (Level A)

Name _____ I.D. _____

Unit 4: Make an Impact Task 3: Essay (B)

'Watching television is bad for children'
To what extent do you agree or disagree with this statement?

Write an essay (about 180 words) on this topic. Use specific reasons and examples to support your opinion.

- ➤ Before you begin writing, you need to decide whether you agree or disagree with the statement above.
- ➤ If you agree, find reasons and examples from sources that show *negative effects* of television. On the other hand, if you disagree, find the evidence to prove that children can receive *positive influences* from watching television.
- ➤ Your essay should start with an introduction that includes your opinion on this topic.
- ➤ Then you can give reasons to support your agreement/ disagreement. Remember to be specific. This will make your argument more convincing.
- ➤ Keep your writing logical and coherent – use some of the connectors learned in class to help organize your thoughts.
- ➤ A proper essay should end with a conclusion. It is an opportunity to summarize the key points you have made and reaffirm your opinion.

Figure 8.3 'Essay' (Level B)

Name _____ I.D. _____

Unit 4: Make an Impact Task 3: Essay (C)

'Watching television is bad for children'
To what extent do you agree or disagree with this statement?

Write an essay (about 180 words) on this topic. Use specific reasons and examples to support your opinion.

Before you start writing, ask yourself these questions:

➢ Do I agree or disagree with the above statement?
➢ What are the reasons to support my agreement/ disagreement?
➢ What kind of information can I include in my writing to make it more convincing?
➢ How do I start the essay? Should there be an introduction? How do I write a good introduction?
➢ Should I state my opinion on the issue from the beginning?
➢ How can I make my writing logical and flowing? How can I make it easy for readers to follow my thoughts?
➢ How do I end my essay? Should there be a conclusion as well? What should be included in my conclusion?

Figure 8.4 'Essay' (Level C)

The complexity of task demands

In order to complete the tasks successfully, learners need to be able to fulfil the task demands and achieve the communicative goals (Willis, 1996; Skehan, 1998). Tasks that impose too many cognitive demands on learners may appear difficult to manage (Brindley, 1987; Skehan, 1996). To assist students with the requirements of multilevel writing tasks, two types of instruction were given. First, the primary instruction, which was identical in all three levels, stated the task demands in terms of topic of writing, text type, word limit, communicative goal and, perhaps, intended audience. Next, the list of secondary instructions, or writing directions, broke down these task demands into practical writing steps. In this sense, the secondary instructions, which varied at each level, helped reduce the cognitive complexity of the task demands for the students. Table 8.1 shows the primary and secondary instructions for an essay task.

Table 8.1   Primary and secondary instructions

Primary instructions	Secondary instructions
'Watching television is bad for children' *To what extent do you agree or disagree with this statement?* Write an essay (about 180 words) on this topic. Use specific reasons and examples to support your opinion.	*Level A* • First, you need to decide whether you agree or disagree with the statement above. • If you agree, find reasons and examples from sources that talk about *bad things* that can happen when children watch television. However, if you disagree with the statement, find other reasons and examples which show *good things* children get from watching television.
	Level B • Before you begin writing, you need to decide whether you agree or disagree with the statement above. • If you agree, find reasons and examples from sources that show *negative effects* of television. On the other hand, if you disagree, find the evidence to prove that children can receive *positive influences* from watching television.
	Level C **Before you start writing, ask yourself these questions:** • Do I agree or disagree with the above statement? • What are the reasons to support my agreement/ disagreement? • What kind of information can I include in my writing to make it more convincing?

The explicitness of information

Also in relation to the cognitive complexity of the task is the degree of explicitness in the information provided to learners. Nunan (2004) asserts that the level of task difficulty can be reduced through explicit input because it minimises ambiguity and cognitive load. In the case of multilevel writing tasks, the main input provided to the students was in the form of task instructions. Accordingly, the instructions written for the three task levels were designed to vary in their degrees of explicitness, especially in terms of recommended language use. To illustrate, Table 8.2 compares the instructions written for the task Postcard to a Friend.

As displayed in Table 8.2, the instructions for Level A tasksheet are the most explicitly written. Instructions at this level suggest both content and language appropriate to the specific text. Additionally, samples of language patterns are given. Meanwhile, Level B tasksheet still offers relatively detailed instructions on how to complete the tasks but omits samples of language patterns. On the other hand, Level C tasksheet provides only guideline questions, implicitly suggesting the language to be used in the writing.

Table 8.2 Instructions written for three task levels of 'Postcard to a Friend'

Level A
- First, you need to think about all the fun things you did or the exciting/surprising/disappointing experiences you had during this trip.
- You can use the guided writing to begin and end your story.
- After a short introduction of where you are and how you feel about the overall trip, you can begin to write about the things you saw, activities you did or people you met etc. – use adjectives and/or adverbs to describe how you feel, such as *beautiful* scenery, *strange* people, meet *unexpectedly* or moving *too slowly*.
- Remember to use Past Tense – you are telling a story that has already happened!

Level B
- You may begin by telling your friend the background information, such as where you are, how you got there, or whom you came with.
- Then you can write about what exactly happened on the trip.
- You should add your thoughts and/or feelings about the trip at the end to conclude.
- You can use Past Tense to talk about events that already happened and Present Tense to talk about general facts.

Level C
Before you start writing, ask yourself these questions:
- How do I begin writing? Do I need to give a short introduction?
- What should I include in my story?
- How should I arrange the information?
- Which tense should I use to tell my story?
- Should I include my feelings and comments or just give the facts?
- How should I end the story?

The syntactic and lexical complexity of instructions

Task levels were not only decided by the degrees of explicitness the instructions offered, but also by the complexity of the language used in these instructions (Ellis, 2003; Nunan, 2004; Duran and Ramaut, 2006). In other words, the vocabulary and language structures for each level of instruction were selected purposely to portray different levels of difficulty. For instance, the Level A tasksheet in Figure 8.2 uses the expressions 'good things' and 'bad things', while the Level B tasksheet in Figure 8.3 refers to 'negative effects' and 'positive influences'.

The degree of control

According to Skehan (1996), task participants usually feel less pressured and consequently perceive tasks as less difficult when they possess some degree of control over the tasks. Therefore, it is ideal that task manageability is assured for all learners. However, previous research findings (Nuangpolmak, 2005) showed different factors leading to the perception of task manageability; namely guidance, assistance, and freedom dependent on the learner's personal traits, such as motivation and self-efficacy. Thus, different measures were employed to vary the degree of task manageability at each level.

In Level A tasks, the students were supported with explicit instructions, language samples and, in some cases, partial texts (see Criteria 1, 2 and 3). Through these features, it was anticipated that even less-proficient learners would be able to successfully achieve the task goals. As for Level B tasks, step-by-step instructions were still provided to guide the students through the production of texts. For those who were not confident enough to complete the writing tasks on their own, these guided instructions were designed to facilitate the fulfilment of task goals. Unlike tasks in Levels A and B, in which control was heightened by precise knowledge of how the tasks were to be executed, the writing tasks in Level C offered a different sense of control in that the students were free to address the tasks in whichever way they wanted to as long as the task goals were achieved. The freedom and flexibility yielded by Level C tasks was likely to appeal to students with a higher writing proficiency.

The amount of support available

Fundamentally, all the measures discussed in Criteria 1–5 were employed to ensure that the students were able to manage the tasks by themselves. The amount of support given within the task (Brindley, 1987; Nunan, 2004), in terms of explicitness of instructions, language samples, and partial texts provided was therefore considered the most important criterion in assigning a particular task to one of three levels. As there were several forms of support embedded within the materials for each task level, it was completely the student's choice to select the task level that offered the kind of assistance they required.

Implementing multilevel writing tasks

Over the course of the 16-week semester, the implementation of the ten multi-level writing tasks was incorporated into the established syllabus and lesson plans. These tasks were designed to supplement the content in the coursebook. For each writing task a prompt was designed as an introduction to the task. The prompt was effective in setting a context for the task, providing a more realistic communicative goal, and suggesting a target audience. An example of a prompt is shown in Figure 8.5. This was a prompt used in the writing task where the students were asked to write about the mysteries surrounding the origin of Stonehenge.

After seeing the writing prompt each student made a decision with regard to the task level he/she would like to perform at. Once decided, each of them collected the tasksheet at the selected level and worked individually to complete

❀**Mysterious MAG**❀

Junior Columnist Awards

Mysterious MAG will celebrate its first anniversary in January next year
On this special occasion, the magazine invites all young writers to participate in the first "Junior Columnist Competition".

To enter the competition, submit a 150-word research-based article entitled ***"The Mystery of Stonehenge"*** to be published in a special "World Wonders" issue. The winner will be awarded 15,000 baht and a chance to become one of the magazine's part-time columnists.

Interested writers can submit their articles via Mysterious MAG's website: www.MMAG.net

Figure 8.5   Writing prompt

the task. The completed writing tasks were commented on, marked, and returned, if possible, before the distribution of the next task. As a requirement of the activity, the students were also asked to fill in a guided reflection form upon completion of the writing task. This reflection form, which was attached to the back of the tasksheet, consisted of eight questions regarding their performance of the task, the knowledge acquired from the task and their plan for future task levels. The guided reflection form embedded as a part of the multilevel writing task is shown in Figure 8.6.

Reflection _____ ✍

In my opinion, this task is ☐ too easy for me ☐ too difficult for me ☐ suitable for my ability

I could do this task ☐ on my own ☐ with my friend's help ☐ by referring to study tips

I think I did this task ☐ very well ☐ quite well ☐ badly because _____
_____
_____

My problem(s) when doing this task was _____
_____
_____

I solved this problem by _____
_____
_____

From this task, I learned _____
_____
_____

I can use what I learned to _____
_____

I will choose level ☐ **A** ☐ **B** ☐ **C** for the next writing assignment because _____
_____
_____

TEACHER'S COMMENT:

Figure 8.6 Guided reflection form

One of the main objectives in designing and implementing a multilevel task approach was to foster autonomous learning behaviours. The best way to do this, as suggested by Nunan (1997), was to have a pedagogical intervention in the actual learning process. Learning situations where autonomy is promoted usually place a great emphasis on training learners in metacognitive strategies such as planning, monitoring, evaluating, and reflecting (Cotterall, 2000), and involving learners in a decision-making process in relation to the self-management of learning experiences, such as selecting materials and determining a learning pace (Lamb, 2003). Accordingly, the reflection form was developed, as a part of multilevel task features, to assist the students in their retrospection. In order to make an informed choice with regard to the future task level, the students would go through the process of monitoring and evaluating their own performance. The reflection form helped highlight this process and, at the same time, raised the student's awareness of their strengths, weaknesses, and needs. During the 16-week implementation of the multilevel task approach, the students were able to plan and choose their task levels based on their own evaluation of previous performances.

Implications for materials development

Where a mixed ability class is concerned, most teachers tend to describe this diversity in terms of student linguistic levels (Jiménez Raya and Lamb, 2003). However, students also vary in their cognitive and affective maturity. These factors in turn will influence their perception of task difficulty. Learning materials which contained simple language structures were not necessarily perceived as the easiest ones. Therefore, materials developers should explore other ways to 'ease' up the learning activities than merely simplifying the language. Furthermore, since the construct of task motivation is influenced by various internal and external factors, such as personal traits, self-efficacy, judgement, and perceived task value (Julkunen, 2001), materials which aim to enhance motivation need to interact with all these factors. It can be argued that no single set of materials can motivate all learners equally. Hence, offering choices to learners seems to be the optimal way that materials can ensure some degree of learner engagement and enjoyment in learning. The concept of multilevel tasks suggested in this chapter illustrates that minor adaptation can be made to the coursebook materials in order to provide choices to the students. These choices do not suggest 'what' the students learnt, but highlight the process of 'how' they learnt (Islam and Mares, 2003). As Allwright (1981) emphasises, materials should be perceived as learning materials rather than teaching materials. Accordingly, materials development should not be focused on the ways in which teachers teach, but on the ways in which learners learn.

As language teachers, we all want to help our students develop their language skills and acquire the language in the best way that they possibly can. Essentially, there are two equal parts in the term language learning, namely language and learning. Therefore, teachers who aim to facilitate language learning must pay attention to these two components equally. The multilevel task approach described in this chapter is an example of a pedagogical intervention where both language and learning can be scaffolded at the same time through the use of learning materials. The design of multilevel tasks, specifically the in-task support features, provides the assistance required for students to complete writing tasks by directing them through the schematic steps of the texts, as well as modelling language features appropriate for such texts. The instructions within the design of the multilevel tasks therefore form a scaffolding to support the students in their production of texts in the class while equipping them with skills to enable the performance of the same tasks without support in the future. Besides scaffolding language ability, the multilevel writing tasks also enable learners to become better at learning. It is believed that learners who utilise metacognitive strategies, such as planning, monitoring, and reflecting, can better manage the learning process and thus become more efficient as learners (Benson, 2001). In turn, these metacognitive skills enable learners to take more active roles in their learning and consequently to develop autonomy (Littlewood, 1996). The implementation of a multilevel task approach can be considered as a support for learners during their transition to becoming fully autonomous.

Concluding remarks

Despite some criticism of teachers as materials developers (for instance Allwright, 1981), McGrath (2002) supports the notion of teacher-developed materials by pointing out that classroom teachers know their own students best and therefore are able to design materials suitable to the levels, needs and interests of their students.

This chapter has provided an example of a teacher-initiated materials development process. It has shown how, through the use of multilevel tasks, teachers can assist their students more meaningfully, both in the present (developing their language abilities) and in the future (becoming autonomous learners). Moreover, the approach outlined here is relatively easy to adapt to the demands of any local curriculum and does not require an unreasonable amount of the teacher's time.

Nevertheless, there are limitations to the multilevel task approach. The limited reading ability of weaker learners may prevent them from fully understanding the instructions given in the handouts. This can result in incomplete tasks or incorrect written products. One solution to this issue would be to include task instructions in the mother tongue, especially in Level A tasks.

In finding ways to improve our practice, there is no need to look further than our own classrooms, as all classrooms have their own challenges and dilemmas. The motivation for creating these multilevel materials was originally fuelled by the constant practical problems of classroom diversity. As it turns out, diversity, like many classroom problems, need not be an issue if we find a way to work with it

Engagement priorities

1. As Benson (2004) claims, language learners should be seen as individuals and their individuality should be embraced in the classroom. What aspect of learner diversity, for example, age, learning styles, first language background, second language proficiency, etc., is common in your practice? How do you plan to address the issue of learner diversity in your classroom?
2. Many students enter a language classroom accepting the fact that they have no control over what and how they learn. The multilevel task approach described in this chapter is an example of a classroom practice where students are given control in terms of learning materials. What else can be done in the classroom to allow students more control?
3. According to Tomlinson (2001), materials take different roles in the learning process. Materials can inform learners about the rules of language, expose learners to language samples, and stimulate language use. Since materials play such an important role in learning, should students get involved in the development of materials? In what ways can students contribute to materials design? In your own context, to what extent do you think student involvement can be achieved?

References

Allwright, R. L. (1981). What do we want teaching materials for? *ELT Journal,* 36(1): 5–17.

Benson, P. (2001). *Teaching and Researching Autonomy in Language Learning.* Harlow: Longman.

Benson, P. (2004). (Auto) biography and learner diversity. In Benson, P. and Nunan, D. (eds), *Learners' Stories: Difference and Diversity in Language Learning.* Cambridge: Cambridge University Press, pp. 4–21.

Brindley, G. (1987). Factors affecting task difficulty. In Nunan, D. (ed.), *Guidelines for the Development of Curriculum Resources.* Adelaide: National Curriculum Resource Centre, pp. 45–56.

Cotterall, S. (2000). Promoting learner autonomy through the curriculum: principles for designing language courses. *ELT Journal,* 54(2): 109–117.

Dörnyei, Z. (2001). *Motivational Strategies in the Language Classroom*. Cambridge: Cambridge University Press.

Duran, G. and Ramaut, G. (2006). Tasks for absolute beginners and beyond: developing and sequencing tasks at basic proficiency levels. In Van den Branden, K. (ed.), *Task-Based Language Education: From Theory to Practice*. Cambridge: Cambridge University Press, pp. 47–75.

Ellis, R. (2003). *Task-Based Language Learning and Teaching*. Oxford: Oxford University Press.

Ellis, R. (2005). Planning and task-based performance: theory and research. In Ellis, R. (ed.), *Planning and Task Performance in a Second Language*. Amsterdam: John Benjamins.

Feez, S. (1998). *Text-Based Syllabus Design*. Sydney: National Centre for English Language Teaching and Research.

Foley, J. A. (2005). English in … Thailand. *RELC Journal,* 36(2): 223–234.

Hemingway, P. (1986). Teaching a mixed-level class. *Practical English Teaching,* 7(1): 18–20.

Holec, H. (1981). *Autonomy and Foreign Language Learning*. Oxford: Pergamon.

Hyland, K. (2004). *Genre and Second Language Writing*. Michigan: University of Michigan Press.

Islam, C. and Mares, C. (2003). Adapting classroom materials. In Tomlinson, B. (ed.), *Developing Materials for Language Teaching*. London: Continuum, pp. 86–100.

Jiménez Raya, M. and Lamb, T. (2003). Dealing with diversity in the modern languages class. In Jiménez Raya, M. and Lamb, T. (eds), *Differentiation in Modern Languages Classroom*. Frankfurt am Main: Peter Lang, pp. 13–20.

Julkunen, K. (2001). Situation-and-task specific motivation in foreign language learning. In Dörnyei, Z. and Schmidt, R. (eds), *Motivation and Second Language Acquisition*. Honolulu: Second Language Teaching and Curriculum Center, University of Hawai'i at Mānoa, pp. 29–41.

Lamb, T. (2003). Individualising learning: organising a flexible learning environment. In Jiménez Raya, M. and Lamb, T. (eds), *Differentiation in Modern Languages Classroom*. Frankfurt am Main: Peter Lang, pp. 177–194.

Littlewood, W. (1996). Autonomy: anatomy and a framework. *System*, 24(4): 427–435.

Long, M. H. and Crookes, G. (1993). Units of analysis in syllabus design – the case for task. In Crookes, G. and Gass, S. (eds), *Tasks in a Pedagogical Context: Integrating Theory and Practice*. Clevedon: Multilingual Matters, pp. 9–54.

McDonough, J. and Shaw, C. (2003). *Materials and Methods in ELT*, 2nd Edition. Oxford: Blackwell.

McGrath, I. (2002). *Materials Evaluation and Design for Language Teaching*. Edinburgh: Edinburgh University Press.

McKay, H. and Tom, A. (1999). *Teaching Adult Second Language Learners*. Cambridge: Cambridge University Press.

Nuangpolmak, A. (2005). *Task Motivation in Writing: A Study of Thai Students*. Unpublished Master Dissertation, Department of Linguistics, Macquarie University.

Nunan, D. (1997). Designing and adapting materials to encourage learner autonomy. In Benson, P. and Voller, P. (eds), *Autonomy and Independence in Language Learning*. London: Longman, pp. 192–203.

Nunan, D. (2004). *Task-Based Language Teaching*. Cambridge: Cambridge University Press.

Prabhu, N. (1987). *Second Language Pedagogy*. Oxford: Oxford University Press.

Prapphal, K. (2008). Issues and trends in language testing and assessment in Thailand. *Language Testing,* 25(1): 127–143.

Skehan, P. (1996). A framework for the implementation of task-based instruction. *Applied Linguistics,* 17: 38–62.

Skehan, P. (1998). Task-based instruction. *Annual Review of Applied Linguistics,* 18: 268–286.

Thai, M. D. (2009). *Text-based Language Teaching.* Cecil Hills, NSW: Mazmania Press.

Tomlinson, B. (2001). Materials development. In Carter, R. and Nunan, D. (eds), *The Cambridge Guide to Teaching English to Speakers of Other Languages.* Cambridge: Cambridge University Press, pp. 66–71.

Vygotsky, L. S. (1978). *Mind in Society: The Development of Higher Psychological Processes.* Cambridge: Harvard University Press.

Willis, J. (1996). *A Framework for Task-Based Learning.* Essex: Longman.

Wing Jan, L. (2009). *Write Ways: Modelling Writing Forms,* 3rd Edition. Oxford: Oxford University Press.

Wongsothorn, A., Hiranburana, K. and Chinnawongs, S. (2002). English language teaching in Thailand today. *Asia-Pacific Journal of Education,* 22: 107–116.

9
Designing Effective, Culturally, and Linguistically Responsive Pedagogy

Josie Guiney Igielski

Introduction

Schooling students in a language that is not their home language has become a responsibility for more and more teachers around the world due to global movements of people. This chapter describes how the author, in a US context, sought to provide access to the curriculum, materials, and learning to the English learners in her classroom.

A significant achievement gap exists in US public schools between native English-speaking students and students whose first language is something other than English. Valdes (1996) posits that factors that contribute to this gap include language barriers, socio-economic status, educational backgrounds, and overall cultural differences. ELLs (English language learners) consistently score below English-speaking peers on academic achievement tests. 'National statistics show that ELLs are three times as likely as native English speakers to be low academic achievers. They are also twice as likely to be held back to repeat a grade' (Freeman and Freeman, 2007: 5). Both educators and society at large need to address these issues in order to provide access to success for all students.

Throughout history, the educational community in the US has tried to address the complex problems of inequality in schooling. Although there is no magical solution or educational programme that addresses all of the factors at play in increasing achievement gaps, one important place to address the gaps is the classroom. The framework for the research described in this chapter was developed using three themes that contribute to student success. The first is a need for culturally responsive teaching (Gay, 2002; Ladson-Billings, 2001; Villegas and Lucas, 2007). The second is the importance of a culturally relevant curriculum and materials for the success of all students (Gay, 2000). The third is the importance of teaching language through thematic and integrated content, and to support all students' first languages and cultures (Freeman and Freeman, 2007; Gibbons, 2002).

Based on the work of these researchers, it became clear that, as a fourth grade (9–10 year olds) teacher with a significant number of culturally and linguistically diverse students, the author could design relevant pedagogy using five main principles: (1) understanding the cultural diversity present in the student population; (2) utilisation of students' funds of knowledge; (3) inclusion of linguistically and culturally diverse content in the curriculum and materials; (4) responsiveness to ethnic and linguistic diversity in the method of instruction; and (5) engagement of students in purposeful language-rich academic tasks (Villegas and Lucas, 2002; Wlodkowski and Ginsberg, 1995; Diaz-Rico and Weed, 1995).

Understanding the cultural and linguistic diversity present in the classroom and utilising students' funds of knowledge

In countries all over the world, teachers design and adapt their curriculum and materials for student populations who have experienced life in a culturally and linguistically different way. Villegas and Lucas (2007: 31) push for teachers to have 'an awareness that a person's worldview is not universal but is profoundly influenced by life experiences, as mediated by a variety of factors, including race, ethnicity, gender, and social class'. Students' cultural identities also play a large role in how they learn (ibid.: 33). Therefore, teachers need to gain more knowledge about the cultures, ethnicities, and languages of the student populations in their classrooms. Without an adequate understanding of students' cultural and linguistic backgrounds teachers will not be able to help all students reach their highest potential.

However, these concepts and understandings only translate into student success when the teacher utilises them in curriculum planning and implementation, while being mindful that each student's worldview is unique and actively evolving. Gay states: 'The knowledge that teachers need to have about cultural diversity goes way beyond mere awareness of, respect for, and general recognition of the fact that ethnic groups have different values or express similar values in various ways. (2002: 107). Teachers must strive to use knowledge of their students in the creation of responsive curriculum design.

Culturally responsive teaching is 'using cultural characteristics, experiences, and perspectives of ethnically diverse students as conduits for teaching them more effectively' (Gay, 2002: 106). When academic knowledge and skills are situated within the lived experiences and frames of references of students they are more personally meaningful, lead to increased engagement, and are learnt more easily and thoroughly (Gay, 2000, 2002; Ladson-Billings, 1995). In this way teachers create space for students' cultures and languages to be represented in the academic domains of school.

No one particular teaching strategy engages all learners all of the time. Instead, teachers must find ways to elicit engagement from students by tapping into student motivation. 'Rather than trying to know *what to do to* students, we must work with students to interpret and deepen their existing knowledge and enthusiasm for learning' (Wlodkowski and Ginsberg, 1995: 17). Teachers must draw on students' cultural perspectives, and at the same time view students as uniquely and actively evolving individuals. Thus, teachers should think not only in terms of general cultural characteristics and traits, but also about what their particular learners bring and know.

Teachers can create a bridge between home culture and school culture by utilising students' funds of knowledge, which Moll and Gonzalez define as 'the idea that people are competent and have knowledge, and their life experiences have given them that knowledge' (2002: 625). Their research also suggests that the documentation of students' funds of knowledge can be used in systematic and powerful ways by teachers to represent and harness personal, familial, and community resources in a school setting. When teachers use the knowledge and expertise that students bring in the service of academic learning, the learning becomes relevant and meaningful.

One important connection between culturally responsive teaching and funds of knowledge is that some knowledge is valued more than other knowledge in institutional contexts such as schools. Historically, the types of knowledge that are validated academically are the funds that exist within white, middle-class culture. This means that the texts, tasks, and even topics that are part of the school curriculum are more familiar to mainstream students than to others, such as English learners, and makes it more difficult for ELLs to succeed in school (Freeman and Freeman, 2007; Moll and Gonzalez, 2002). Thus it is important to consider the materials through which content is presented.

Including ethnically and culturally diverse content in the curriculum and materials

'Students need to understand that the history of the United States is not about the life events and accomplishments of one culture. It is an extraordinary chronicle of many different cultures each determining their place and purpose in history' (Montgomery, 2000: 36). Teachers can accomplish this goal by using texts and information that are diverse in content and theme. It is especially important for ELLs learning in English to have the additional support of materials that make a connection with their lives. However, finding quality literature that meets this criterion can be difficult because some texts perpetuate stereotypes instead of addressing issues from the perspective of an individual. Researchers Freeman and Freeman (2007: 13) have created rubrics and assessments to help educators establish a repertoire of resource materials that respect and value individuals. When using stories, a key resource material for all learners, they suggest that teachers consider whether the characters presented in the story have cultural or linguistic characteristics similar to those of the student population. They prompt educators to consider whether the material will provide parallels or connections to the students' lived experiences. One final consideration is the setting and context of the story. Culturally responsive content utilises 'literacy that builds on linguistically and culturally diverse students' existing knowledge, [and] draws on their families, communities, and the world around them to make sense of the world' (Gaitan, 2006: 156).

A vital aspect of culturally and linguistically relevant teaching is the inclusion of content that is written in the student's first language (Freeman and Freeman, 2007). Even if teachers do not share the students' languages, they can infuse their curriculum with first language materials, like books and classroom print, letting students use their first languages where possible in writing, and bringing in school and community members who speak the students' language. An important consideration for culturally and linguistically relevant content is the creation of what Montgomery (2001) calls a 'Culturally Complex Atmosphere', which incorporates relevant and current news and events, a diverse classroom library, cross-cultural literature discussions, and cooperative learning. This atmosphere helps students to begin to understand and appreciate the range of human experiences and cultural backgrounds. Culturally responsive content also directly addresses controversy. Gay states:

> responsive curriculum addresses controversy by studying a wide range of ethnic individuals and groups; contextualizing issues within race, class, ethnicity, and gender; and including multiple kinds of knowledge and perspectives. (2002: 108)

With an approach that explicitly engages students in thinking and talking about controversial issues, students are given the opportunity to see issues as complex and to engage in critical analysis.

Responding to ethnic and linguistic diversity through the methods of instruction

Teachers are responsible for providing access to academic success for all learners. The goal is to design learning that serves students from non-dominant cultures equitably. There are many ways teachers can provide access to students within the method of instruction of their curriculum.

Participation patterns

The term participation patterns refers to the way in which students are asked to participate in the act of learning. Students' learning styles vary. Some are culturally or linguistically specific. For example, some cultures have individualistic approaches to learning and others have communal approaches (Pransky and Bailey, 2002). The use of different participation patterns helps teachers organise learning so that all students within a multicultural classroom can experience success. Setting up activities that include a variety of modes of engagement helps students from non-dominant cultures succeed and excel in content area instruction. In classrooms where teachers allow flexible grouping, there is greater flexibility in the flow and acquisition of information. Useful participation patterns implemented in response to this knowledge are cooperative groups, guided discussions, and homogenous linguistic pairings, in addition to more traditional teacher-fronted approaches (Hawkins and Katz, 2008).

Themed units

Themed units provide scaffolding and meaningful connections for all learners, but specifically for ELLs. 'Organizing curriculum around themes supports ELLs as they learn English and learn academic content in English. Themes help students make sense of instruction.' (Freeman and Freeman, 2007: 78). Interdisciplinary themes are effective because they encourage students to participate in meaningful reading, writing, listening, and speaking tasks. Freeman and Freeman refine the concept of themed teaching by focusing organisation of instruction around 'big questions' like 'Why do people immigrate or migrate?', which give ELLs and other culturally diverse learners a context within which to interpret learning. Students are able to organise their thinking and analysis within a lesson by considering how they fit into the larger organising question. For example, the big question above enables students to better analyse a lesson on illegal immigration to the United States from Mexico.

Native language support

Mainstream monolingual teachers are most effective in teaching multilingual students if they design instruction that draws on students' first language and cultural knowledge. Freeman and Freeman (2007: 92–96) list several methods for supporting first languages in a mainstream classroom. These include: using a preview/view/review approach; accessing cognates; bilingual tutoring; allowing ELLs to talk in their first language; using first language storytellers; arranging for students to read in their first language; and publishing books written in first language. They also stress the importance of allowing students, ELLs in particular, time to reflect on the materials presented and practise the skills taught within the content.

Assessment

ELLs undergo a range of formal assessments in US schools. These include standard state, district, and classroom assessments, as well as assessments of language proficiency. However, these assessments are usually used for accountability purposes and are not necessarily useful for the classroom. Useful assessments provide teachers with accurate feedback about a student's proficiency with language and understanding of content that helps them create a responsive curriculum. Such assessments include 'teacher observations of interactions, teacher student interactions, outcomes of listening, reading, speaking, and writing tasks, portfolios of work, and students' self-assessments' (Gibbons, 2002: 124). They offer an alternative to traditional assessment approaches that can be effective but are limiting due to possible bias, issues with content validity, and practicality of implementation (ibid.). Teachers use assessment measures that include analysis of student work and interactions to pinpoint what students can do with language, and what they are learning, thus enabling them to plan a more responsive curriculum that is tailored to student levels and needs.

Engaging students in purposeful language-rich academic tasks

A key component of culturally responsive teaching is to teach language through the content areas and not in isolation. 'If second language learners are not to be disadvantaged in their long-term learning, and are to have the time and opportunity to learn subject-specific registers of school, they need access to an ongoing language-focused program across the whole curriculum.' (Gibbons, 2002: 5). This type of curriculum is designed with both language and content objectives in mind. Content objectives for ELLs function as they do for main-stream students, and identify the content area knowledge students are to gain, which usually aligns with state and school standards. Language objectives identify the language that students will need to participate successfully in a content lesson, the forms, features and functions of language specific to what they are learning and being asked to do. Language objectives operate on many levels, including individual words and vocabulary, sentence structures, and whole texts, seeking to increase the level of academic language used by learners within the curriculum.

Content specific vocabulary is an important component of a language-focused curriculum, and academic vocabulary words need to be purposefully selected and meaningfully experienced. However, teachers also have to be skilled in finding the language features within the curriculum. Language-focused instruction focuses on usage of formal and informal language structures, syntax, tense, first language interference, note taking, summarising, asking questions, use of appropriate connectives, word choice, and vocabulary. In planning instruction teachers first inventory the language needed for student success, and then tailor the language objectives to fit the current proficiency levels and needs of their students. Beginning with just one or two language-focused goals for each lesson is an effective way to begin to see all of the ways in which language can infuse content instruction.

Culturally and linguistically responsive learning in a fourth grade classroom

I am a fourth grade teacher in an elementary school in a city with a population of 230,000. My school is a high poverty school; ELLs are a significant percentage of its population with the largest group coming from Spanish-speaking families. The second largest ELL group is Hmong-speaking. Various other languages are present at our school including African-American Vernacular English, Bhutanese, Vietnamese, and Chinese. According to school district data, in the 2008–2009 school year, 74 per cent of the school's population were low income, and 38 per cent were ELLs.

When I began to research my fourth grade inclusive mainstream classroom of sixteen students, nine of whom were ELLs, I could not see all my students' histories valued and validated in the curriculum. I did not see my students making enough connections between the texts and themselves. I saw the language and vocabulary of the texts and curriculum as being prohibitive for my ELLs (and all my students) instead of being a vehicle for expanding students' current knowledge and vocabulary. In response to the lack of responsive pedagogy in my classroom, I conducted a study based on two fundamental questions:

1. How can explicit attention to language, culture, and identity in the curriculum and practice affect students' sense of themselves as learners in school?
2. How can the curriculum and pedagogy validate and value what students bring in service of academic learning?

In order to answer these questions I designed a curriculum unit that utilised a framework of culturally and linguistically relevant pedagogy, as described above and summarised in Table 9.1.

Table 9.1 Framework for culturally and linguistically relevant pedagogy

Big question(s) for the unit:

Access to and utilisation of funds of knowledge	Content goals	Language objectives	Diverse content	Relevant delivery method
Students as experts and resources; Families and communities as experts and resources; Prior knowledge activation	State and district standards for social studies, reading, writing, maths, oral language, and inquiry research; Textbook goals and vocabulary	Students' language needs/goals	Teacher resources and student resources; Content presented that confronts controversy	Participation patterns; Assessments used; Information exchange format and style; Primary language support

The goal of the framework was to create a structure that would push me to be more purposeful, and culturally and linguistically relevant in the implementation of content and use of materials. This structure and ideology held me accountable for providing students with multiple entry points and better access to the content and language of the unit. These key factors are addressed for every lesson in the organising headings of the framework, which was an effective tool for leveraging students' funds of knowledge, language, and cultural capital in the service of academic learning.

I designed a study that compared a traditional, commercially-designed curriculum unit to one that I developed using the framework. I taught the traditional unit (the theme was mapping) according to the teaching guide with no modifications. It included fourteen social studies lessons, and several writing lessons. After the completion of the traditional unit, I identified shortcomings for my student population: the text was too lengthy, the vocabulary was not repeated and integrated within the unit, and the concepts were not presented in a way that was relevant to the lives of my students. I also identified the ways my students' success as learners was limited within the curriculum. The traditional unit never tapped into my students' funds of knowledge or asked me, their teacher, to modify a lesson based on what I knew about their lives. Students also looked for connections that were never made within the traditional unit, and their misconceptions continued. For example they asked me, 'Where is Puebla, Mexico? Is it in Texas?'

Within the traditional unit, in terms of responsive delivery methods, during paired activities students produced work that better met the requirements of the assignments. Students paired with others who shared a common first language met the requirements of more lesson objectives, something I considered when designing delivery methods for the modified unit. With regard to diverse modes of assessment, student work indicated that most students were searching for, and not finding, relevance in the traditional unit. One student's final reflection was, 'Why do maps even matter?' Regarding the richness of language within tasks, students used some specific vocabulary within discussions, but not independently within oral and written responses. This feedback confirmed that the modified curriculum unit needed to be guided by a unifying theme, and supported by essential, inquiry style questions.

The end of unit test scores and student feedback served as clear evidence that students had not gained essential content goals nor developed a meaningful understanding of key vocabulary. This data and reflection on the implementation of the traditional unit led to the responsive planning and linguistic scaffolding of content and language goals for the modified unit.

The content theme of the modified unit was immigration and migration to our state. I designed the modified unit utilising several different materials, including the district-issued, fourth grade social studies text chapter, and picture books, web resources from the Historical Society, guest speakers, student and family stories, and photographs of immigrants and migrants throughout US history. It was a month-long unit consisting of fourteen social studies lessons, daily writing lessons, and a non-fiction book study within reading. Each lesson varied from thirty to sixty minutes in length. Maths and science lessons were integrated in a more indirect way to the unit.

Practitioners' diverse knowledge base

Prior to the design and implementation of my modified unit I knew that assessing my own bias and worldview would be an important step towards success. Self-assessment using the questions in Table 9.2 helped me identify my weaknesses and strengths. personally and professionally. It made me re-evaluate how I would initiate the unit with my students, and how adept I would be at responding to and identifying their cultural and linguistic needs.

Knowledge of my students, their families, their first languages, their cultural and ethnic backgrounds, and the community in which they lived was the basis for my curriculum design. I worked hard not to essentialise my students' experiences by focusing on the identity of students as individuals. Each year deepening this knowledge base is an adventure for me, and I purposefully take the opportunity to engage students and families in non-school environments. Some strategies I have found successful are going to students'

Table 9.2 Teacher diversity self assessment

- What is my definition of diversity?
- Do the children in my classroom and school come from diverse cultural backgrounds?
- What are my perceptions of students from different racial or ethnic groups? With language or dialects different from mine? With special needs?
- What are the sources of these perceptions (including friends, relatives, television, movies)?
- How do I respond to my students, based on these perceptions?
- Have I experienced others making assumptions about me based on my membership of a specific group? How did I feel?
- What steps do I need to take to learn about the students from diverse backgrounds in my school and classroom?
- How often do social relationships develop among students from different racial and ethnic backgrounds in my classroom? What is the nature of these relationships?
- In what ways do I make my instructional programme responsive to the needs of the diverse groups in my classroom?
- What kinds of information, skills, and resources do I need to acquire to effectively teach from a multicultural perspective?
- In what ways do I collaborate with other educators, family members, and community groups to address the needs of all my students?

Source: Montgomery (2001).

sporting events, shopping at neighbourhood businesses, discovering parents' places of employment, participating in community events, and volunteering at neighbourhood resource organisations. These activities help me find links between the school curricula and my students' lives. For example, I learnt that a student's father was struggling with immigration issues after conversing with the family several times at a weekly soccer game. We had built enough trust for them to feel comfortable sharing this aspect of their lives, and this in turn affected how I presented immigration issues in my unit.

Funds of knowledge

The deep knowledge base I have about my students' lives helps me to situate their learning in experiences that relate to and celebrate the cultural capital that they bring in the service of learning. Harnessing students' funds of knowledge gives me the opportunity to design a curriculum that validates what is historically undervalued or omitted from traditional curricula. Several students in my classroom had parents that were first generation immigrants. This knowledge proved valuable in my search for guest presenters. These connections became empowering sources for students to interview, record, and map immigration stories.

The use of primary language guest presenters in the unit enabled speakers of Spanish and Hmong to be viewed as possessing expert knowledge. The guest speakers also provided an authentic way for Mexican, Hmong, and Native American cultures to be viewed as valuable parts of history. The immigration or migration stories I selected from the textbook were featured because of their content, and the likelihood that students would connect to them personally, or within a historical context. In addition, several lessons provided opportunities for peer to peer mentoring and first language scaffolding, which placed value on the student's primary language as opposed to English.

Include linguistically and culturally diverse content

The texts utilised throughout the unit were selected to reflect the cultural, ethnic, and linguistic diversity present in the classroom. In the unit each student had access to a story that closely related to their own lived experience with immigration and/or migration. Where the texts fell short, or posed a developmental challenge, guest speakers from the community, and in some cases the families of students themselves, were incorporated as primary language storytellers. Students were also given opportunities in discussions and assessments to respond in both oral and written forms in their primary language.

Montgomery's (2001) 'Culturally Complex Atmosphere' became a way in which students contextualised the complex issues that are involved in the topic of immigration and migration. In particular, a trusted and respected guest speaker from our school staff spoke about her immigration story from Mexico to the United States. Her story presented the marginalised point of view on the topic of illegal immigration. This trusted source, and the focus on essential questions, helped students deal with a controversial topic while engaging in content and language specific goals. This presentation was a catalyst for incorporating current events, and it helped validate the complexity of historical immigration and migration stories from the Holocaust, slavery, war refugees, and religious persecution. Evidence from my study showed that several students shifted their original thinking, and began to see the validity of the marginalised perspective on illegal immigration.

Respond to ethnic and linguistic diversity in the method of instruction

Themed units

The essential questions that focused my integrated immigration and migration unit created open-ended opportunities for student to engage meaningfully in the content and process of the unit. These questions were: Why do people (im) migrate?; What factors push them from their home?; What factors pull (im) migrants to a particular location?; How does (im)migration affect the culture and identity of the (im)migrants?

Unlike the unmodified unit, students were provided with questions that guided their thinking, and also enabled them to interpret objectives and make connections. Several of my ELL students came back to the vocabulary words and concepts of push and pull in a later science unit to describe the movement of fauna in our local watershed. The big questions drew not only on the state's history, but also on the histories of my students and their families. In this way the unit's theme and driving questions were relevant to my students' lives and could be modified to include and respond to all students' diverse needs.

Participation patterns

Flexibility in grouping increases the flexibility of the flow of information in the learning environment. Students engaged in varied participation patterns are given more opportunities to demonstrate their skills, and for developing richer meaning. For example, students were asked to first map immigration stories of guest speakers as a class, map stories from supporting texts in small linguistically heterogeneous groups, record their own stories at home, and finally to translate their research into a personal immigration or migration capstone project with a linguistically homogeneous peer. These groups served not only as content scaffolds, but also as opportunities for linguistic and cultural leverage points to be negotiated and given meaning.

My research showed that cooperative groups offered the most responsive academic structure for students whose cultures value the collective over the individual. Within this format students were expected to engage in listening, writing, and speaking in English. The goals of these groups were attainable for all students because of peer mentoring and because the project's success was determined by the efforts and abilities of the group as a collective.

The guided discussions of read aloud texts and guest speakers' stories provided opportunities for students to negotiate meaning and share their own opinions and reflections. This is evidenced by one ELL student's comment that, '[presenter's name]'s push factors are like [an immigrant from our read aloud]'s because they wanted to get away from bad laws. They were brave to leave.' A non- ELL responded, 'Those laws were unfair. People should leave places where they aren't safe. Like in my book for reading group [a holocaust story].' Discussions like this were key factors in rich language development and the exchange of ideas. They provided students with access to the wide variety of texts and materials available to them throughout the unit.

As a responsive curriculum designer I felt that there were times when linguistically homogeneous groups were necessary scaffolds for the success of the project. These groups gave students opportunities to engage in peer mentoring, translation, and primary language clarification. For example, students were grouped this way when working on creating a map of the immigration or migration story for their final project. In one pair of Spanish speakers, one student helped the other translate sections of her interview (which was conducted and recorded in Spanish) as they discussed how to address all of the requirements of the project using a graphic organiser. I found these pairings to be very useful during planning phases and before sharing. These groups were transformative in terms of building confidence for my ELLs. One pair of Hmong girls spoke entirely in Hmong for their planning process, and when it came time to share they helped each other find the words for their all-English presentation. One stated that, 'It felt good to have [the other girl] think too. Sometimes it hard not to get messed-up.' These two girls rarely volunteered to speak in class, but after this experience frequently requested time to think together and then share.

Scaffolding

The concept of scaffolding (Wood, Bruner and Ross, 1976) is to provide supports that help students work beyond their current level, then gradually remove them, enabling the student to work independently at a more advanced level. The entire unit was designed in this manner. Students were first provided with teacher-led and text-based examples of their unit projects and goals. Then guest speakers contextualised and made these projects and goals more relevant. Students then engaged in projects as members of cooperative groups with the support of other ELLs and native English speakers. Finally, students were asked to complete projects about their own immigration or migration stories. This final step was a self-directed and open-ended approach to achieving the unit goals.

Engage students in purposeful language-rich academic tasks

The unit was designed with language development at the root of each lesson. There were direct vocabulary objectives: specific terms (culture, identity, push, pull, immigration, migration, affect, food ways, refugee, integrate), use of comparisons and contrasts (like/unlike, same/different), and using content specific vocabulary when discussing a text. There were also language function and form objectives: presenting opinions (I'd like to say, I'd like to add, in my opinion), asking interviewees questions in an appropriate manner and voicing disagreement politely (I don't agree with you, in my opinion, did you think about). Language function objectives included: recounting a story in writing, using appropriate connectives of time (first, next, afterwards, finally and past tense), formulating questions for an interview, and determining importance of questions.

Finally, students were asked to present their projects orally to several different audiences. The projects were posters detailing their own im/migration story, or that of a family or community member. The posters included a map of the subject's im/migration route, a timeline of their life, a short history of the places the subject had lived, and the reasons why they had left a location or decided to live in a new location. The oral presentations were the culmination of all the unit's language objectives. Each student demonstrated mastery of language use and form by writing a speech for the different audiences that would be present at our celebration.

Within the culturally and linguistically relevant unit, I was looking to validate and value the culture and knowledge of all students in the classroom. My prior knowledge of the students as learners at school, and my willingness to recognise them as possessors of valuable cultural capital were the building blocks of the unit's design. Each lesson built on the strengths of the students, and targeted specific objectives to expand their content knowledge and understanding of language. Students engaged in lessons that were designed to create a connective web of language and content that pushed them to engage meaningfully in learning. In this way access to content was scaffolded and the learning reflected students' varied cultural and linguistic needs. Students were valued and validated because the unit was designed in response to their expertise and needs.

Assessment

Student mastery of content and language goals was evaluated through a portfolio assessment. I had conferences with individuals in which they presented evidence of their learning throughout the unit in both oral and written formats. Students had to explain how they met the objectives in a one-on-one meeting where they led the discussion, and also submitted a one page, written version. This combination helped all students, but especially ELLs, prepare for their oral one-on-one meeting. Students also completed self-assessments of the work in their portfolios, their participation in discussions and groups, and their overall growth in the unit's goals. The portfolios allowed students to meet criteria in a more open-ended manner than a traditional unit test could. Student success was determined using multiple factors and modes of expression. This type of differentiation gave my ELLs many different entry points to demonstrate understanding and mastery of language and content objectives.

I also utilised check-ins, which are mini one-on-one conferences designed to quickly assess each students' success with a specific language or content goal. These informal check-ins were documented in an ongoing and systematic way, and helped clarify progress during the unit, and identify strengths and weaknesses at the unit's conclusion. Formal assessments of student portfolios, vocabulary inventories, and content and language specific objectives were based on pre-established rubrics.

Conclusion

'Perhaps the greatest challenge for teachers is to offer students academically challenging curriculum while, at the same time, helping them catch up with both English and content.' (Freeman and Freeman, 2007: 15) The responsive curriculum framework detailed in this chapter demonstrates that students achieve success and are validated when they are provided with academic, social, and emotional access to a curriculum that is designed and implemented with the intention of valuing and accommodating their perspective. By remaining focused on who participated and how they participated, by utilising both formal and informal assessments, I was able to keep the unit grounded in my students' funds of knowledge and further develop my knowledge base about the diversity present in my classroom. Educators will find greater success in these efforts when they find support in their colleagues, students' families, school and district administrators, and the larger community.

It is the responsibility of mainstream practitioners to increase their knowledge of cultural ways of knowing and being, and their knowledge of effective teaching for ELLs while still supporting non-ELLs. A responsive curriculum implemented in a classroom with small student to teacher ratios offers the best educational environment for all students, but specifically for ELLs. Culturally and linguistically relevant pedagogy implemented by knowledgeable practitioners could revolutionise curriculum design and help put an end to the achievement gaps that exist. This type of unit design and ways of using materials not only specifically addresses the needs of ELL populations in mainstream classrooms, but also has relevance in English medium classes.

It takes continuous effort, collaboration, and self-evaluation to develop a knowledge base of the diversity in the learning environment, and an awareness of how language and culture affects our interactions with the world and our meaning making processes. This project serves as proof that time and effort invested in designing the curriculum and materials that engage students in language-rich, culturally aware, and personally validating educational experiences leads to students' increased academic success, increased emotional connection to learning, and more widespread social understanding and appreciation for each other. The responsive framework provides access for a wide range of learners and accommodates the needs of the individual and the collective. Educators engaged in this difficult and complex work will be catalysts for change, but educational systems will never truly work until our social, political and environmental systems reflect the evolving needs of our global society.

Engagement priorities

Providing a curriculum that is responsive to student language and culture is important for the success of all learners. The way in which the curriculum is designed will be unique to each educational setting, and implemented differently for specific students. The framework described in this chapter presents accommodations and curricular considerations applicable to all learning settings and is designed to help you begin, or continue, this difficult and complex work in your own educational setting. Here are some areas for further exploration:

1. What steps can you take to deepen your knowledge and understanding of your students' roles as learners and possessors of rich funds of knowledge?
2. How do the curriculum and the materials in your classroom provide entry points for your students' lives to be valued and validated?
3. What restrictions are present in your school/classroom environment that would prevent the implementation of a responsive curriculum? What resources and tools do you need to overcome these barriers?

References

Diaz-Rico, L. and Weed, K. (2002). *The Crosscultural, Language, and Academic Development Handbook: A Complete K-12 Reference Guide,* 2nd Edition. Boston: Allyn & Bacon.

Freeman, D. E. and Freeman, Y. S. (2007). *English Language Learners: The Essential Guide.* New York, NY: Scholastic.

Gaitan, C. D. (2006). *Building Culturally Responsive Classrooms: A Guide for K-6 Teachers.* Thousand Oaks, CA: Corwin Press.

Gay, G. (2000). *Culturally Responsive Teaching: Theory, Research, and Practice.* New York: Teachers College Press.

Gay, G. (2002). Preparing for culturally responsive teaching. *Journal of Teacher Education,* 53(2): 106–116.

Gibbons, P. (2002). *Scaffolding Language Scaffolding Learning: Teaching Second Language in the Mainstream Classroom.* Portsmouth, NH: Heinemann.

Gonzalez, N. and Moll, L. (2002). Cruzando el Puente: building bridges to funds of knowledge. *Educational Policy,* 16(4): 623–641.

Hawkins, M. and Katz, A. 2008. *Language Matters: A Framework for School-Based Language and Classroom Teaching.* Madison WI: WIDA Consortium.

Ladson-Billings, G. (1995). Toward a theory of culturally relevant pedagogy. *American Educational Research Journal,* 32(3): 465–491.

Ladson-Billings, G. (2001). *Crossing Over to Canaan: The Journey of New Teachers in Diverse Classrooms.* San Francisco: Jossey-Bass.

Montgomery, W. (2001). Creating culturally responsive, inclusive classrooms. *The Council for Exceptional Children,* 33(4): 4–10.

Montgomery, W. (2000). Literature discussion in the elementary school classroom: developing cultural understanding. *Multicultural Education,* 8(1): 33–36.

Pransky, K. and Bailey, F. (2002). To meet your students where they are, first you have to find them: working with culturally and linguistically diverse at-risk students. *The Reading Teacher,* 56(4): 370–383.

Valdes, G. (1996). *Con Respeto: Bridging Distances Between Culturally Diverse Families and Schools.* New York: Teachers College Press, Columbia University.

Villegas, A. M. and Lucas, T. (2002). *Educating Culturally Responsive Teachers: A Coherent Approach.* Albany, NY: State University of New York Press.

Villegas, A. M. and Lucas, T. (2007). The culturally responsive Teacher. *Educational Leadership,* 64(6): 28–33.

Wlodkowski, R. and Ginsberg, M. (1995). A framework for culturally responsive teaching. *Educational Leadership,* 20(1): 17–21.

Wood, D., Bruner, J. S. and Ross, G. (1976). The role of tutoring in problem solving. *Journal of Child Psychology & Psychiatry & Allied Disciplines,* 17(2): 89–100.

Part III
Materials and Technology

10
English Language Learning through Mobile Phones

Arifa Rahman and Tanya Cotter

Introduction

With the advent of the 21st century, there has been a growing realisation, particularly in developing countries, that an ability to use the English language is necessary to participate fully in global economic and social opportunities. As a result, there has been a proliferation of national and international initiatives to channel English language teaching (ELT) endeavours into directions that might lead to more effective outcomes. The past two decades have also ushered in innovative practices that have had an impact on ELT and its interrelated areas like course design, materials development, teaching/learning methodology, and the use of resources provided by ever easier access to technology.

This chapter is set within the context of this growing trend for using technology for language learning, in this particular case, the ubiquitous mobile phone. It is an attempt to add to the growing understanding of the educational value and impact of mobile technology by investigating to what extent it has the potential to be an effective tool for developing English language skills and for fostering self-directed learning.

The chapter starts with a brief overview of the setting in Bangladesh and recent English teaching initiatives adopted there. It then moves on to a discussion of mobile phone language learning services in developing contexts, before focusing on a current English learning project in Bangladesh. This mobile phone initiative is discussed in terms of planning, design, and implementation followed by an analysis and evaluation of its educational impact. The final section deals with changes that have been incorporated to adjust to the learning culture and the local context, providing some useful insights for a wider audience embarking on similar projects.

English language learning initiatives in Bangladesh

Bangladesh has a population of approximately 150 million (Bangladesh Bureau of Statistics, 2012) making it one of the most densely populated nations in the world. As a developing country with a large population the government faces many challenges in providing access to quality education for all and levels of English tend to be low, especially outside the capital, Dhaka, which may be attributed to historical, sociolinguistic, and educational management factors (Hamid and Baldauf, 2008; Seargeant and Erling, 2011).

English has become the universally accepted international language with many developing countries, like India and Bangladesh, seeing English as necessary to their economic development. The importance of being able to communicate in English in today's globalised world is one of the major reasons why the number of ELT initiatives in Bangladesh has grown since the mid-nineties. There has been a plethora of state-run directives and a succession of donor-aided ELT projects including PEDP II, TQI, ELTIP, SEQAIP, and ETTE[1]. Perhaps the largest to date is English in Action (EIA), a nine-year programme with primary, secondary, and adult initiatives funded by UKaid[2].

The overall objective of EIA is to raise the English language skills of 25 million people in Bangladesh by 2017 by initiating innovative ways of learning English. The assumption is that improved English language skills will ultimately provide Bangladeshis with more prospects for participating in ever growing opportunities. With regard to the economic benefits of learning English, a BBC Media Action (2009) baseline survey for the adult initiative of the project revealed that 87 per cent (of 8,300 respondents surveyed) thought that knowing English would help them earn more money.

One of the strategies that EIA has applied is to increase access to English language learning resources and to improve English language skills through the use of mobile technology. With 95.528 million mobile phone subscribers in Bangladesh at the end of August 2012 (BTRC, 2012), access to a handset is increasingly commonplace, even among poorer and harder to reach communities.

Mobile technology and English language learning

With increasingly widespread accessibility to mobile technology, its potential to transform where, when, and how people learn is widely recognised and the technology is being harnessed to provide educational content in both formal and non-formal learning environments. Learning through mobile technology, commonly referred to as m-learning, provides the opportunity to learn anytime, anywhere since learning can take place on personal, portable devices at no fixed time or location and can support face-to-face, blended, distance, or self-directed learning.

With regard to English language learning, numerous multidimensional and memorable ways to practise and improve English language skills are available through applications which can be downloaded from the Internet to the latest smartphones. However, this is at the high end of the market and accessible only to those who can afford the most up-to-date mobile technology. While mobile cellular subscriptions reached almost 6 billion in 2011, with developing countries largely responsible for this growth, mobile broadband penetration in the developing world was only 8 per cent compared to 51 per cent in the developed world (ITU, 2012). However, even simple handsets are equipped to deliver learning resources via SMS text messages, audio formats, and Interactive Voice Response (IVR) quizzes which require users to respond to questions delivered in SMS or audio by pressing numbers on the keypad. Moreover, many less sophisticated handsets are increasingly able to support multimedia content, such as games.

SMS through mobile

In English language learning, there have been several studies to assess the impact of SMS. For example, Cavus and Ibrahim (2009) used SMS to send vocabulary messages to first year volunteer students in Cyprus studying computer information systems. The students received short text messages, at timed intervals during the day, with English words and their L1 meanings related to their academic field of study. Participants reported learning new words and enjoying the learning experience.

In Mongolia SMS technology has been used to provide English learning modules to those otherwise unable to afford or access computer-based distance education programmes. Students involved in this initiative also responded positively to this kind of learning (UNESCO, 2012).

Other initiatives that use SMS have targeted far greater numbers of learners in non-formal learning environments. Since 2009, Nokia Life Tools has been providing a range of services for people outside urban areas in India, Indonesia, China, and Nigeria, including an English language learning service through SMS supported by local languages at beginner, intermediate, and advanced levels. In 2012, Nokia Life Tools relaunched an enhanced and more interactive service.

In November 2011 the US State Department, in partnership with the US Embassy in Tunis and the largest mobile network operator, Tunisiana, launched an English learning mobile service also using SMS technology. By dialling *136#, subscribers answer interactive multiple-choice questions related to 50 everyday situations (US State Department, 2011).

Wang, Cheng and Fang (2011: 92) argue that mobile learning investigations 'have centered on two cell phone functions, text messaging and web access'. Given the low penetration of the websites in developing countries, it is not surprising that, in trying to reach less urban areas, providers of ELT content have opted to maximise the benefits of SMS technology. However, low cost, easily accessible content can also be provided to users with basic handsets through audio lessons. These can be made available through mobile network operators, can be preloaded onto a handset, or can be loaded onto a handset through micro SD cards[3]. According to a GSMA Development Fund survey (2012: 5) on young people in Ghana, India, Morocco and Uganda:

> Although smart phones and data enabled devices are beginning to make an impact in emerging markets, voice calls remain the most used and favoured service: 85% of young mobile users made voice calls every day, and 67% of respondents believe that calls would be the most desirable method for receiving content such as educational information.

Audio through mobile

One example of an initiative using audio through mobile is English Seekho (translated as Learn English) launched in India in 2009 by IL&FS in association with Tata Indicom (2012). The service provides five-minute audio lessons in conversational English together with interactive quizzes and SMS lesson summaries. Another example is the mobile service developed by BBC Media Action for the adult initiative of EIA, which launched in 2009 in Bangladesh and provides three-minute audio English lessons and interactive quizzes supported by the first language, Bangla.

Multimedia content through mobile

Although mobile broadband penetration is still low in developing countries, the number of people with mobile phones that support multimedia content, such as games, is increasing. In India this kind of mobile device is used by the Mobile and Immersive Learning for Literacy in Emerging Economies (MILLEE) project to deliver English language learning to children from low income families in rural India. The educational games have been designed to model the traditional games that these children play and thus provide enjoyable, alternative, and culturally appropriate ways to learn English. According to MILLEE, devices which can support multimedia content 'are perfect for new kinds of out-of-school language learning, which can occur at places and times that are more convenient than school' (MILLEE, 2012: 1).

Not only is there anecdotal evidence on the educational value and impact of mobile English language learning, but there is also a growing body of research, the results of which have been largely positive, where users claim that they enjoy the experience and are able to learn from it. For example, BBC Media Action's midline survey (2012) for the adult initiative of the EIA project revealed that more than two-thirds of those who had used the audio lessons and IVR quizzes found them useful as a way of learning English. A typical mobile audio lesson presents a short two-line dialogue, which is then broken down. Users are encouraged to repeat the language they hear and answer questions. One example of a dialogue for a beginner level user is:

A: Hello. Nice to meet you.

B: Nice to meet you too.

BBC Janala: an English learning, mobile initiative in Bangladesh

BBC Media Action is responsible for the adult learning initiative of the EIA project. In 2009, a nationwide baseline survey of 8,300 respondents who were mobile users/cable and satellite viewers, aged 15–49, revealed that around 84 per cent of people in Bangladesh viewed learning English as a top priority for their future, with 99 per cent reporting that they wanted their children to learn English (BBC Media Action, 2009).

BBC Janala (translated as BBC Window) was developed as part of the wider EIA project to enable Bangladeshi adult learners, from a wide range of socio-economic groups (with a focus at the lower end), to learn English affordably through mass media. Mobile technology, television, websites, CDs and print lessons are used to deliver accessible and affordable ELT materials to adults who are unable to access face-to-face tuition or who may need extra practice resources to support their learning. The aim is to change perceptions of, and reduce barriers to, learning English among the adult population. BBC Media Action's baseline survey (2009) revealed that 64 per cent of those surveyed felt embarrassed to speak English, 47 per cent considered English to be too expensive to learn, and 44 per cent felt English was difficult to learn. Thus, the most significant barriers at the time of the survey were confidence, cost, and the perceived difficulty of learning English.

Since its launch in 2009, the mobile phone service has been providing three-minute pre-recorded English audio lessons that focus on different aspects of language (such as vocabulary), and different situations in which language is used (as in English for work). The target language is presented in context in the form of a short dialogue and a Bangladeshi presenter uses L1 to introduce the lessons, set the scene, and give instructions. The target English is repeated several times in different ways and learners are encouraged to listen, repeat, and answer questions aloud. They can also record their stories, give feedback, and participate in IVR quizzes, thus fulfilling a fundamental element of m-learning: 'its ability to deliver learning resources to those who may otherwise be unable to attend traditional learning environments such as classrooms and provide a practical and personal way to learn' (GSMA Development Fund, 2010: 6).

The BBC Janala mobile service transforms a simple handset into a low-cost educational device, which can be used anytime and from anywhere in Bangladesh since all six operators provide the service at a reduced tariff of less than half a penny per minute plus VAT. By end July 2012, BBC Janala had 6.4 million users of this service.

Developing mobile audio lessons and quizzes

There are limitations to developing educational content for less sophisticated mobile devices since it cannot support images or video and interactivity is limited. However, audio lessons and IVR quizzes can be provided at low cost in a context whereby the learner, who may have had negative experiences of education, is not threatened by the abilities or opinions of others and can begin to build their confidence.

In m-learning there is a need to ensure that the technology does not obstruct access to the learning content and that it can be navigated with ease on less sophisticated mobile devices. This is especially important for those who may have no experience of the technology or may be new adopters. In addition, it is essential to develop content that takes into consideration the needs, wants, and abilities of the target learners, engages them and helps them to learn through the technology and not in spite of it. Sharples, Milrad, Sanchez and Vavoula (2009: 6) claim that:

> The design of mobile learning activities should be, like the design of any learning activity, driven by specific learning objectives. The use of (mobile) technology is not the target; rather, it is a means to enable activities that were otherwise not possible, or to increase the benefits for the learner(s).

As for all ELT materials, in the development of audio English lessons and quizzes for mobile phones, factors such as level, topic, relevant language, and the local context need to be considered. As the content is likely to be used for self-directed learning, it is also important to consider what support can be provided to help learners understand the lesson. Moreover, if audio is to be central to the delivery method, the voice requires special attention and pitch, tone, intonation, style, and speed will all need to be tested in the development process. This is important because many learners' feelings of anxiety can be reduced and their confidence built up 'through a "voice" which is relaxed and supportive' (Tomlinson, 2003: 8).

In the BBC Janala project, in order to understand the needs and context of the target audience, to create the mobile phone service together with the content, and to assess what impact the service has had, BBC Media Action's researchers have drawn on a wide range of research methods to collect and analyse data. Their studies have included:

- investigating needs and context to guide development;
- pre-testing and piloting of media products to provide feedback on audience responses;
- monitoring audience reactions;
- evaluating the impact.

In order to evaluate the effectiveness of mobile phones as a tool for developing communication skills in English by listening to the mobile audio lessons and participating in IVR quizzes, information was collected from a panel of representatives from the target audience and a full report was produced (BBC Media Action, 2011a). It is from this report that the overview and the project impact have been extracted and presented in the following section.

Evaluating the educational impact of the project

This impact assessment study extended over ten months (April 2010 to February 2011) during which time a panel of users were tracked in terms of:

- Engagement: by assessing users' motivation to use lessons, their opinion of lessons and whether they were driven to discuss and recommend the lessons to others.
- Language development: by evaluating the users' ability to retain and use the specific information taught in the lessons, and by assessing their capacity to apply the learning to everyday life.
- Learning English in other ways: by determining whether users were practising English with others and were involved in further engagement.

The panel

In order to ensure a wide representation from the target audience, respondents were recruited and invited to an English testing session according to a set of criteria that included a balance in terms of gender, age, socio-economic class, education, and occupation (including unemployed).

Grouping of panellists

Respondents underwent speaking and writing tests based on the descriptors of levels A1 to B2 of the Council of Europe's Common European Framework of Reference (CEFR). Taking into account the results of the tests and their interest in learning English, 46 panellists, consisting of 23 males and 23 females, were selected initially and divided into three groups:

- Those at beginner level (A1) with moderate levels of interest in learning English were assigned the Beginners Basic Package (BBP) which required them to listen to one lesson per week and take part in a quiz.
- Those at beginner level (A1) but with high levels of interest in learning English were assigned the Beginners Full Package (BFP) which required them to listen to three lessons a week.
- Nine panellists with higher levels of English (A2 to B1) were assigned the Intermediate Package (IP) with three, higher level lessons to listen to each week.

The panel decreased to 32 during the study due to dropouts. In order to avoid losing the statistical significance of the data, four additional females (boosters) were recruited in November 2010. This means that a total of 50 panellists took part in the study, though not all together at any one point in time. In addition, new intermediate mobile lessons ceased to be published and the intermediate panel stopped operating in November 2010.

The cost of the airtime used by panellists was compensated weekly by mobile credit top-ups to ensure that financial pressures did not interfere with the project.

Panel assigned tasks

Participants agreed to undertake the following activities:

- Use mobile lessons: dial and listen to each of the assigned lessons according to the package allocation. The respondents were told to listen to each lesson as stipulated to ensure uniform exposure.
- Fill in diaries: all panellists were provided with self-completion forms called diaries, to be filled in immediately after listening to the lesson. In these diaries, panellists recorded their immediate feedback about the effectiveness and drawbacks of the lessons.
- Undergo regular face-to-face interviews and lesson tests: these interviews took place every four to six weeks and were designed to track how effective the lessons were in teaching English and increasing confidence and motivation to learn.

Face-to-face interviews

The interview questions covered the degree to which the panellists understood the lessons; whether they could recall the key learning points; and whether they could reproduce the English they had learnt from the lessons. The interviews explored levels of motivation for learning English and the barriers faced during learning to see how this changed over time while using the mobile phone lessons. In the first interview, respondents were also asked a series of questions to determine their preferred learning styles, such as whether users were primarily auditory, visual, or kinaesthetic learners.

Quarterly English tests

Every three months, the users were tested on their English speaking and writing skills. These tests, based on CEFR descriptors, were assessed by ELT experts. Scores from the pre-test (during recruitment) and from the following rounds were compared to reveal whether the mobile phone lessons had an impact on the users' English writing and speaking skills.

Previous experience of learning English

Most panellists had learnt English at school or college. A few had also learnt English through newspapers and/or television. Male panellists tended to have more previous English learning experience and had more exposure to English content. Many of the panellists did not have a favourable experience of learning English. They criticised the education system, which tends to focus on rote learning, getting good grades, and passing exams rather than communicating in English. Many stated they had found grammar the most difficult aspect of English, particularly sentence structure, followed by vocabulary and spelling. However, users believed that learning English through mobile lessons was entertaining compared to their previous experience of learning, which they had found uninteresting, even frightening.

Results of the evaluation

Some common features emerged from an analysis of the information collected from panellists in the study. These have been grouped under the following:

1. attitudes towards the mobile lessons;
2. motivation and confidence;
3. learning practices;
4. aspects of language use.

Attitudes towards mobile lessons

Panellists were generally positive about the mobile phone lessons for various reasons. Firstly, they appreciated the convenience in accessing the lessons anytime and from anywhere. Most of them listened to the lessons at home and some also used them while travelling. A few of the panellists listened to the mobile lessons together.

It is good because it is convenient; can dial anytime; especially because people have the freedom to dial when I am in the appropriate mood and no obligation when I am not. (Male, 20 years, IP)

Secondly, all the panellists found the content useful and relevant. They thought the lessons were life oriented and the phrases they learnt could be used in everyday situations. One male user of the BBP stated, 'I can learn to use English in daily life.' Panellists also appreciated learning certain phrases/words and how to apply them in different situations.

It is good because it has shown when and where we may apply English and the way we should apply it. (Female, 18 years, BBP)

One user mentioned that, although the words introduced were already familiar, he had learnt how to pronounce them well through the lessons.

Thirdly, panellists found the mobile lessons easier and more interesting than their traditional English lessons. All except two said they preferred mobile phone learning to conventional methods. One female user of the BBP described lessons as 'very interesting, amazing and grammar seems a lot easier now'. Panellists pointed out that they learnt English in schools and colleges only to pass written English examinations rather than in order to speak and listen to English.

At school, college, it is for passing the exam and after that people forgot their learning but here [mobile] they are free from this tension [passing exam]. (Female, 27 years, BBP)

Finally, some also felt it was a cheaper way of learning than taking private tuition or going to a coaching centre.

There were, however, aspects of learning English through mobile phones that some panellists were not very comfortable with. Some complained that they did not receive any tuition in grammar, which their previous educational experience had led them to expect. Some missed the presence of a teacher with whom they could speak when they could not understand, or when they wanted further explanation or clarification.

It was clear in school life because someone was there to make me understand if I can't, but I am alone and I find it hard to understand. (Male, 21 years, BFP)

Moreover, 37 per cent stated that they had problems understanding all the content. Some felt the pace of the lessons was fast, while others found the

British accents daunting. This was particularly true for those with a limited exposure to spoken English prior to the study.

> Lessons were very good, but the problem is to understand the British accent. I had to listen to it for five to six times. (Male, 19 years, IP)

Over the course of time, and with more exposure to the mobile phone lessons, the attitudes of some of the less satisfied panellists changed. They came to realise the importance of learning English and found the lessons beneficial.

> Earlier, I didn't realise how much important it is to learn English language, so, wasn't much interested. Now, I realise the importance. (Female, BBP).

Motivation and confidence

Motivation has been identified as a key factor in successful language learning (Ellis, 1997). Panellists were asked to rate their motivation to learn English, on a scale of one to ten, at six-month intervals. Out of 32 panellists, 40 per cent reported increased motivation to learn English over the course of ten months. On the other hand, 60 per cent reported no increase. Interestingly these latter panellists were the ones who were highly motivated to begin with and remained equally motivated after exposure to the BBC Janala service. Therefore, in the case of these users, motivation was a key factor in learning. In addition, listening to the mobile lessons enabled learners who were over-confident about their own English ability to identify weaknesses and the areas they needed to focus on to improve their English.

The panellists reported two common reasons for learning English: a realisation that there was an increased need for English; and that knowing English would bring more respect from peers. Other factors included a desire for self-development, interaction with foreigners, coping in society, going abroad, increasing world knowledge, using the Internet, and increasing ability to use technology.

Panellists stated that, whereas previously they had been nervous about communicating in English, they felt more confident and less fearful after exposure to the lessons. When asked to rate their confidence about their ability to learn English, 73 per cent of panellists reported increased confidence in learning English over the study period, and the 23 per cent who felt confident at the start remained confident until the end. Reasons for increased confidence were attributed to interesting lessons, frequent practice, positive feedback, fairly good results, and access to useful learning tools.

Learning practices

Most panellists tried to adhere to the stipulated number of lessons per week, but worked through lessons at their own convenience. Interestingly, although they had agreed to use only the mobile lessons at the outset of the study, some of them started employing additional means of learning English, including using BBC Janala's website, print and television content.

A significant aspect that emerged, which appeared to impact on learning in a positive manner, was the further engagement factor. Panellists using the Beginners Basic Package and who had more involvement in the lessons, learnt better than those with less involvement. Further involvement included: extending the lesson by reviewing it, repeating it, making and reviewing notes, or practising; seeking further practice by talking about the lessons with others or going to coaching centres/tutorials; or applying learning to real life by becoming teachers at neighbourhood elementary schools, watching English television programmes, helping children or younger siblings with English homework or studies, reading English medium newspapers, listening to English pop music, or writing more SMS/text messages in English.

The further engagement factor also appeared to be at variance with the VARK learning styles model (Fleming and Mills, 1992). It would seem that auditory learners would be at an advantage when using mobile lessons, yet the degree of learning appeared to be almost independent of the learning style, with a high success rate comparable among all four types of learners with equivalent levels and forms of further engagement. On the other hand, the success rate was medium or low among those who only listened to the lessons *without* further engagement, regardless of their preferred learning style. To sum up, individual learning styles did not impact significantly on learning. On the other hand, learners who were more involved and had engaged further in additional modes of learning appeared to learn better.

However, it is pertinent to note that for intermediate learners further engagement was not a significant factor. The data shows six out of the eight intermediate learners improved their English-speaking and writing skills purely as a result of the exposure to the mobile lessons and reported not to have engaged in other means of learning English.

Overall, what appeared to impact on learning was:

- compliance: listening to the three-minute lessons;
- confidence: in their ability to learn;
- learning in other ways: further engagement;
- motivation: the higher the motivation level, the more successful the learning. Those with higher levels of English at the outset were generally more motivated.

Aspects of language development

The panellists were tested for their speaking and writing skills over the project period. Out of the 35 learners tested, seven improved significantly, 11 improved moderately and five improved slightly. Eleven of the learners showed no improvement and one learner, who had been in a road accident, showed a decline. Progress was confined to those belonging to the two higher levels using the Beginners Full Package and the Intermediate Package.

Language analysis of writing and speaking tests (pre-test at the beginning, tests administered throughout the ten-month period, and a post-test) indicated the following:

Writing skills

Whereas at the pre-exposure stage panellists were answering questions with single words, after mobile lesson exposure some started to use complete sentences. For example,

> Where do you live?
> Mirpur (pre-exposure)
> I live in Mirpur (after mobile exposure)

Grammatical accuracy also increased to some extent. In the pre-exposure stage, the degree of inaccuracy sometimes blocked communication (for instance, I song). However, on subsequent rounds, users produced answers which, despite grammatical inaccuracies, were able to convey meaning (such as, I like watch TV).

Additionally, it was found that during the pre-exposure tests almost all the users avoided using complex sentences. However, in post-exposure rounds, intermediate users attempted to write more complex sentences which, despite some inaccuracies in word order, were reasonably acceptable in terms of grammar (for instance, I have no free time as I am all time busy).

With regard to vocabulary, some of the users' answers reflected their increase in vocabulary and a growing confidence in using more expressive words (such as bonding, challenging, bonanza, heritage site). At the same time, even after exposure to the mobile lessons, there was still an inaccurate use of vocabulary (for instance, people self-working, oftenly I go).

With more mobile lesson exposure, there was a more frequent use of connectors (such as first, then, finally, and, but, also). Although spelling and punctuation errors were frequent, especially among users of the Beginners Basic Package, there was evidence of improved control during the later stages.

Speaking skills

The panellists improved in the following areas:

- Fluency: users were comparatively more forthcoming and more fluent in the later rounds of speaking tests. Although not always grammatically accurate,

answers became more spontaneous over the course of time (for instance, Yes, I like live Rajshahi. It is peace city).
- Accuracy: there was a relatively greater degree of grammatical accuracy during the later rounds.
- Using comparisons: in the earlier sessions, panellists were unable to use comparative and superlative adjectives when required (as in: This is big. This is small), while during the later sessions some were able to use comparative adjectives (bigger, smaller). However, there were some cases of over generalisation, such as biggest being used to compare two objects.
- Extended speech: during later rounds, some panellists attempted to extend their language output by providing more information when answering questions (When I need essential goods, I go to market. I usually go to market at noon).
- Taking risks: users in later stages attempted to use words which are less frequently used by Bangladeshis (like exciting, interesting). Although these words were not always used appropriately, the propensity to use them can be taken as an indication that panellists had started taking risks with language.
- Improvement in pronunciation: all eight intermediate users demonstrated improvements in their pronunciation, especially in terms of intonation and word stress. However, levels of improvement varied.

  > I learnt that unimportant words are usually unstressed and are almost silent. They are almost merged with the preceding or following words while pronouncing. (Male, 25, IP)

- A similar improvement was also observed among some beginner level users, particularly when they were conscious of pronunciation, improvement.
- There was some development in aspects of discourse and communicative effectiveness. This was evident through relevant content and a sense of engaged meaning, despite considerable grammatical and lexical errors such as, 'I can see the picture another overbridge and it is used walking one side to another side. Who don't use this overbridge they maybe accident on the road.'

Mobile language learning revisited: a response to context and culture

Fullan (2007), in his seminal work on educational innovation, speaks of 're-culturing' as the kind of psychological acceptance required of users when faced with new or changed modalities of delivery. Wedell (2009) takes this concept a step further and argues that this same sense of 're-culturing' also needs to be undertaken by the change agent as a response to an understanding of the culture and the context within which the users operate. Subsequent developments in the BBC Janala project can be analysed in the light of this concept of 're-culturing'. In response to the findings of this study – and several other research studies that took place prior to, at the time of, and after the study period – lessons for the BBC Janala mobile phone service have been modified extensively.

Level, amount and relevance of content

During the first phase BBC Media Action responded to learner feedback by lowering the level and reducing the amount of content, reducing the length of the lessons, and ensuring that the content was more relevant to learners' lives. This last was achieved by introducing topics like cricket and Bangladeshi festivals, which learners could relate to more easily. BBC Media Action (2011b) reports that much of the success of the service is due to making the content relevant to the users' lives. This had been earlier reported by Lotbiniere (2010).

Accents

There was a transition from using L1 speakers of English with British accents to using fluent Bangladeshi speakers of English with accents more familiar to users. This change was due not only to the feedback, but also to the realisation that there is a need for Bangladeshi speakers of English to understand Asian English for trade and commerce with neighbouring countries. This use of English as an International Language (EIL) and as a Lingua Franca (ELF) can be linked to the strong advocacy initiated by Jenkins (2000) in terms of English being used today by around 1.5 billion non-native English speakers worldwide for whom intelligibility across multilingual groups is more important than native speaker accents.

Teacher figure

Another significant change has been the introduction of a teacher figure across all media platforms, including the mobile service. User feedback about the teacher has been positive, with the majority feeling that the teacher helps them learn. This is significant since the idea for using a teacher figure came from the initial research into how the lessons could be improved. The teacher plays an important role in a context such as Bangladesh, where there is little experience of self-directed learning and where there is a high regard for an authoritative teacher figure, and it may well be that the presence of a teacher can help learners adapt to this new kind of learning by offering tangible and recognisable support and by meeting learner expectations. When asked about the teacher in the mobile phone lessons, one user stated, 'he doesn't seem like a teacher to a student, but a teacher to a friend. If I meet the teacher, he will be very friendly ... It is impossible to learn anything without a teacher'.

Repetition

Another feature of the lessons which has been modified and has subsequently received positive feedback is the increase in the amount of repetition. Within the lesson, the English is repeated several times and the listener is encouraged to repeat aloud. This may well be a popular feature of the lessons since the Bangladeshi education system is still quite traditional and rote learning is a fairly common practice (Rahman, 2009), although there have been attempts to change this and introduce more communicative approaches. It is also worth mentioning that Bangladesh is a country with a strong oral tradition and a nation that prides itself on its traditions and the art of storytelling and poetry. Moreover, the majority religion is Islam and the recitation aloud of the Quran plays a central role in religious practices.

This context may result in learner perceptions that when language is being memorised and repeated, learning is taking place. Moreover, sufficient repetition in the lessons appears to be a factor in building confidence and reducing fear. One user reported, 'the repetition is a good idea, especially for people like me who are weak in English. The repetition helps me understand'.

Use of L1

The use of L1 in the lessons has featured from the outset of the project, since this support was considered necessary in a culture with little experience of self-directed learning. It can be argued that through L1 support learners are put at ease, anxiety is reduced, and confidence is built. In an audio mobile lesson, where there is no scope for a demonstration or a picture, the use of the mother tongue to convey meaning becomes more important. Moreover, the fact that these lessons require a financial commitment, however low, from the low income groups they are aimed at, means it is essential that meaning is conveyed in the shortest time possible.

One significant modification to the lessons has been the development of a style of Bangla more easily accessible to users. To achieve this Bangla copywriters and copyeditors with experience of writing for mass communications were brought in to develop a style appropriate to the target audience. Users report that the more accessible Bangla helps them to understand the lessons more easily and that they no longer have any problems in following Bangla instructions and explanations, which were previously of a more pedantic nature.

Conclusion

In light of the panel study and subsequent discussion, it can be argued that a mobile learning service for English language learning has the potential to be an effective learning tool, not only for developing English language skills but also for increasing confidence and levels of motivation, and encouraging learners to engage further in additional modes of learning.

However, in order to do this, the service needs to be developed with the assumption that context and culture have a significant influence on human behaviour and that reality is seen as being constructed by the subjective perceptions of those involved within that context. The implications in this particular case appear to be not just the introduction of m-learning for developing English language skills, but how far and to what extent this technology is realistically appropriated by local users.

Another parameter which needs to be built into educational delivery programmes is the provision for ongoing research that functions as a watchdog and assists in assessing, monitoring, and developing the delivery system. These two perspectives are likely to provide useful insights into the sustainability of English language learning projects, particularly those using technology, that are being initiated all over the developing world.

Engagement priorities

1. The materials developed for the BBC Janala mobile phone lessons were adapted in response to research carried out with the target audience. What can teachers do to ensure that the materials they are using are appropriate to their context and relevant to their learners' needs and interests?
2. In what ways is classroom learning different from self-directed learning? What implications does this have for the development of classroom and self-directed learning materials?
3. In the evaluation of the educational impact of the mobile phone lessons presented in this chapter, a significant aspect that emerged, which appeared to impact on learning in a positive manner, was the *further engagement* factor. Can teachers encourage their learners to engage further or is it a matter of the learner's motivation and interest? What role could technology play in the *further engagement* factor?
4. '*Re-culturing*' is the kind of psychological acceptance arising from sensitivity to local context and culture. The BBC mobile learning project revised some of the content and the modality of delivery due to this re-culturing awareness. Can you identify some re-culturing processes in language development situations you are familiar with? What were the outcomes of the steps that were taken? Were they sustainable?

Notes

1. Primary Education Development Project II (PEDP II), Teacher Quality Improvement Project (TQI), English Language Teacher Improvement Project (ELTIP), English for

Teaching: Teaching for English Project (ETTE), Secondary Education Quality and Access Improvement Project (SEQAIP).
2. English in Action (EIA) involves a consortium of partners including BMB Mott MacDonald, Open University UK & BBC Media Action (formerly BBC World Service Trust). BBC Media Action is responsible for the adult initiative of the project.
3. Micro SD cards are very small flash memory cards which store data (e.g. audio and video material) and can be used in mobile phones or other portable devices that support them.

References

Bangladesh Bureau of Statistics (2012). Welcome to Bangladesh Bureau of Statistics. *Bangladesh Bureau of Statistics* [website]. Available at http://www.bbs.gov.bd/Home.aspx [Accessed 13/08/12].

Bangladesh Telecommunication Regulatory Committee (BTRC) (2012). Mobile Phone Subscribers in Bangladesh. *BTRC* [website]. Available at http://www.btrc.gov.bd/index.php/telco-news-archive/599-mobile-phone-subscribers-in-bangladesh-january-2012 [Accessed 13/08/12].

BBC Media Action (formerly BBC World Service Trust) (2009). *English in Action BBC Janala Baseline Research Synthesis*. Dhaka: BBC Media Action.

BBC Media Action (formerly BBC World Service Trust) (2011a). BBC Janala Mobile Phone Learners Panel Report: *How Effective is the Mobile Phone As a Tool to Learning English?* Dhaka: BBC Media Action.

BBC Media Action (formerly BBC World Service Trust) (2011b). *BBC Janala Mobile Content User Testing Report*. Dhaka: BBC Media Action.

BBC Media Action (formerly BBC World Service Trust) (2012). *The Impact of English in Action Media Products: Midline Survey Report*. Dhaka: BBC Media Action.

Cavus, N. and Ibrahim, D. (2009). m-Learning: an experiment in using SMS to support learning new English language words. *British Journal of Educational Technology*, 40(1): 78–91.

Ellis, R. (1997). *SLA Research and Language Pedagogy*, 1st Edition. Oxford: Oxford University Press.

Fleming, N. D. and Mills, C. (1992). Not another inventory, rather a catalyst for reflection. *To Improve the Academy*, 11: 137–155.

Fullan, M. G. (2007). *The New Meaning of Educational Change*, 4th Edition. New York: Teachers College Press.

GSMA Development Fund (2010). *m-Learning: A Platform for Educational Opportunities at the Base of the Pyramid*. London: GSMA.

GSMA Development Fund (2012). *Shaping the Future: Realising the Potential of Informal Learning through Mobile*. London: GSMA.

Hamid, M. O. and Baldauf, R. B. Jr. (2008). Will CLT bail out the bogged down ELT in Bangladesh? *English Today*, 24(3): 16–24.

ITU (International Telecommunication Union) (2012). Key statistical highlights: ITU data release June 2012. *International Telecommunication Union* [website]. Available at http://www.itu.int/ITU-D/ict/statistics/ [Accessed 01/08/12].

Jenkins, J. (2000). *The Phonology of English as an International Language*. Oxford: Oxford University Press.

Lotbiniere, M. (2010). Language reaches poor by mobile phone. *The Guardian* [online newspaper]. Available at http://www.guardian.co.uk/education/2010/dec/07/language-lesson-mobile-phones-lotbiniere [Accessed 17/04/12].

MILLEE (2012). Mobile and Immersive Learning for Literacy in Emerging Economies: Overview. *Human Development Lab @ Carnegie Mellon University* [website]. Available at http://www.cs.cmu.edu/~mattkam/lab/millee.html [Accessed 01/08/12].

Rahman, A. (2009). College teachers' perceptions of ELT: relevance to teacher training. In Mansoor, S., Sikander, A., Hussain, N. and Ahsan, N. (eds), *Emerging Issues in TEFL: Challenges for South Asia*. Oxford: Oxford University Press.

Seargeant, P. and Erling, E. J. (2011). The discourse of 'English as a language for international development': policy assumptions and practical challenges. In Coleman, H. (ed.), *Dreams and Realities: Developing Countries and the English Language*. London: British Council, pp. 248–267.

Sharples, M., Milrad, M., Arnedillo Sanchez, I. and Vavoula, G. (2009). Mobile learning: small devices, big issues. In Balacheff, N., Ludvigsne, S., De Jong, T., Lazonder, A. and Barnes, S. (eds), *Technology-Enhanced Learning: Principles and Products*. Netherlands: Springer Netherlands, pp. 233–249.

TATA Indicom (2012). English Seeko. *Mobile Learning* [website]. Available at http://www.tataindicom.com/tata-zone-mobile-learning.aspx [Accessed 12/08/12].

Tomlinson, B. (ed.) (2003). *Developing Materials for Language Teaching*, Illustrated, Reprint Edition. London: Continuum.

UNESCO (2012). *Turning on Mobile Learning in Asia: Illustrative Initiatives and Policy Implications*. Paris: UNESCO.

US State Department (2011). Mobile English: @ State Dept Pilots Language Learning Program in Tunisia. *U.S. Department of State Official Blog* [online blog]. Available at http://blogs.state.gov/index.php/site/entry/mobile_English_statedepts_first_pilot_in_tunisia/ [Accessed 8/08/12].

Wang, F., Chen, X. and Fang, W. (2011). Integrating cell phones into a Chinese high school EFL classroom: Students' attitudes, technological readiness, and perceived learning. *Journal of Educational Technology Development and Exchange*, 4(1): 91–102.

Wedell, M. (2009). *Planning for Educational Change*, 1st Edition. London: Continuum.

11
Using Interactive Fiction for Digital Game-based Language Learning

Joe Pereira

Introduction

The concept of learning spaces has moved beyond the walls of the classroom and language learning is now, more than ever, in the hands of the learner. Teachers must accept that their role in the learning process has changed, in many situations, becoming that of facilitator. As facilitators, they should promote the use of learning materials that are motivating, engaging, and useable in both the classroom and in autonomous learning contexts. A valid alternative to traditional language learning materials can be found in digital game-based language learning (DGBLL), which offers a means for all four language skills to be practised in a flexible, highly empowering and engaging way. This chapter proposes and evaluates the use of the text-based video game genre of Interactive Fiction (IF) as an authentic learning material in line with the principles of second language acquisition (SLA). Furthermore, it describes how IF, in addition to creating conditions in which reading, writing, speaking, and listening skills may be practised, can be a particularly useful tool for improving reading for fluency and promoting reading for pleasure.

The learning context

The majority of students at the British Council in Porto, Portugal, are young learners between the ages of 13 and 17, many of whom are preparing for Cambridge ESOL exams. Young Portuguese learners of English often have a good level of comprehension of spoken English and good pronunciation, in large part due to the fact that foreign movies and television shows are not dubbed in Portuguese but subtitled, and music sung in English is widely marketed and appreciated. Nearly all the classes are monolingual with lesson instruction taking place solely in English, in order to provide opportunities for learners to develop their communicative competence, described by

Larsen-Freeman (1986: 131) as 'being able to use the language appropriate to a given social context'. The acquisition of communicative competence is also the primary goal of Communicative Language Teaching (CLT), the teaching approach officially promoted by the British Council. The main principles of CLT include the following (Richards, 2006):

- learners need to be engaged in meaningful and authentic interaction and communication;
- content must be relevant, purposeful, interesting and engaging;
- language learning is facilitated by inductive discovery of language rules;
- the process of language learning involves creative use and trial and error – language is learnt by using it;
- intrinsic motivation results from authentic interest in what is being communicated with the language;
- the use of authentic language and materials is fundamental;
- fluency is strived for over accuracy.

In this teaching context, speaking and listening skills are prioritised in classroom tasks in order to help learners achieve the goal of acquiring communicative competence. This often involves students participating in speaking tasks in pairs or groups, where they are encouraged to share experiences and opinions. However, despite this focus on speaking and listening in the classroom, reading and writing skills are not neglected, but are linked mostly to grammar-focused activities. Reading texts, usually from coursebooks, are used mainly to test basic comprehension and to introduce vocabulary and grammatical structures. Thus, reading for fluency and, by extension, for pleasure, is not often actively promoted by teachers, due to the need to follow an established syllabus. Many young learners do not think of reading for pleasure, especially in a foreign language, as a necessary way to improve their language skills, and even less as a worthwhile way to spend their free time. I therefore began to use IF initially as a means of motivating students to engage in extended reading outside the classroom.

Digital game-based learning

Video games are currently the most lucrative entertainment industry in the US (ESA, 2012) and have become a pervasive element in modern society. Not only have they made their mark on the public consciousness, but they have also become accepted as serious educational tools. In parallel, the field of study pertaining to using video games for education, known as digital game-based learning (DGBL), has seen enormous growth in the last decade. Gee's (2007a) seminal work presented thirty-six learning principles inherently found in good video games, based on theories of situated cognition and semiotic domains. Gee (2007b: 43) points out that the motivating and engaging elements of video games are precisely why they make such good tools for learning:

> When we think of games, we think of fun. When we think of learning we think of work. Games show us this is wrong. They trigger deep learning that is itself part and parcel of the fun. It is what makes games deep.

Some recent research on using video games for foreign language learning (Reinders, 2012; Cornillie et al., 2012) has examined critically whether the learning principles and affordances of video games can be used for structured language learning, and the results indicate that there is potential for their implementation, with some necessary pedagogical considerations and reservations. DGBL has even begun to be represented in mainstream foreign language learning publishing, with a pioneering teacher development book on how to use video games in the language classroom (Mawer and Stanley, 2011).

An introduction to interactive fiction (IF)

> You are standing at the end of a road before a small brick building. Around you is a forest. A small stream flows out of the building and down a gully.
> (Crowther and Woods, 1976).

With this passage a new literary genre, the text adventure, was born[1]. A text adventure is both a video game and a form of participatory storytelling where the reader/player is the protagonist of the story (usually presented in the second person) and must provide input in natural language in order to interact with it. As text adventures began to transcend the staple fantasy theme to become more varied in setting and more complex in scope, the genre began to be marketed by its more prominent creators as Interactive Fiction, thus denoting its enhanced interactive qualities and literariness. Montfort (2003) defines IF as being:

1. A text accepting and generating computer program;
2. A potential non-linear narrative;
3. A simulation of an environment or world;
4. A structure of rules, with which an outcome is sought and played voluntarily: a game.

In order to reach the goal of the game, which is often unknown or unclear at its beginning, the player needs to command the protagonist to explore the game world and interact with the characters and objects within it.

Frotz 2.50 – Bronze.zblorb

Entrance Hall
Main Castle
Rooms searched: 2/55   S

When the seventh day comes and it is time for you to return to the castle in the forest, your sisters cling to your sleeves.

"Don't go back," they say, and "When will we ever see you again?" But you imagine they will find consolation somewhere.

Your father hangs back, silent and moody. He has spent the week as far from you as possible, working until late at night. Now he speaks only to ask whether the Beast treated you "properly." Since he obviously has his own ideas about what must have taken place over the past few years, you do not reply beyond a shrug.

You breathe more easily once you're back in the forest, alone.

Bronze
A fractured fairy tale by Emily Short
Release 11 / Serial number 060503 / Inform 7 build 3K27 (I6/v6.30 lib 6/10N)

Have you played interactive fiction before? > y

If you have not played Bronze before, you may still want to type HELP to learn about special commands unique to this game.

Drawbridge
Even in your short absence, the castle has come to look strange to you again. When you came here first, you stood a long while on the drawbridge, unready to cross the moat, for fear of the spells that might bind you if you did. This time it is too late to worry about such things.

An iron-barred gate leads north.

> examine me
You are nontrivially the worse for your journey – hungry, dirty, and tired. But all that can be seen to later.

> n
(first opening the iron-barred gate)
You shouldn't be able to open it, heavy as it is, but it swings aside lightly at your touch. The Beast said that it knows friend from enemy; and the castle, at least, still regards you as friend.

Entrance Hall
There is no fire in the big fireplace, and no one is waiting for you here; the air is very cold. Over the gate, the old familiar warning sign is painted.

Various passages lead deeper into the castle: north towards the central courtyard, southwest to the guard tower, east and west into the libraries, the offices, the galleries. Somewhere in this maze, he waits; and he should be told as soon as possible that you did return.

An iron-barred gate leads south to the drawbridge.

> read sign
You read: *Those who seek to leave the castle depart at peril of their lives and souls, unless another servant be provided in exchange, or a fixed term of absence be granted by their master.*

> w

Figure 11.1   A screenshot of *Bronze* by Emily Short (2000)

As an example, in *Bronze* (Short, 2000), an alternative version of the *Beauty and the Beast* fairytale, the reader plays the part of Belle returning to the Beast's castle after a week's leave as per their arrangement. After being given the initial description of the immediate location, the Drawbridge, the player is given total freedom to explore the game world and experiment with commanding Belle. The EXAMINE ME command produces some non-essential, but nevertheless interesting, information. Navigation, in this case by using the N command (an abbreviation for GO NORTH), takes Belle into another location in the game world, the Entrance Hall. The description of the Entrance Hall provides more information on the setting of the story and gives the player the first indication of a goal: to find the Beast. The descriptive text of the Entrance Hall also indicates the possible exits from the room and points out that there is an object in the area which may be of some importance and can be manipulated by Belle. The sign, as expected, can be read, and the command READ SIGN provides more backstory. The W command moves Belle west into another part of the castle, where both she and the player will continue to explore the environment and discover what needs to be done in order to find the Beast. However, this is only the beginning of the story and the player's many subsequent actions can lead to three different endings to the tale.

In IF, through exploration of the game world, the reader is not merely a passive observer, but is also an instigator of change in the story, dictating how the narrative unravels. By deciding what to do and by giving the necessary commands to perform those actions, the narrative is co-constructed by the reader. However, one of the challenges in IF is to discover not only what to do and what actions to take, but also to discover what words are necessary to embody these actions, in a way that the computer will understand. The element of IF that understands natural language (known as the parser), cannot understand every word. It chiefly recognises the most common words needed to function within the specific world/story being experienced. An example of common verbs and commands understood and needed to play IF can be seen in Andrew Plotkin's (2010) *IF for Beginners guide*:

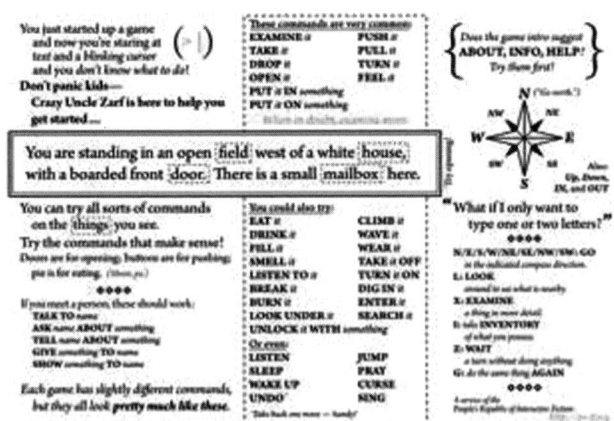

Figure 11.2   IF for beginners guide by Plotkin and Albaugh (2010)

Most commands in IF are given by using a verb plus noun construction, such as 'GET THE SILVER BELL AND RING IT' or 'LOOK UP FATHER IN THE CONTRACT BOOK.' Giving the game a command that is not understood will require the player to paraphrase the idea or follow a different line of thought.

While the main goal in IF is to reach the end of the story, achieving it is not as straightforward as simply typing 'GO NORTH', reading the textual descriptions and occasionally interacting with the environment. In addition to the linguistic challenge of discovering how to communicate with the story, the game element of IF provides logical puzzles that need to be solved in order for the narrative to open up. Pereira (2011: 3) notes that:

> Puzzles in IF act as a challenge and force exploration of the game world. They should not be considered as an add-on to the narrative experience – they are an integral part of the interactive process between the reader and the author, which generates the narrative.

As an example of this, many puzzles in *Bronze* require the use of a specific object in a specific location, such as climbing a stool to reach a higher point or wearing a magical helmet to allow Belle passage into hitherto inaccessible parts of the castle.

In this way, in addition to being a form of participatory storytelling, IF is also a challenging game. As such, IF has the potential not only to motivate and engage learners to read, thus giving them the opportunity to improve their reading fluency, but also to actively promote language learning awareness and acquisition, due to the deep engagement and interactivity required to play it.

Language learning with IF

Because of its textual nature and relationship to literature, IF is a natural tool for practising reading skills. As reading is a vehicle for introducing vocabulary, grammatical forms and cultural notions, its role in SLA is acknowledged (Day and Bamford, 1998). The initial reason for using IF in a teaching context was to help learners improve their reading fluency by offering an alternative source of reading material to traditional texts, which might empower them to become autonomous readers. Taguchi et al. (2006: 1) define 'reading fluency' as the ability

> to identify words in a text quickly and accurately with a minimal amount of attention. Word recognition is done efficiently and effortlessly and consequently, readers can read connected text silently or orally with speed and good comprehension.

It is generally accepted that the 'extensive reading' approach – providing large quantities of texts to learners which they find enjoyable – is a means of improving the decoding and comprehension of texts (Alyousef, 2006). However, the real difficulty lies in providing learners with large quantities of texts that they find captivating, especially if they are to be read outside the classroom in their own time. Lancy and Hayes (1988: 42) note that

> in helping students to learn how to read, it is clear that half the task is to teach the students how to read while the other half involves getting them to use that ability often enough to become fluent.

Because IF offers challenge and is dependent on user interaction, it is potentially more motivating to engage with than a traditional text, as reported in the results of a study by Lancy and Hayes (1986: 9):

> students with no more than average interest in reading will spend large amounts of time engaged in interactive fiction that requires heavy amounts of reading.

This potential for creating intrinsic motivation to begin reading, and providing prolonged engagement to continue with it, are two reasons why IF can be used to promote the practice of reading for fluency and extensive reading both in and outside the classroom.

The evaluation of IF

While my own research (Pereira, 2013) has shown that learners perceive IF to be an engaging and useful tool for practising English language skills, Tomlinson (1998: 3) maintains that 'it is not necessarily enough that the learners enjoy and value the materials'. In order to determine if IF is an appropriate form of learning material, I framed the argument using the criteria from Chapelle's Judgemental evaluation of CALL[2] framework (Chapelle, 2001):

> Language learning potential: The degree of opportunity present for beneficial focus on form.
>
> Learner fit: The amount of opportunity for engagement with language under appropriate conditions given learner characteristics.
>
> Meaning focus: The extent to which learner's attention is directed towards the meaning of the language.
>
> Authenticity: The degree of correspondence between the CALL activity and target language activities of interest to learners out of the classroom.
>
> Impact: The positive effects of the CALL activity on those who participate in it.

Practicality: The adequacy of resources to support the use of the call activity.

Furthermore, the evaluation criteria must be applied not only to the computer application itself, but also to the specific task being done with it (Chapelle, 2001: 53). The task involved learners playing a 45-minute session of *9:05* (Cadre, 2000), as part of a 90-minute lesson using the following procedure:

1. Pre-reading/playing phase: difficult vocabulary is clarified through a non-contextualised matching activity. Learners are given a list of possible (but not all) verbs and commands understood by the game. (20 minutes)
2. While-reading/playing phase: learners play the game in pairs. Learners are encouraged to replay the game after reaching one of the multiple endings in order to see how IF allows the reader to make different choices and take different paths (and in this case, especially to corroborate the 'bad' ending). (45 minutes)
3. Post-reading/playing phase: this involves a class discussion of what students really think happened in the story, some classroom practice on the third conditional (taking examples from happenings in the story), and the setting of a composition based on the story for homework (a letter to a loved one explaining the actions taken by the protagonist). (25 minutes)

Language learning potential

Because most IF is authentic and unscripted for language learners, no specific focus on form is provided by the game during play. As when using traditional literature for language learning, the main focus of IF is on meaning and not on form. Understanding the words and the rules that govern the world model and the protagonist's place in it is mandatory in order to advance through the narrative. However, because the player needs to provide input in a way that the game understands it, some focus on form, specifically related to verbs and prepositions is required by the player, otherwise progress in the game cannot be made. Despite not focusing specifically on form, IF can nonetheless provide learners with opportunities for incidental language learning. The existing body of research on using IF for foreign language learning has thus focused on the incidental learning of vocabulary (Cheung and Harrison, 1992; Cornillie et al., 2011). However, in my view, the language learning potential of IF goes well beyond focus on form and incidental learning. Through the implementation of Pre-, While-, and Post-tasks, it can be used as material that allows for the practice of all four language skills.

```
Bedroom                                               Time:  9:07 am
```

The phone rings.

Oh, no – how long have you been asleep? Sure, it was a tough night, but– This is bad. This is very bad.

The phone rings.

--

9:05 by Adam Cadre
Version 1.01 (10 February 2000) / Serial number 9502
Written in Inform 6.21, library 6/10

--

Bedroom (on the bed)
This bedroom is extremely spare, with dirty laundry scattered haphazardly all over the floor. Cleaner clothing is to be found in the dresser. A bathroom lies to the south, while a door to the east leads to the living room.

On the endtable are a telephone, a wallet (which is closed) and some keys.

The phone rings.

> examine me
You're covered with mud and dried sweat. It was quite an exhausting night – no wonder you overslept! Even making it to the bed before conking out was a fairly heroic accomplishment.

The phone rings.

> answer phone
You pick up the phone. "Hadley!" a shrill voice cries. "Hadley, haven't you even **left** yet?? You **knew** that our presentation was at nine o' clock sharp! First the thing with the printers, now this – there won't even be enough left of you for Bowman to fire once he's done with you. Now get the hell **down** here!!"

Click.

>|

Figure 11.3 A screenshot of 9:05 (Cadre 2000)

The pre-reading/playing phase

During the pre-reading phase, any difficult vocabulary should be clarified using non-contextual activities, such as a meaning matching task, so as not to give away plot information or clues linked to puzzles and their solutions. During this phase, the learners' schemata (Carrell and Eisterhold, 1988), or personal knowledge of the topic or theme, can be activated through discussion and other activities, as long as elements of surprise in the narrative are not ruined.

However, if the topic of the story is known, as in the adapted fairytale *Bronze*, activating schemata during this phase can scaffold learners during the while-reading phase and can also be exploited during tasks in the post-reading phase (such as comparing the different versions, creating a new version, and so on).

The while-reading/playing phase

While playing most IF, because turns are not taken in real time, there are natural pauses for reflection, allowing learners to find support for clarifying difficult language, either from the teacher or from discussion with a partner (if played in a classroom setting), or from a dictionary or the Internet (if played in an autonomous learning context). Some IF interpreters also have built-in text to speech options, which may enhance learner support for unfamiliar vocabulary by providing examples of pronunciation. During the while-reading phase in IF, the use of comprehension questions is not necessary as progress in the game is inherently linked to the player's understanding and synthesis of the text. If a passage or word is not understood, the player may be unable to solve a puzzle when confronted with it at a later time, and will remain stuck until that text is revisited and assimilated. Progression through the game clearly shows that the reader understands the meaning of the words and how the words affect the narrative and the world model that is being simulated.

Paralleling its major role in SLA, feedback and learner modification of output is integral to playing IF successfully. The process of 'noticing' mistakes in output (Schmidt and Frota, 1986) involves the learner becoming aware of a linguistic difficulty, followed by an attempt to modify that output, which potentially facilitates SLA. It is this cycle of input/output which creates the narrative in IF. Player input in IF can result in two types of output by the game: error messages, or the presentation of new narrative text. Feedback in IF is not yet adaptive and thus upon executing an unsuccessful command, learners need to consider if their error is:

> spelling related: PUT THE *CANDEL* ON THE STOOL;
>
> syntax related: PUT THE CANDLE *TO* THE STOOL;
>
> vocabulary related: *POSITION* THE CANDLE ON THE STOOL;
>
> that their command is simply not possible: *EAT* THE CANDLE;
>
> or irrelevant to the story: PUT THE CANDLE *UNDER* THE STOOL.

The writing skill is thus being practised during these exchanges and there is some opportunity for the noticing and repairing of written errors. During this while playing phase it also possible to implement tasks involving varied group dynamics, such as information gap type activities, or giving each member of a group a specific role (taking notes, mapping, and so on).

The post-reading/playing phase

In the post-reading phase, all of the language skills may be revisited through follow-up activities and a focus on form can be implemented through tasks on discrete language points.

Computer-mediated collaborative learning

Given the textual nature of the medium the learning affordances of IF may seem restricted to reading and writing skills. However, speaking and listening skills can also be practised and a much greater possibility for noticing and repairing errors is possible when playing IF in pairs or small groups. The act of two or more people working at a single computer and communicating with each other in order to accomplish a given task is known as computer-mediated collaborative learning (CMCL). In CMCL the computer-provided task becomes a source of generating language between users. The greatest opportunity for SLA during CMCL occurs when the discourse between learners allows for 'negotiation of meaning', defined by Pica (1994: 495) as the:

> modification and restructuring of interaction that occurs when learners and their interlocutors anticipate, perceive, or experience difficulties in message comprehensibility.

Ortega (1997: 87) further stresses the importance of pairing learners when using CALL by positing that CMCL:

> may provide for an instructional context that generates opportunities for communicative practice of the target language and opportunities for meaningful learner output to a significantly greater degree than more traditional arrangements in the L2 classroom.

Learner fit

The subject of learner fit is certainly an important consideration when selecting language learning materials. For the most part, IF is authentic material and thus needs to be carefully selected, with consideration of the level of linguistic difficulty being paramount. Any IF considered for use with learners needs to be played through, and more than once, in order to experience alternate endings and different paths. While a recommended pre-reading phase will consist of the clarification of difficult vocabulary and possibly further schemata-activating activities, the majority of words in the text (99 per cent, according to Nuttall, 1982) need to be familiar to the learner in order for them to understand the text and be able to interact with the game. In addition to evaluating the level of linguistic difficulty, one needs to think about the appropriateness of the language itself and the narrative content. Game-specific considerations, such as genre, puzzle difficulty, and geographic complexity of the game world, have been suggested by Pereira (2012). However, because of its authentic nature, and because the vast majority of modern IF has been written by adults for adults, it is difficult to find IF that can be used with low-level learners. The need to have an active imagination and some puzzle-solving ability in order to successfully interact with puzzle-based IF further restricts who will be able to play it satisfactorily. Notwithstanding, by offering a higher level of support through vocabulary lists and hint sheets, in addition to using text adventures from the 1980s with sparser text descriptions and less complex language, it may still be possible to use IF with these learners. Further support can be given by getting learners to play IF in pairs which, in addition to offering conditions for negotiation of meaning and SLA, also offers scaffolding for learners with weaker linguistic and cognitive skills.

Meaning focus

When reading/playing IF understanding the meaning of the language and responding to it with meaningful input, based on a conceptual model of the narrative and the game world, is what characterises it as a both a narrative and a game and ultimately, as a unique form of participatory storytelling. The main goal when playing IF is a meaningful one: to reach the end of the story, co-authoring it along the way. Further to this inherent focus on meaning, IF is completely in line with the principles of the CLT approach to language learning:

- reading for fluency is seen as a process instead of a product and is valued more than the accuracy of discrete language points.
- the target language needs to be used to interact with the game;
- finishing the story and problem-solving constitute meaningful tasks;
- solving puzzles requires using knowledge and language, which can often be transferred to the real world;
- it is an authentic text.

Authenticity

The principles mentioned in the previous section stress the authentic nature of IF both as a material and as a learning activity. The language tasks involved in playing IF require the use of the target language in a meaningful way, as represented in the following cycle:

- decoding the language presented in the text;
- synthesising the information and re-contextualising it;
- thinking of the words needed to express a desired action;

- creating the input following the conventions of IF;
- adapting the words or actions upon negative feedback.

However, in addition to engaging in this cycle of creating comprehensible input/output to create the narrative, the vast majority of IF includes a further element of challenge in the form of logic puzzles. Solving puzzles in IF often requires not only a clear understanding of the text and the subtle clues hidden within it, but also the ability to hypothesise how things work and how they are connected in the real world and in the game world.

As an example, in *Bronze*, the solution to some of the major puzzles in the game involves acquiring a candle by first summoning a ghostly servant following the mythology of the game world through a process requiring, among other objects, a bell and a magical helmet. The links between the servants and these objects can be found in the narrative and need to be discovered and acted upon by the reader in order to progress in the game. However, the player also needs to know:

1. What a bell and helmet do and how they are used;
2. The exact language involved in using bells and helmets.

Thus, in order to solve these puzzles, the player is challenged in five distinct ways:

1. Piecing together the information that explains how the game world works (servants, bells, mirrors, magical clothing);
2. Discovering and acquiring these objects in the game;
3. Understanding that a bell can be used to make a noise and a helmet worn to reduce, or in this case, amplify it;
4. Knowing that the verb 'ring' collocates with bell and 'wear' collocates with helmet;
5. Producing the correct input at the right time and in the right location.

While the example described here is based in a fantasy world with elements of magic, many puzzles in *Bronze* and in IF in general, no matter what the setting, are based on knowledge of real world concepts and the manipulation of real world objects. Gee (2007a: 105) posits that situated and embodied learning, also called 'learning by doing' can 'lead to real understanding and the ability to apply what one knows in action'. Another concept related to schema theory, which is also strongly relevant to playing IF, is that of 'script', described as 'a pre-determined, stereotyped sequence of actions that defines a well-known situation' (Schank and Abelson, 1977: 41). Scripts, like schemata, are cultural not universal. Playing IF, because it is experiential and implements situated cognition, can be an excellent source for broadening learners' schemata and scripts, thus extending their own content and cultural knowledge, which may be transferable to real world situations.

Positive impact

As well as the language learning affordances of IF, because it is a form of literature, it encompasses all the advantages of using literature for language learning, such as developing content knowledge and cultural awareness, and appealing to imagination and creativity (Van, 2009).

Furthermore, IF is known to activate the following cognitive skills:

- problem-solving and lateral thinking (Shelton, 2005);
- critical thinking (Seitan, 2010);
- spatial orientation (Gander, 2004);
- metacognitive strategies (Kozdras et al., 2006).

All of these cognitive skills are transferable to the learners' real lives beyond the game and beyond the classroom, where further learning may take place. After playing IF in a classroom setting, learners may become interested in playing/reading IF on their own. Encouraging learners to play IF outside of class time, possibly even as a homework assignment, might motivate them to become more autonomous learners and readers.

Practicality

The three elements needed to play IF are a computer (or mobile device), an interpreter (the software that runs IF game files), and a game file. Because IF is completely text-based, it can run on computers that are decades old. Game files are cross-platform and interpreters to play them can be found for nearly every computer operating system and mobile device. The vast majority of IF games and interpreters are distributed for free by their developers and can be found at the Interactive Fiction Database (http://ifdb.tads.org). IF is also extremely portable, with large and complex games requiring only half a megabyte and the interpreters themselves less than ten megabytes. It is therefore quick and easy to set up on multiple machines, even by teachers themselves, provided administrator access rights are not required. In learning contexts where the software cannot be installed, hundreds of IF games can be played online in Java applets or, preferably, through the browser-based Parchment interpreter (http://parchment.toolness.com). While this may be convenient, the main disadvantage of using a browser-based interpreter is a more limited ability to save and restore one's progress or to save a transcript of the game session for post-play analysis.

IF can be implemented in a variety of different learning scenarios. It can be used with one computer and a data projector in a whole class setting, or with students at individual machines, alone, in pairs, or in small groups. IF is also perfectly suited as an autonomous learning tool to practise reading for fluency, as the presence of a teacher is not required. Advancing through the narrative by solving the linguistic and logic puzzles that act as barriers to progress is clear evidence of the reader's comprehension of the text. Desilets (1999: 7) posits that the 'pause' in the flow of text, created by the existence of a puzzle in IF,

> adds an evaluative dimension of considerable instructional power, an element that operates even when the teacher isn't around ... The aesthetically-placed pauses for problems thus become, among other things, compelling and integrated reading comprehension tests, perhaps the only such tests that most kids will take voluntarily. (Desilets, 1999: 8)

In the absence of a pre-reading, vocabulary clarification phase during autonomous play, a dictionary should be consulted while playing. Additionally, help related to playing the game and solutions to puzzles are available for most games as in-game hints (implemented in many of the higher quality games), and maps and walkthroughs (step-by-step guides) can be found on the Internet.

Evaluation results

Evaluating the benefits of using IF for SLA using Chappelle's Judgemental CALL evaluation framework has produced the results shown in Table 11.1.

The results show that despite there not being a strong focus on form when playing IF, there is still the possibility for incidental language acquisition in both classroom and autonomous learning scenarios. Furthermore, adding a CMCL component to the classroom setting can create significant opportunities for noticing and negotiation of meaning, in addition to extending reading and writing skills practice to include listening and speaking. Additionally, the

Table 11.1   Results of IF CALL evaluation

Chappelle's criteria	Classroom setting	Autonomous learning
Language learning potential (form)	POSSIBLE+	POSSIBLE−
Learner fit	POSSIBLE	POSSIBLE−
Meaning focus	STRONG	STRONG
Authenticity	STRONG	STRONG
Impact	MEDIUM	MEDIUM
Practicality	STRONG	STRONG

recommended implementation of Pre-, While- and Post-reading tasks, can provide opportunities for specific focus on form.

The question of learner fit requires some consideration since finding suitable IF for use with lower levels, while possible, may be both a time consuming and difficult task. With regards to the other criteria, IF more than meets the requirements for both learning scenarios.

In conclusion, I believe that IF has very clear language learning affordances and that reasons for its consideration as valid language learning material have been evidenced through judgemental evaluation. The following section reports on the validity of IF as language learning material from the perspective of the learner.

Results of students playing IF: a case study

In a recent case study on the perceptions of using IF for language learning (Pereira, 2013), ten upper intermediate learners of English as a foreign language were observed while playing *9:05* for a period of 45 minutes, followed by *Lost Pig* (Jota, 2007) for 60 minutes. The students were then asked to fill out a questionnaire with Yes/No and open-ended questions on their perceptions of the usefulness of IF as a language learning tool and their opinions on whether playing IF was a fun and engaging experience. The results of the observation show that the students were totally engaged during the playing sessions and actively practised the four language skills. Results from the questionnaire revealed that while nine of the ten students stated that they found playing IF to be a pleasurable activity, they were unanimous in recognising its language learning affordances, and many students commented on how playing IF exercised their imagination and problem-solving skills. Questions pertaining to whether students viewed IF as a potential tool for the autonomous practice of reading fluency outside the classroom were met positively, with seven of the ten students replying that they would play IF at home to practise English.

Conclusion

Despite having reached its peak of popularity three decades ago and not having state-of-the-art graphics or cinematics, IF continues to be a potentially motivating and engaging DGBLL tool. Because it is text-based, its language learning affordances are clear both to students and teachers and this is evidenced by the judgemental evaluation of IF as valid CALL material described in this chapter. IF can offer engaging language practice for all skills in the classroom, as well as offering a more challenging and interactive alternative to static text for improving reading fluency in an autonomous learning context. However, there are challenges in using IF in the language classroom, mostly related to finding IF that can be played by lower-level learners and the fact that playing IF requires that learners have above average imagination and problem-solving skills. Nonetheless, these challenges can be overcome by providing adequate support. Teachers who wish to use IF with their learners are given this support through the *IF Only: Interactive Fiction and teaching English as a foreign language* website (http://www.theswanstation.com), which provides in-depth lesson plans for carefully selected IF games covering most levels of language proficiency. In-class support for learners when playing IF can be given by using pair/group interaction and supplying vocabulary lists, maps, and quick hints if they get stuck in the game.

The implementation of DGBLL in the classroom will become more prominent as language teachers become more aware of the affordances of digital games and as they overcome their reluctance in accepting them as valid language learning material. It is my hope that IF, and the growing body of teachers who have begun to use it with their learners, will help make DGBLL a widespread addition to traditional language learning materials.

Engagement priorities

1. IF has been criticised for not having a clear focus on form, due to its authentic nature. Is this a determining factor in deciding whether to use IF with your learners? Can you think of ways to provide this focus on form in the while- or post-reading phases?
2. One of the main challenges of using IF with learners is their need to be imaginative and able to apply critical and lateral thinking in order to solve puzzles. While IF itself serves as a tool to give learners practice in problem-solving, it may be useful to prepare learners to think in these terms before playing. How can we get our learners to be more imaginative and to think outside the box?
3. Beyond the walls of the classroom, IF is an excellent source of alternative (and potentially more engaging) material to practise autonomous reading fluency. In addition to recommending IF works for learners to read/play, how else can we help them get the most out of this resource on their own?
4. The next step after having your learners play IF is to get them to create their own IF in the classroom, using freely available authoring software such as Inform 7 (http://www.inform7.com) or Quest 5 (http://www.textadventures. co.uk/quest/). How might writing their own stories sway those learners who are put off by the extensive reading or puzzle-solving to value IF from a creative writing and collaborative perspective?

Notes

1. The original text adventure game, 'Adventure', was the first form of electronic literature to accept natural language input and would spawn hundreds of imitators on home computers throughout the 1980s.
2. Beatty (2003: 7) defines computer assisted language learning (CALL) as 'any process in which a learner uses a computer and, as a result, improves his or her language'.

References

Alyousef, H. S. (2006). Teaching reading comprehension to ESL/EFL learners. *Journal of Language and Learning*, 5(1): 63–73.

Beatty, K. (2003). *Teaching and Researching Computer Assisted Language Learning*. Harlow: Pearson.

Cadre, A. (2000). *9:05*. [Video game]. Available at http://adamcadre.ac/if.html [Accessed 01/01/2013].

Carrell, L. P. and Eisterhold, C. J. (1988). Schema theory and ESL reading pedagogy. In Carrell, L. P., Devine, J. and Eskey, D (eds), *Interactive Approaches to Second Language Reading*. Cambridge: Cambridge University Press, pp. 73–92.

Chapelle, C. (2001). *Computer Applications in Second Language Acquisition: Foundations for teaching, Testing and Research*. Cambridge: Cambridge University Press.

Cheung, A. and Harrison, C. (1992). Microcomputer adventure games and second language acquisition: a study of Hong Kong tertiary students. In Pennington, M. C. and Stevens, V. (eds), *Computers in Applied Linguistics: An International Perspective*. Clevedon: Multilingual Matters Ltd: Avon, England.

Cornillie, F., Thorne, S. L and Desmet, P. (2012). ReCALL special issue: Digital games for language learning: challenges and opportunities. *ReCALL*, 24: 243–256.

Cornillie, F., Jacques, I., De Wannemacker, S., Paulussen, H. and Desmet, P. (2011). Vocabulary treatment in adventure and role-playing games: a playground for adaptation and adaptivity. In De Wannemacker, S., Clarebout, G. and De Causmaecker, P. (eds), *Interdisciplinary Approaches to Adaptive Learning: A Look at the Neighbours. First International Conference on Interdisciplinary Research on Technology, Education and Communication, ITEC 2010, Kortrijk, Belgium, May 25–27, 2010*. Revised Selected Papers. Springer, pp. 132–148.

Crowther, W. and Woods, D. (1976). *Adventure*.[Video game]. Available at http://ifdb.tads.org/viewgame?id=fft6pu91j85y4acv [Accessed 01/01/2013].

Day, R. R. and Bamford, J. (1998). *Extensive Reading in the Second Language Classroom*. New York: Cambridge University Press.

Desilets, B. (1999). Interactive fiction vs. the pause that distresses: how computer-based literature interrupts the reading process without stopping the fun. *Currents in Electronic Literacy*, (1). Available at http://www.cwrl.utexas.edu/currents/spr99/desilets.html [Accessed 01/01/2013].

Gander, P. (2004). Spatial mental representations in interactive fiction – what is particular about the interactive text? In Porhiel, S. and Klingler, D. (eds), *L'Unitétexte Pleyben*, France: Perspectives, pp. 96–124.

Gee, J. P. (2007a). *What Video Games Have to Teach Us About Learning and Literacy*, 2nd Edition. New York: Palgrave Macmillan.

Gee, J. P. (2007b). *Good Video Games and Good Learning: Collected Essays on Video Games, Learning and Literacy (New Literacies and Digital Epistemologies)*. New York: Peter Lang Publishers.

IF Only: *Interactive Fiction and Teaching English As a Foreign Language* [Website]. Available at http://www.theswanstation.com [Accessed 01/01/2013].

Inform 7 [Software]. Available at: http://www.inform7.com [Accessed 01/01/2013].

Interactive Fiction Database [Website]. Available at http://ifdb.tads.org [Accessed 04/28/2012].

Kozdras, D., Haunstetter, D. and King, J. (2006). Interactive fiction: 'New Literacy' learning opportunities – empowering learners through engagement. *E-Learning*, 3(4): 519–532.

Lancy, D. F. and Hayes, B. L. (1986). Building an anthology of interactivefiction. Paper presented at symposium, *The Computer as an Environment for Learning, American Education Research Association, San Francisco, CA, April 16–20, 1986*. Available at http://www.eric.ed.gov/ERICWebPortal/contentdelivery/servlet/ERICServlet?accno=ED2759 91 [Accessed 01/01/2013].

Lancy, D. F. and Hayes, B. L. (1988). Interactive fiction and the reluctant reader. *English Journal*, 77(7): 42–66. Available at http://www.jstor.org/stable/818936 [Accessed 01/01/2013].

Larsen-Freeman, D. (1986). *Techniques and Principles in Language Teaching*. Oxford: Oxford University Press.

Jota, A. (2007). *Lost Pig* [Video game]. Available at http://www.grunk.org/lostpig [Accessed 01/01/2013].

Mawer, K. and Stanley, G. (2011). *Digital Play Computer Games and Language Aims*. Peaslake: Delta Publishing.

Montfort, N. (2003). *Twisty Little Passages: An Approach to Interactive Fiction*. London: MIT Press.

Nuttall, C. (1982). *Teaching Reading Skills in a Foreign Language*. London: Heinemann Educational Books Ltd.

Ortega, L. (1997). Process and outcomes in networked classroom interaction: defining the research agenda for L2 computer-assisted classroom discussion. *Language Learning & Technology*, 1(1): 82–93.

Parchment. Available at http://parchment.toolness.com [Accessed 03/28/2012].

Pereira, J. (2011). A narrative at war with a crossword – an introduction to interactive fiction. In Görür-Atabaş, H. and Turner, S. (eds), *Expectations Eclipsed in Foreign Language Education: Learners and Educators on an Ongoing Journey*. İstanbul: Sabancı Üniversitesi, pp. 87–96. Available at http://digital.sabanciuniv.edu/ebookacik/3011200000287.pdf [Accessed 01/01/2013].

Pereira, J. (2012). *Choosing an Interactive Fiction Game for Use in the Classroom.*[Blog]. Available at http://www.theswanstation.com/wordpress/2011/12/choosing-an-interactive-fiction-game-for-use-in-the-classroom [Accessed 01/01/2013].

Pereira, J. (2013). Beyond hidden bodies and lost pigs: student perceptions of foreign language learning with interactive fiction. In Baek, Y. and Whitton, N. (eds), *Cases on Digital Game-Based Learning: Methods, Models and Strategies*. New York: IGI Global.

Pica, T. (1994). Research on negotiation: what does it reveal about second-language learning conditions, processes, and outcomes? *Language Learning*, 44: 493–527.

Plotkin, A. and Albaugh, L. (2010). *IF-for-Beginners Card*. Available at http://pr-if.org/doc/play-if-card [Accessed 01/01/2013].

Quest 5 [Software]. Available at http://www.textadventures.co.uk/quest/ [Accessed 01/01/2013].

Reinders, H. (ed.) (2012). *Digital Games in Language Learning and Teaching*. Basingstoke: Palgrave Macmillan.

Richards, J. (2006). *Communicative Language Teaching Today.* Available at http://www.professorjackrichards.com/pdfs/communicative-language-teaching-today-v2.pdf [Accessed 01/01/2013].

Schank, R. and Abelson, R. (1977). *Scripts, Plans, Goals, and Understanding: An Inquiry into Human Knowledge Structures.* Hillsdale, NJ: Lawrence Erlbaum.

Schmidt, R. and Frota, S. (1986). Developing basic conversational ability in a foreign language: a case study of an adult learner of Portuguese, In Day, R. (ed.), *Talking to Learn.* Rowley, MA: Newbury House.

Shelton, (2005). *Designing and Creating Interactive Fiction for Learning.* Available at http://archive2.nmc.org/content/gaming/pdf/shelton2005.pdf [Accessed 01/01/2013].

Short, E. (2000) *Bronze.* [Video game]. Available at http://emshort.wordpress.com/my-work [Accessed 01/01/2013].

Seitan, C. (2010). Minds in need of training: how interactive fiction exercises student's critical thinking skills. Available at http://www.docstoc.com/docs/89462042/Composition-Final-Paper [Accessed 01/01/2013].

Taguchi, E., Gorsuch, G. and Sasamoto, E. (2006). Developing second and foreign language reading fluency and its effect on comprehension: a missing link. *The Reading Matrix,* 6(2): 1–17. Available at http://www.readingmatrix.com/articles/taguchI_gorsuch_sasamoto/article.pdf [Accessed 01/01/2013].

The Entertainment Software Association (ESA) (2012). Available at http://www.theesa.com/facts/pdfs/ESA_EF_2012.pdf [Accessed 01/01/2013].

Tomlinson, B. (1998). *Materials Development in Language Teaching.* Cambridge: Cambridge University Press.

Van, T. T. M. (2009). The relevance of literary analysis to teaching literature in the EFL classroom. *English Teaching Forum,* 3: 2–9.

12
Using Web 2.0 Tools in CLIL

Fabrizio Maggi, Maurizia Cherubin and Enrique García Pascual

Introduction

The purpose of this chapter is to show how the use of Web 2.0 tools in foreign language learning CLIL situations, besides increasing foreign language exposure and use, enhances the levels of student satisfaction, motivation, and confidence, all of which are crucial for communicative, lifelong foreign language learning. We will illustrate how the use of Web 2.0 technology can connect students across grade levels and schools as collaborators and peer tutors of school subject matter in English. Learners are generally used to traditional, individual activities such as reading articles, books or short stories, but may be unfamiliar with the type of collaborative learning activities that Web 2.0 supports. By preparing material to teach each other and assessing or reworking peer output, students experience a variety of cognitive and communicative activities that stimulate reflection, critical thinking, and self-directed, self-organised learning. This chapter describes ways to motivate learners to get involved in these new Web 2.0 activities.

What is CLIL?

The CLIL acronym (Content and Language Integrated Learning) has become a very familiar term in European school contexts. The term was coined and launched by David Marsh in 1994[1]. According to Marsh: 'CLIL refers to situations where subjects, or parts of subjects, are taught through a foreign language with dual-focussed aims, namely the learning of content, and the simultaneous learning of a foreign language.' The concept was taken up and developed in the Eurydice Report, *CLIL at School in Europe* (Eurydice, 2006), which stated: 'The acronym CLIL is used as a generic term to describe all types of provision in which a second language (a foreign, regional or minority language and/or another official state language) is used to teach certain subjects in the curriculum other than the language lessons themselves.' Of major significance in the development of CLIL is the fact that the CLIL languages are not limited to traditional foreign languages, but also include minority languages, regional languages, or other officially recognised languages. Thus, CLIL is not only a language policy tool for the promotion of foreign languages, especially of English, but can also serve to promote languages that are spoken by very few people.

There are many advantages to the CLIL approach, both for learning subject matter and for learning language. Because of the dual focus on language and content, 'CLIL induces the learner to be more cognitively active during the learning process' (Van de Craen et al., 2008: 197). In addition to developing academic cognitive processes and communication skills, it develops confident learners. CLIL 'can be very successful in enhancing the learning of languages and other subjects, and developing in the youngsters a positive "can do" attitude towards themselves as language learners' (Coyle, 2010: 30). CLIL encourages intercultural understanding and community values. Research also shows (Braun, 2007; Sierra, 2008; Zydatis, 2009) that learners become more sensitive to vocabulary and ideas presented in their first language, as well as in the target language, and they gain a more extensive and varied vocabulary. In the target language learners reach proficiency levels in all four skills (reading, writing, listening, and speaking).

In this chapter we provide practical examples to confirm the ways CLIL develops learner confidence, enhances their understanding of the target content, and increases communication skills in the target language.

ICT in education

Information and communication technologies (ICT) have evolved dramatically in the last decade and the use of ICT in education (Internet, WWW, search engines, digital videos, digital audios, PPT, spreadsheets and so on) is leading to change in the practices, methods and content of teaching, and in assessment processes. In order to increase knowledge of the effectiveness of ICT in education and training, over the past ten years research has analysed, among other things, the extent to which access to these technologies (including Internet connections) can improve learning and what kind of learning will be positively affected. The data collected from the international surveys IEA-TIMSS 2007 (http://www.iea.nl/timss_2007.html) and OECD-PISA 2009 (http://www.oecd.org/pisa/pisaproducts/pisa2009/pisa2009keyfindings.htm) show a population of learners, especially young people, fully engaged in a multimedia world, both inside and outside school. A large number of young people are using computer technology and its derivatives, such as fifth generation digital devices (iPods, tablets, smart phones), for a variety of purposes. For the younger generation, in particular, the use of computers is part of normal daily activities. The integration of ICT within the sphere of education and vocational training therefore reflects these trends.

In 2000 the European Commission adopted a specific plan of action, called *eLearning*, to determine the central issues for development in the following decade, in particular to examine the effective integration of ICT in education and training. In this document, *eLearning* has been defined as 'the use of new multimedia technologies and the Internet to improve the quality of learning by facilitating access to resources and services'.[2]

The subsequent strategy *i2010 one-inclusion*,[3] on the one hand has identified specific areas directly related to the use of ICT to improve teaching effectiveness, and, on the other hand, has emphasised the need to promote education and training in the use of ICT. From this perspective, educational technology has become one of the four crosscutting themes of the Lifelong Learning Programme (Council of the European Union, 2008), and a priority in the four vertical programmes (Erasmus, Comenius, Leonardo da Vinci and Grundtvig).

Web 2.0

One area in particular that has been the focus of interest in education is that of Web 2.0. This term, introduced at a conference in 2004 by Tim O'Reilly, refers to the second generation of the World Wide Web (WWW). The new generation of the Web contains features and functionality that were not previously available. Web 2.0 does not refer to a specific version of the Web, but rather to a series of technological improvements.

Some examples of features considered to be part of Web 2.0 are:

- *Blogs*: also known as Web logs, allow users to post thoughts and updates about their life on the Web.
- *Wikis*: sites like Wikipedia, Wikispace, enable users from around the world to add and update online content.
- *Social networking*: sites like Facebook and MySpace, allow users to build and customise their own profiles and communicate with friends.
- *Web applications*: a broad range of applications such as Vimeo, Delicious, Skype, Dropbox, make it possible for users to run programs directly in a Web browser.

Web 2.0 technologies provide a level of user interaction that was not available before. Websites have become much more dynamic and interconnected, producing 'online communities' and making it even easier to share information. In other words, the WWW has evolved from Web 1.0, which, according to

Berners-Lee, Hendler and Lassila (2001), could be considered the 'read-only web', towards becoming a 'read/write platform' where users can engage with others, contribute and publish information in several formats including text, graphics, animation, audio, and video.

Today the term Web 2.0 is used to describe applications that take full advantage of the networking nature of the Web; they encourage participation, are inherently social and open and distinguish themselves from previous generations of software by a number of principles:

- Web 2.0 enables and facilitates the active participation of each user;
- Web 2.0 applications and services allow publishing and storing of textual information, by individuals (blogs) and collectively (wikis), of audio recordings (podcasts), of video material (YouTube), of pictures (Flikr, Picasa), and so on.
- Web 2.0 services typically focus on usability and aim to simplify the interactions as much as possible by concentrating on the task or service the application provides.

Web 2.0 and language learning

The WWW has become an environment for personal and collective productivity, and this opens up great opportunities for learning and teaching. Unlike traditional Web 1.0 technologies, social software, such as social networks, wikis, and blogs, have opened up new opportunities for interaction and collaboration between teachers and learners, and among learners. The 'distributed knowledge' (Roelofsen, 2006; Bonifacio et al., 2003) available, regardless of place and time, now uses the same applications and does not depend on a particular computer, operating system, or on specific software and the compatibility of file formats they produce. Web applications allow you to create and edit text, presentations, graphics, photographs, mental and conceptual maps, slideshows, sound effects, video, video seminars, hypertext, and websites.

A learner can, for example, watch a clip from a new foreign language movie, comment on it in the target language in a blog and thereby start a discussion about the movie in a social network with his or her peers or even beyond the classroom context with native speakers. All this is possible without, at any stage, having to change tools or technologies: the Web is the platform throughout. The fact that each user can generate their own content on the Web and practise their right to communicate represents another benefit of Web 2.0 for language learning and teaching, both culturally and linguistically.

We now have access on the Web to a vast and constantly growing range of content in the form of text, audio, and video files, provided by users with different motivations and of different age groups, social, local, and linguistic backgrounds. For language learning and teaching this can only be considered beneficial, insofar as it helps to fulfil one of its main aims, namely to create communication situations for the learner which are as authentic as possible. These advancements of Web 2.0 in terms of interactive communication, collaboration, and user participation open up new potentials for enhancing each of the four language skills, as all of the commonly discussed social software applications mentioned above can be employed both for receptive and productive purposes.

Collaborative learning and Web 2.0

We use the term collaborative learning to refer to a method of education through which students at various performance levels work together toward a common goal; a collaborative activity is not only a socially distributed activity, but also an activity in which the objectives of each individual depend on those established and shared by other participants in the learning situation. Collaborative learning is a democratic model of class management, which mainly focuses on working in heterogeneous groups that give each member an equal opportunity to achieve success. For this reason, the first and fundamental aim of those who intend to apply this teaching method is certainly the creation of an educational, non-competitive, highly empowering, and collaborative environment.

When weak students work with the best students in cooperative situations it increases the use of higher order reasoning strategies: strategies for producing more detailed analysis and criticism, more creative answers, more elaborate levels of explanation. The cognitive processes induced by having to talk, discuss, and explain to others, often in different ways, improve memory retention and promote the development of reasoning strategies based on the elaboration of the content (Johnson and Johnson, 1987). In general, the research suggests a superior cognitive level in cooperative groups of students who provided elaborated explanations to others. In particular, students who received elaborated explanations learnt more than those who worked alone, but not as much as those who provided explanations (Webb, 1985).

Web 2.0 tools have immense potential for fostering collaborative learning. The Internet allows the free exchange of information, the circulation of ideas, and interaction between participants (synchronous and asynchronous). It makes the written word, which at school is considered to be a tool for composing texts later subjected to the judgement of the teacher, a means of interpersonal communication, discussion of ideas and experiences and, ultimately, a social tool. As Kaye (1994: 19) puts it:

Working through the computer means working together, which implies a sharing of tasks and an explicit intention to add value in order to create something new or different through a collaborative process. A broad definition of collaborative learning could be the acquisition by individuals of knowledge, skills or attitudes that are the result of a group action or said more clearly, individual learning as a result of a group process.

Thus, collaboration is a deliberative and structured process that stands in sharp contrast to a simple exchange of information or instruction execution.

Prior to Web 2.0, ICT supported online teaching models that were essentially focused on the learners, or, as Isidori (2003: 47) puts it, 'the online didactic learning environment aims to create systems focusing attention on the learner'. With the advent of Web 2.0 the focus has shifted from teaching learners to creating ways for learners to work together autonomously so that they can learn from and with each other. Thus, when we talk about learning environments planned in a manner typical of Web 2.0, we mean those virtual places in which students can study and help each other to learn, equipped with 'tools that facilitate the active participation' and

> make the place where you study a rich environment of solicitations, capable, said in behaviourist terms, of providing quality inputs so that learning can take place. (Rosati, 1999: 67)

Collaborative learning is the educational model used in educational online activities because it allows students to work on issues, projects, or products interacting among themselves and with the teacher. Using all the tools of Web 2.0 it is possible to guide the students to meet their specific interests and realise their own purposes so that they can see and understand all the possibilities of the new learning environment, which they can later use as tools to perform and carry out their own personal projects.

This is the case of webquests[4], for instance, which are very popular with CLIL teachers. Webquests make effective use of the vast information resources available on the Web and promote higher order thinking through authentic assignments that emphasise enquiry-based learning. They provide a model for teachers searching for ways to incorporate the Internet into the classroom on both a short- and long-term basis. Webquests can be designed within a single discipline or they can be interdisciplinary, and are most likely to be group activities. For example, a webquest on human rights violations for high school students focuses on the task of persuading people to take action against human rights abuses (http://www.aacps.org/aacps/boe/instr/curr/comed/HSwebquest/frick/index.html). *Viva Espana* is a role play-based webquest in English for students who wish to learn about Spain. Webquests have been a part of project-based learning and teaching in mainstream education for some time, but they also have a multitude of applications in language classes that are focused on content or theme-based learning.

Another concrete example is the use of Google Docs, a free Web-based application in which documents can be created, edited, and stored online then accessed from any computer with an Internet connection. It allows users to create and edit documents online while collaborating in real time with other users. For this reason it is an ideal tool for collaborative projects in which multiple authors (students) work together in real time, possibly from diverse locations. All participants can see who made specific document changes and when those alterations were done, facilitating collaboration. Moreover, the revision history included in the service allows teachers to see the additions made to a document, with each student distinguished by colour (although the entire document must be manually searched to find these changes). Because documents are stored online as well as on users' computers, there is no risk of total data loss.

A case study: the Vertical Transversal CLIL project

We now want to show a practical application of how the use of some of Web 2.0 tools can increase student interaction, participation, and motivation, and provide peer tutoring and teaching. The project *Vertical Transversal CLIL: the student protagonist of their own learning* follows CLIL methodology by using only the second language, English, to communicate, listen to, and learn from others, using integrated technology.

The project focused on a science unit that involved two schools in two different towns: a third class of a middle school in the province of Milan; and a third class of a secondary high school in Pavia, aged 14 and 17 respectively. The authors had different roles in the project: Maurizia was directly involved as a middle school teacher of English; Fabrizio took care of the organisation of the whole project; and Enrique provided the necessary theoretical pedagogical background.

The project can be considered a vertical project because it involved students from two different grades of school. They exchanged information, documents, and presentations using the second language, the Web 2.0 tools, and by video-conferencing; they experimented with peer education and tutoring, showing what they learnt using the interactive whiteboard (IWB). In this way students became the protagonists of their own learning, while teachers were facilitators and, in a certain sense, learners too. The project can be considered a transversal project because the subjects it dealt with – cells, meiosis, mitosis, Mendel's Law – are part of the curricular programme for science for both grades. Middle school students study the cell in English, while high school students study Mendel's Law in the same language.

The assessment was based on peer evaluation. The students cooperated and collaborated to create presentations, documents and videos to post and share on their blog and on the school website. Moreover, the high school students, using shared Google documents, checked the results of a quiz they created for the middle school students, explained the mistakes made and provided feedback through a final videoconference.

The aims of this project focused on language, content and learning to:

- improve overall target language competence;
- diversify methods and forms of classroom practice;
- provide opportunities to study content from different perspectives;
- access subject-specific target language terminology;
- develop oral communication skills;
- develop social abilities to build up knowledge using the Web 2.0 tools;
- improve learning in a student familiar environment;
- increase learner motivation.

Project development

In this section we describe the different phases of the project, and the ways in which ICT was integrated in each phase (highlighted in bold). The project was developed over a span of six months.

Phase 1: Planning

English and science teachers from the two different schools agree on the goals, the topics, the phases, the time, and the methodology to follow using *Google docs* and *Google Calendar* to set the deadline of each phase. Both schools use *IWB* for presentations and for surfing the Internet. They also select *YouTube* videos (for example this video on mitosis: http://www.youtube.com/watch?v=VlN7K1–9QB0) and use *Skype* for videoconferencing. The purpose of using these videos or animations is to provide a visual contribution to the text students are working on, for example to make evident and clear the mechanism of functioning of a cell.

Phase 2: Setting up the project

Middle school English and Science teachers prepare some interactive activities to do in class using the IWB multimedia software; they give students a list of specific vocabulary and documents simplified according to the students' language level. For example, middle school students are provided with vocabulary related to the cell and asked to organise key points on the IWB, as shown in Figure 12.1.

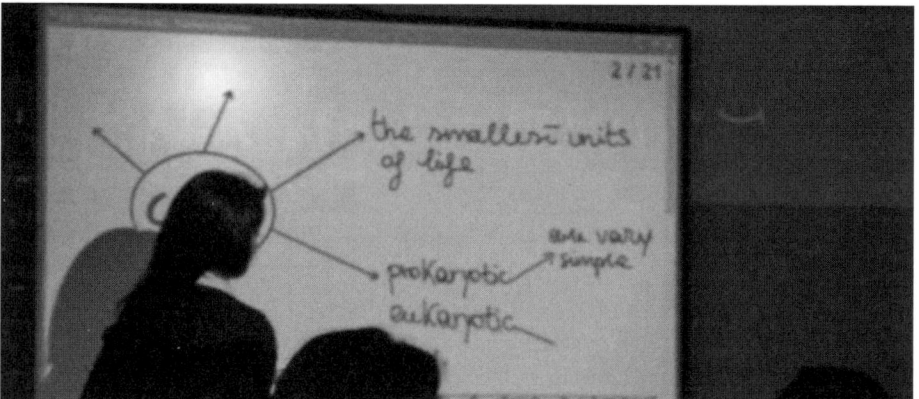

Figure 12.1   Middle school students using the IWB to brainstorm vocabulary related to the cell

Phase 3: Working organisation

Middle school teachers divide students into working groups of 4/5 people according to students' interest in the topics: cell, meiosis, mitosis, DNA, reproduction. In the IT laboratory students surf the Internet for materials, documents, videos, and images to insert in their presentations. Each group assigns a specific task and a different role to each of its members: each group has a leader (he/she is the group representative, interacts with the teachers and enforces time); an editor; an Internet surfer and so on.

Phase 4: Presentations

Teachers open a *gmail* account for the middle school classes involved in the project to share documents and presentations with the secondary school students. At the end the middle school students present meiosis/mitosis in English to their peers in their own class, as in Figure 12.2, and, through *Skype*, to the secondary school students. The materials shown in Figure 12.2 are a patchwork of information taken from the Internet.

Phase 5: Peer education and student tutoring

By means of videoconferencing the secondary school students explain Mendel's law in full detail through a PowerPoint (PPT) presentation with graphs and drawings and show the experiment carried out in the science laboratory to the middle school students (see Figure 12.3). In order to make Mendel's Law simpler to understand, students provide very practical examples. In Figure 12.4 they are explaining the theory of the green pea using plasticine of different colours.

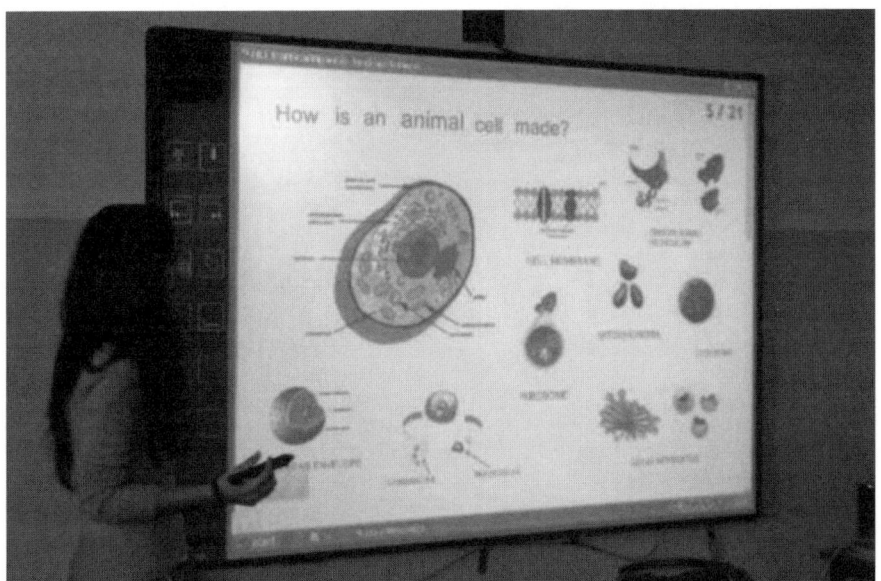

Figure 12.2 Middle school students explain the cell

Figure 12.3 Videoconference. High school students explain Mendel's Law

Figure 12.4   Students provide very practical examples

Phase 6: Peer assessments

Secondary school students prepare an online multiple-choice test in English about Mendel's Law. Using *Google docs*, the test is administered to each middle school student, who carries out the test underlining the correct answers in light gray, as in Figure 12.5. The tests are checked by the older students who highlight the mistakes in dark gray and underline the correct answer in mid gray. At the end older students give a mark according to the number of right answers, using a range from excellent to insufficient. The corrected tests are immediately sent back to the middle school students, once again employing *Google docs*.

Phase 7: Feedback

Through a final videoconference, the older students provide feedback on correct and incorrect answers and correct the wrong ones, and the younger students provide feedback about the secondary school students' presentation in areas such as: the topic is easy to understand; the students are confident with the topics; the language and vocabulary are appropriate.

Phase 8: Storing materials

All the materials produced are then posted to the virtual *Dropbox* store in order to create a repository from which students can download the files they are interested in, whenever they want. The products are also posted on the

Name.   Data...6/6/11
                    BIOLOGY TEST

1.
2. A pea flower has:
   • neither pollen norovules
   • both pollen and ovules
   • pollen but not ovules

3. Pollen carries:
   • father's information
   • mother's information
   • the anthers

4. In pea plants Mendel identified some characters easy to study. How many?
   • ?
   • 10
   • 22

5. One of the characters studied by Mendel was seed colour which could be:
   • either yellow or white
   • either green or white
   • either green or yellow

6. In cross pollination:
   • pollen meets some other pollen
   • Mendel transfers pollen from one flower to another
   • Mendel transfers voules from one flower to another

7. The first generation of children is called:
   • P
   • F1
   • F2

8. After the cross polination between two pure lines for the flower colour Mendel obtained:
   • all red flowers
   • all white flowers
   • some red flowers and some white ones

9. The red flower trait is dominant:
   • over the seed colour
   • over the white flower colour
   • only in F1

Figure 12.5   Example of multiple-choice test questionnaire

'Vertical and Transversal CLIL' *Blog* (http://madaenglish.blogspot.it/2009/11/prophase-metaphase-anaphase-i.html).

Evaluation

Evaluation and assessment in CLIL is complex owing to its duality: language and content. Not only are teachers supposed to assess the skills and knowledge acquired by students, but also consider the process, namely how students achieved certain results (Serragiotto, 2006). According to the project objectives the focus of evaluation is on learners' knowledge in relation to content, the level of language acquisition, and how students passed on information to their peers. The evaluation of this project was carried out as follows:

- Content was evaluated through tests similar to the one shown in Figure 12.5. Mainly multiple-choice, cloze tests, wh- questions. The questionnaire was checked and marked by older students, who also prepared complete feedback on the mistakes made.
- Assessment of language acquisition was, on the contrary, only a task for teachers. They evaluated the quality of language interchange and interaction in the groups and during videoconferences. The final editing of the materials and documents prepared by students was also checked by teachers to evaluate both content and language.
- The quality of interaction and the role and involvement of students in the oral exchanges was also considered. Employing an observation grid, teachers were able to form a fair idea of the relationship between students within the group, the figure of the leader within the group, how students came to a final decision, the effectiveness of presentations during a videoconference, and how older students were able to pass information on to younger students.

The Vertical and Transversal CLIL project is based on peer education using Web 2.0 tools, so evaluation and assessment also took into consideration the quality of learning achieved by students using Google Docs and blogs. Moreover, assessing other students' work allows students to learn by doing. When a student judges a peer's outcome he or she has the opportunity to revise what he or she learnt, to develop autonomy, and to improve higher order thinking skills through the processes of assessing and evaluating.

Reflections on the project

As teachers, we understand that the use of some Web 2.0 tools can be very useful in stimulating collaboration to increase the motivation and involvement of the students. For example, the use of Google Docs was of paramount importance. With this tool, students worked closely with each other, arriving at the production of a common text shared within the group, always working at a distance, interacting, exchanging ideas and eventually producing a common document.

This would have been impossible to achieve in the traditional classroom. The documents were then placed in PPT and illustrated through the use of the IWB.

Another positive aspect was the combination of the IWB and videoconferencing through the use of Skype. Having to explain what they have learnt to their peers, the students, with great care, did their best to prepare clear and thorough materials. They rehearsed their presentation to be sure not to make mistakes. This high level of involvement and effort undoubtedly contributed to the success of the initiative. Motivation therefore played a key role because the students had to face a new and challenging situation, impossible in the context of the traditional classroom.

Another activity not possible in a traditional classroom was the activation of practices of peer teaching and peer tutoring when working vertically (across middle and high schools). These were, without doubt, the most exciting activities of the project. This being a vertical project that involved students of different ages (4 years apart), we saw a significant interaction and a great effort by the two groups of students to explain the topics learnt in the clearest, simplest way. Both sets of students prepared materials on the cell, mitosis, meiosis and Mendel's Law and then explained the content to their companions. We think they really succeeded and this fact has been very satisfying for both teachers and students.

A final consideration concerns peer evaluation. We think it has been very rewarding for the high school students to assess the knowledge of their middle school companions. Preparing the test required a great deal of cooperation and reliability in processing. The correction was accurate, the students catalogued the errors, and prepared explanations for mistakes that were illustrated in the last videoconference.

Selecting and adapting materials

At present, there are relatively few published materials for CLIL teaching and so one of our project tasks was the selection and adaptation of materials. Based on our experience, we have provided a set of criteria to serve as a point of reference for evaluating, selecting, and adapting materials which can be found on the Internet and used as a basis for collaborative and cooperative work through suitable Web 2.0 tools (wiki, Google Docs and so on). These criteria can also serve as a guideline for adapting materials to meet local requirements, as CLIL courses need to be compatible with local curriculum frameworks and, moreover, student needs vary from year to year.

For example, in Phase 2 of the project, the teachers provided students with some materials, in particular concerning the cell. On the Internet and in the scientific literature there are countless papers on this topic, but you cannot just copy and paste, you have to select and adapt them for the cognitive level of the students. This may seem obvious, but it is particularly difficult, if not impossible, to find materials that are appropriate. In order to accomplish this task, we used the following criteria:

a. The aim and sequence of the materials should include both content and language objectives. They may also include plans for the teaching of learning strategies and higher order thinking skills (HOTS). In the case of the cell materials, our content objectives focused on the learning of the main topics concerning the cell: mitosis and meiosis. Our language objectives focused mainly on the acquisition of a basic technical vocabulary for younger students (Figure 12.2), on the understanding of principles and processes and on explaining the results of a process to the older students. Our learning strategies addressed how students acquire information. They included strategies for learning how to paraphrase critical information, picture information to promote understanding and remembering (Figure 12.4), asking questions and making predictions about text information, and identifying unknown words in text. We also employed strategies to help students express themselves (Figure 12.3), write sentences and paragraphs, monitor their work for errors, confidently approach and take tests (Figure 12.5) and pass information to peers.
b. Materials should be appropriate to the students' age and grade level.
c. Adequate support should be provided to compensate for gaps in the students' cognitive and linguistic resources. If necessary, comprehension can be supported and reinforced through timelines, semantic webs, Venn diagrams, maps, graphs, drawings, photos and other visuals. As shown in Figures 12.1, 12.2, and 12.3, we employed mind maps, pictures, drawings, and handmade diagrams to help students understand the content.
d. Textual materials should be clearly written. We chose simple and clear materials that explained thoroughly the cell and its features. In some cases we adapted the materials.
e. Materials should provide a purpose for using the language. Students should feel they are learning new information and language should be used as a tool for carrying out meaningful tasks. For example, Figure 12.1 shows students using English to organise and learn the vocabulary related to cells. When they had fully learnt the active vocabulary, students were asked to explain to their peers the main characteristics of a cell.
f. Activities should include multiple opportunities for working in pairs or in small groups (collaborative learning).
g. Materials should require students to reason, solve problems, and make decisions. There should be practice in analysing, inferring, predicting, hypothesising.

Adapting materials

Adapting materials is largely a matter of simplifying the language of a text without distorting or diluting the meaning, but, unless teachers are confident of being able to do this successfully, it might be better to choose a different text. The aim is to make the materials more accessible by eliminating a few linguistic features that can impede comprehension. In doing so, the teacher provides students with a bridge to their reading linguistically more complex materials in a specific area. This was particularly evident in Phase 5 when students had to prepare materials on Mendel's Law suitable for middle school students. With the help of the English teacher they selected documents, simplified grammar (they transformed passive forms into active forms), added a glossary, added drawings and pictures, and produced a video to better clarify the law.

Conclusion

The services and applications of Web 2.0 can help teachers to exploit their resources in class and help students to improve their English level. So many resources exist that we can now choose activities specifically related to our curriculum that are also related to topics of most interest to teenagers. Moreover, most Web 2.0 tools are really user friendly and do not require highly sophisticated technical competence in order to manage them.

However, there are drawbacks. We do not have enough time to surf Internet, to find and prepare new activities and tasks for our students. Furthermore, the new technologies do not always work so well in our schools, for instance, when you switch on the computer, you may encounter problems and waste a lot of time. Moreover, there are not always enough computers for all the students in the school laboratory.

As English teachers, one of our main aims was to help students to be more autonomous in the process of learning a foreign language while also teaching them to develop communicative competence in English and to learn new content. We think Web 2.0 is a tool that can help us teach English and achieve these objectives, although it may not always be easy. However, the benefits to students are great. In our experience, these are the skills acquired by our students during this project:

- use a second language to pass on information;
- improve searching skills: both broad and narrow;
- develop thinking skills: analyse, evaluate, justify, deduce, hypothesise, compare and contrast;
- use online resources to share documents and exchange information, also using chats and videoconferences;

- use Web 2.0 tools to communicate effectively;
- develop relational skills;
- implement peer teaching/tutoring and peer assessment.

All of these are important transferable skills that go well beyond the classroom.

Engagement priorities

1. What Web 2.0 tools do you currently use in your classroom? In your experience, have they increased student motivation and participation? What are the advantages and drawbacks for you as a teacher? For your learners?
2. In what ways do Web 2.0 tools create authentic target language use? In what ways do they enhance content learning?
3. In addition to ways described in this chapter, what are other ways Web 2.0 tools can be used for peer assessment?
4. In what ways do Web 2.0 tools foster both autonomy and collaboration?
5. Do you think Web 2.0 will eventually replace print materials in the classroom?

Notes

1. From McMillan resource: http://www.animalexplorers.com/AnimalExplorers/page/clil
2. eEurope 2002 Action Plan: http://ec.europa.eu/information_society/eeurope/2002/documents/archiv_EEurope2002/actionplan_En.pdf
3. The *i2010 strategy* was presented in the i2010 Communication in June 2005. Since then, it has been reviewed through Annual Reports and most recently updated through the *Europe's Digital Competitiveness Report.*
4. You can find theoretical explanations and concrete examples of webquests in Isabel Torres's wonderful website: http://www.isabelperez.com/webquest/

References

Berners-Lee, T., Hendler, J. and Lassila, O. (2001). The semantic web. *Scientific American*, 284(5): 34–43.
Bonifacio, M., Bouquet, P., Mameli, G. and Nori, M. (2003). *Peer-Mediated Distributed Knowledge Management*. University of Trento. Department of Information and Communication Technology. Available at http://www.dit.unitn.it [Accessed 6/12/13].
Braun, A. (2007). Immersion et compréhension en lecture. In Puren, L. and Babault, S. (eds), *L'Éducation au-delà des frontières*. Paris: L'Harmattan, pp. 215–257.
Coyle, D., Hood, P. and Marsh, D. (2010). *CLIL: Content and Language Integrated Learning*. Cambridge: Cambridge University Press.
Council of the European Union (2008). 2008 Joint Council/Commission Report on the implementation of the Education & Training 2010 work programme, 'Delivering

lifelong learning for knowledge, creativity and innovation' Available at: http://ec.europa.eu/education/lifelong-learning-policy/doc/nationalreport08/council_En.pdf [Accessed 6/12/13].

Eurydice (2006). *Content and Language Integrated Learning at School in Europe.* Available at http://ec.europa.eu/languages/documents/studies/clil-at-school-in-europe_En.pdf [Accessed 6/12/13].

Isidori, M. V. (2003). *Apprendimento in rete. Innovazioni e sperimentazione psicopedagogica e didattica.* Pisa: Edizioni ETS.

Johnson, D. W. and Johnson, R. T. (1987). *Learning Together and Alone: Cooperative, Competitive, and Individualistic.* Englewood Cliffs, NJ: Prentice Hall.

Kaye, A. (1994). Apprendimento collaborativo basato sul computer, TD Tecnologie Didattiche n.4, Menabò Editore.

Rosati, L. (1999). *Lezioni di Didattica.* Roma: Anicia.

Serragiotto, G. (2006). La valutazione del prodotto CLIL. In Ricci Garotti (a cura di), *Il futuro si chiama CLIL: Una ricerca interregionale sull'insegnamento veicolare.* Trento: IPRASE del Trentino.

Sierra, J. (2008). Assessment of bilingual in the Basque Country. In Cenoz, J. (ed.), *Teaching Through Basque: Achievements and Challenges.* Clevedon: Multilingual Matters, pp. 39–47.

Van de Craen, P., Mondt, K., Allain, L. and Gao, Y. (2008). Why and how CLIL works. Available at anglistik.univie.ac.at/fileadmin/user_upload/dep_anglist/weitere_Uploads/Views/Views_0703.pdf [Accessed 6/12/13].

Webb, N. (1985). Student interaction and learning in small groups: a research summary. In Slavin, R., Sharan, S., Kagan, S., Hertz-Lazarowitz, R., Webb, C. and Schmuck, R. (eds), *Learning to Cooperate, Cooperating to Learn.* New York: Plenum.

Zydatis, W. (2009). *Deutsch-Englische Züge in Berlin. (DEZIBEL): Eine Evaluation des bilingualen Sachfachunterrichts an Gymnasien.* Frankfurt a M.: Peter Lang.

Part IV
Materials and Teacher Education

13
The Story Reading Project: Integrating Materials Development with Language Learning and Teaching for NNES Teachers in Training

Bonny Tibbitts and Patricia Pashby

Introduction

The young English teacher from Korea stands in front of the classroom, a book open to a colourful page held for the audience to see. '[A]nd starts kneading the dough'[1], he reads aloud. Looking up, he asks, 'What is kneading?' Puzzled sounds come from the audience. He sets the book face down on the desk behind him, rolls up his sleeves, and grinning, says, 'Okay, stretch your arms like this!' He pushes the heels of his palms forward, while chanting 'kneading the dough'. The audience imitates his rhythmic movements and chants along, placing stress on the first syllable in 'kneading' and a strong rising/falling intonation on 'dough'. 'Softly', whispers the teacher, and the audience whispers the chant. 'Loudly!' he shouts, as the audience screams the chant and then bursts into laughter.

This is Anderson, a participant in our four-week training programme in the US for elementary school English teachers from South Korea. The scene took place during his final project presentation in the last week of the programme.

Language teachers enrolled in this or similar programmes often have a need to develop language skills while also developing language teaching skills. Perceived deficiencies in language ability can affect a teacher's effectiveness, especially in the area of confidence. When teachers lack confidence, they often hesitate to engage in activities that would benefit their language learning community (Braine, 2010; Cullen, 2002). Susan Lavender (2002: 246), in her study on the perceptions of teachers in short, in-service programmes, found 'teachers consistently, and over a range of instruments, viewed language improvement as the single most important component of their course'. At the same time, teacher training programmes are required to address much more than language skills.

219

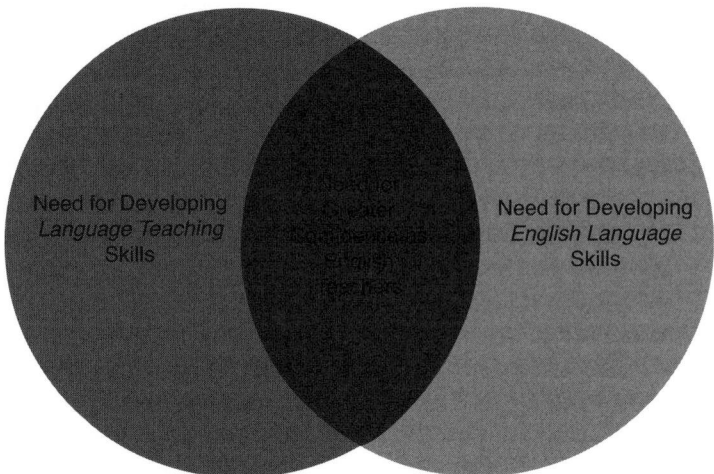

Figure 13.1   Needs of language teachers in short-term training programmes

They are expected to include teaching methodology, techniques, practice, and reflection. Teacher educators find it challenging to address both language and language teaching needs adequately in the very short time they have in development programmes. Incorporating these two aims in a single project allows trainers to address both language teaching and language learning simultaneously, thus saving time and allowing participants to develop some of the language that they perceive necessary for success in their classrooms.

Context

Like many other East Asian nations, South Korea has gone through a number of educational reforms over the past two decades aimed at improving English language instruction, which include beginning instruction in elementary grades with greater emphasis on oral skills (Butler, 2007). As part of in-service training for public school elementary teachers responsible for English language instruction, the Ministry of Education in South Korea is sending groups of teachers for four-week sessions in the US. Before arriving, each group, varying from 20 to 45 teachers from all over South Korea, spend six months at a Korean national university studying English language and language teaching. The goals set by the Ministry of Education for the culminating four-week session at a US university are to improve the Korean English teacher's communicative competence in the US setting and gain some practical experience teaching English.

Our participants have from one to 25 years teaching experience and come from a wide variety of teaching settings, many of which have set curricula in which the teachers are not able to freely choose their materials. Some teachers teach all subjects to their students, including English, while others teach only English. Classes are usually 45 minutes in length. Some teachers have proprietary classrooms while others must move from room to room. We have had participants with teaching situations as varied as a one-room school on a small island with grades one through five in the same room and very few resources, to large city schools with hundreds of students and many resources. The teachers work long hours, sometimes into the evening, and seldom get a choice as to which class they will be assigned, often changing classes each year.

Providing training to meet the needs of such a varied group presents numerous challenges. How do we provide valuable learning experiences for teachers who come from such diverse situations in terms of teaching assignments, freedom to choose materials, motivation level of students, and access to resources? How do we work effectively with participants who vary in their level of teaching experience and English skills? What materials can we use to meet the needs of all participants? We found the solution to these challenges in a project-based approach in which participants develop materials based on storybooks.

Theoretical framework

Our main goal for each participant is that he or she returns to the classroom with a greater level of confidence in both English and language teaching skills. Four components, all driven by a materials development project based on storybooks, work together to achieve this. First, project-based learning and teaching (PBLT) is implemented in a materials development project, including a final presentation demonstrating all that has been learnt. Second, communicative language teaching (CLT) is taught and modelled; participants receive instruction through a series of workshops targeting language skills, materials development, and teaching skills. A third component is creating autonomous language learners by directly teaching new language skills and providing multiple opportunities for reflection, practice, and repetition. The final

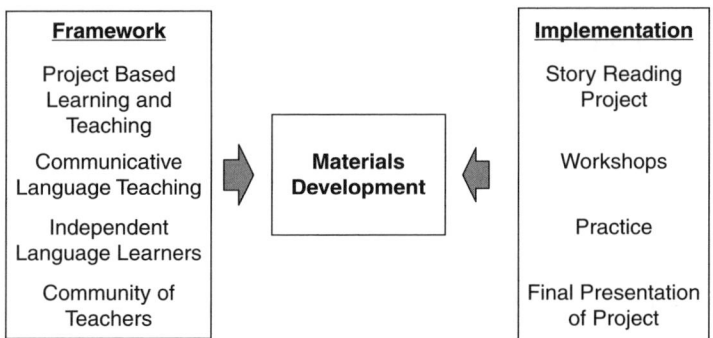

Figure 13.2   The structure of The Story Reading Project

component is community building among peers through modelling of collaborative teaching and effective interaction and feedback. These components work together as layers rather than steps or separate parts.

Approaches to language teaching and language teacher training

Our participants vary in their English language proficiency, and most can benefit from a focus on their language development. Language proficiency directly affects language teaching, especially when there is avoidance of engaging in communicative language with learners (Braine, 2010; Cullen, 2002). In Lavender's study, teachers in training reported the following activities as most useful:

- active language production from all participants;
- work outside the classroom;
- language input towards an end;
- interim tutor feedback;
- hard work;
- a tangible, permanent outcome.

(Lavender, 2002: 245)

When thoughtfully approached, all of the above can be combined into a materials development project for professionals that incorporates language learning.

Project-based learning and teaching

Our teacher training programme models a project-based learning and teaching approach. The programme curriculum is organised into a series of workshops with activities and tasks leading to a culminating project. Stoller (2006: 20) summarises the commonly reported benefits of PBLT for language learners as including 'improved language skills, content learning, real-life skills, sustained motivation, and positive self-concepts'. Project-based learning effectively incorporates meaningful communication, experiential learning, individual strategy building, and a sense of accomplishment. With the focus on the culminating product, language learning becomes incidental because the whole project incorporates both language learning and teaching. We use a project-based approach for instruction of both language and teaching methodology because it incorporates multi-faceted learning while allowing participants to find a level of challenge that is individually appropriate.

Communicative language teaching

Within this project-based approach, our general framework is best described as communicative language teaching (CLT). We understand this methodology may not be congruent with the curriculum of the settings in which our participants teach, and we must 'address how the local context contributes to affecting the teachers' instructional practices' (Kamhi-Stein, 2009: 97). While CLT is well-known in the literature, most of our participants have not experienced it directly and have not incorporated it into their teaching style; therefore, we find it important to give them an active experience with CLT so they can consider which aspects may enhance their teaching in order to add these elements to their teaching approach. Modelling this approach in our workshops gives participants the chance to practise being part of a language learning community where they can make mistakes, ask questions, critique rather than criticise, and see the gains made as they engage in extended practice each day.

Our approach to communicative language teaching and language teacher education is guided by learning and teaching principles described by Douglas Brown (2007). These include: the cognitive principles of automaticity, meaningful learning, intrinsic motivation, and autonomy; the socioaffective principles of language ego, willingness to communicate, and language–culture connection; and the linguistic principles of native language effect, interlanguage, and communicative competence. We make these explicit to participants in a workshop during the first week and ask them to connect all training experiences back to these and/or other principles they use to guide their teaching.

Independent learners

Also central to our approach to both language teaching and language teacher training are our efforts towards creating self-directed language learners. Brown (2007: 259) asserts that language teachers have a 'mission of enabling learners to eventually become independent of classrooms – that is, to become autonomous learners'. Throughout the programme, we provide explicit instruction in language learning strategies, along with time and opportunities to apply and practise them. Participants have time to reflect on their strengths and weaknesses as language learners and teachers, and adjust as necessary while they work towards successful completion of their projects. In turn, we trust that our participants will apply this experience to the teaching skills they bring back to their classrooms and find ways to enable their learners to develop strategies for autonomous learning. We also hope that they apply this experience of independent learning to their continued professional development as language teachers, finding ways not only to continue building their English skills but also to strengthen the knowledge and skills needed to be effective language teachers.

Community

An excellent way to encourage and sustain lifelong learning is through peer support. Collaborative teacher development (Johnston, 2009) effectively helps teachers work together as equals to strengthen teaching and bring improvements to the field in general. As strong believers in the benefits of collaboration, we model teaching as a team and demonstrate how we make choices about methodology, techniques, and materials in unrehearsed dialogues in front of the participants. Furthermore, we consider the participants our language teaching peers. In our workshops, we demonstrate the effectiveness of clear, non-judgemental feedback, and we show that respect and care for our fellow teachers worldwide allows us to be more effective.

Materials

To meet the needs of our participants, we introduce materials that have great flexibility and can be used in a wide variety of teaching situations. We encourage the use of supplementary materials and creating projects that will enhance classroom experiences. Tomlinson (2010: 89) argues that in selecting materials we must 'prioritize the potential for engagement by [using]...a text or task that is likely to achieve affective and cognitive engagement'. Materials should encourage a variety of actions, reactions, and interactions, and stimulate creativity that allows learners to experience with their hearts and minds. When materials tap into emotions, there can be real responses from the learner, encouraging authentic communicative language use. For these reasons, well-chosen storybooks are engaging materials.

Choosing storybooks

The foundation of the Story Reading Project is children's picture books. According to O'Donoghue and Hales (2002: 185), it is important to empower teachers to work with authentic materials. We need to provide opportunities for them to 'examine authentic instances of language...and consider themselves as researchers of language'. We choose to use books written for native speakers because: they have authentic sentences, providing context for vocabulary; they have examples of language and situations illustrating the culture of the target language; and they give us the chance to practise the target language. Participants utilise the project to explore authentic language and culture in storybooks.

   We look for visually appealing books in which pictures represent vocabulary in the story, and we are also careful to choose books that are culturally enlightening and appropriate for elementary students. We choose books with vocabulary that introduces cultural concepts, is interesting for frequency or idiomatic reasons, and is suitable for pronunciation practice. We avoid those with nonsense words since these represent a stumbling block for non-native speakers. We favour books with natural, conversational rhythms, over books that have a rhythmic aspect that would not occur in conversation or prose. We also eliminate books that might be too long or overwhelming, for reasons such as complexity of grammar, so that the project can be accomplished within our programme's timeframe.

For the project to be successful, participants must select books that are appealing to them. We supply a large variety of books that we have pre-selected, and participants are able to choose one with the English level and content they want to work with. This allows individuals to decide how much they want to challenge themselves.

Overall, this Story Reading Project is attractive to participants as it provides intrinsic motivation by addressing participants' language learning needs in ways that appeal to language teachers through providing intense language practice and production with 'a tangible, permanent outcome' (Lavender, 2002). The project also has significant extrinsic motivation as not only are participants expected to complete a worthwhile project, but must also perform it well for an audience of peers. In the end, they take home with them: a portfolio of materials (storybook, lesson plans, and support materials) developed during the programme that they can potentially use immediately in their classrooms; the ability to read and interact with materials in a fluent manner; and peer feedback as to how to make the materials work in their classrooms.

The training programme

Our training programme is housed in the American English Institute at the University of Oregon. We are staffed with a director, teacher training faculty, tutors, and activity assistants. Starting in 2007, we began offering four-week training sessions which included 80 hours of instruction and 40 hours of observation and skills practice. The programme consists of workshops and lectures on teaching methods, site visits, class observations, English communication, fluency, discussion, and reflection. Following is a description of how we incorporated all of these elements into a project addressing language competence within a methodology course.

The Story Reading Project

In the Story Reading Project, participants: (1) select a storybook from among books that have been carefully chosen for their language development possibilities; (2) learn to read it with appropriate pronunciation and prosody; (3) develop parts of the storybook for target students, such as characters, storyline, vocabulary, idioms, or grammar; (4) gather or create realia materials to support teaching the book in a classroom; and (5) devise a lesson plan exhibiting communicative language teaching principles. After three weeks of workshops, practice sessions, and peer input, the participants conduct their lessons for each other and for invited teachers from our English programme. This lesson must include a dramatic reading of the storybook which engages the audience and an interactive lesson using materials developed to support the language learning objectives.

The first few days of the training programme are filled with activities aimed at creating a collaborative atmosphere and an understanding of the materials development project. The primary goal is to give enough background about the framework so that participants have direction for their projects, a clear understanding of what is expected of them, and also an understanding of what they will gain by participating fully. Workshops in the first two days cover: a review of communicative language teaching; a description and demonstration of a complete project and samples of past projects; a workshop on dramatic reading and reasons for reading aloud; and beginning workshops on pronunciation and prosody.

Motivation for a reading project

Through a series of workshops on building pronunciation skills, developing principled lessons and activities for the storybook reading materials, and practising teaching these materials, the Story Reading Project focuses on instructing language teachers to read aloud a children's storybook. A learner's ability to read quickly and accurately with correct pronunciation and prosody usually increases his or her comprehension. Motivated fluent readers can concentrate on meaning instead of decoding (National Reading Panel, 2000). Our participants read aloud so that we can directly address their pronunciation, phrasing and intonation.[2]

In addition to addressing oral production, the Story Reading Project aims to increase fluency through practice. Practising reading a storybook several times strengthens skills in decoding, pronunciation. and expressive reading. Multiple repetitions of the text increase the chance for language learners to move beyond the initial efforts required for decoding and pronunciation to more fluent speech and reading, because these skills increase the connection between the written and spoken word. The National Reading Panel (2000: 28) reports: 'Repeated and monitored oral reading improves reading fluency and overall reading achievement.' The project workshops and practice sessions provide the tools and feedback for monitoring repeated reading. In her research brief on reading fluency, Penner-Wilger (2008: 6) states, 'the [repeated] practice generalized to new passages', so practising a reading passage should have a long-term effect.

Another effective method for increasing reading fluency is listening to fluent reading (Rasinski, 1989). Participants are encouraged to practise outside of workshops, listen to each other, and to find fluent models to read their stories aloud. More importantly, the project trains participants to be models for their own students.

The most important effects of the project become evident in the final presentations, where we see well-rehearsed, confident teachers reading aloud in

English in front of their peers. This presentation is a concrete way for the participants to bring together all the different parts of the programme – teaching methodology, reading aloud, materials, and lesson plans they have developed – while providing extrinsic motivation to improve oral production, pushing participants to take full advantage of the workshops and the practice schedule set up for them. It also serves as an event for this community of peers to recognise the accomplishments of each teacher.

Workshop overview

The Story Reading Project is conducted through a series of workshops that develop participants' understanding of the story material and their ability to read it aloud. Workshops cover pronunciation, expressive reading, vocabulary development, and understanding of cultural and other meaning. All workshops address the participants' language needs while exploring a particular focus in language teaching and learning. By the end of the programme the participants have developed well-rehearsed classroom activities with accompanying learner exercises and materials.

All workshops are experiential in nature so that the participants can understand what their students might experience from similar activities, and they illustrate materials and methods that can be used by participants to develop their projects. Workshop leaders work within the CLT approach, creating a safe environment for participants to explore not only workshop content, but also their own language learning and teaching. A variety of formations for group work and debriefing activities are used. Whenever possible, the leaders engage in collaborative teaching to illustrate respectful and supportive team teaching. The participants are also given multiple opportunities for reflection about the ways in which the presentation, ideas, and content of workshops can be adapted for their projects and for their individual teaching and learning situations.

Because the workshops and project serve the dual purposes of training teachers and of enhancing language skills, the goals of the workshops can be seen from two points of view. Participants experience the workshops as both language learners and teachers, so a goal such as choosing vocabulary from a story can be seen as both a teaching and a language learning skill. Much the same is true of the reflection activities. Participants may find that they have more to learn from reflecting as teachers than as learners, or vice versa. It is important that workshop leaders remain aware of this duality and design workshops so that both experiences are available to the participants. In keeping with the CLT approach, a skilled workshop leader, by encouraging participation and communication, can help participants use their own experiences and background to gain from the workshop. Participants often find they learn far more than language teaching concepts because they are communicating in the target language about concepts that they have never discussed before, or only discussed in their first language.

The workshops within our training programme most directly related to the Story Reading Project are Dramatic Reading, Realia, Story Comprehension, Reading Expression, Vocabulary, and four pronunciation workshops.[3] Each is two hours in length. Sequencing these workshops generally follows the order we provide here. Most important is that the first pronunciation workshop (on stress, rhythm and intonation) should come before the Reading Expression Workshop. Below is a description of two workshops giving a general idea of how we develop the project. For each, we describe a brief rationale, goals, a summary of the content and process, reflection questions and follow-up assignments.

The Dramatic Reading Workshop – Rationale

Reading aloud dramatically can engage people, young and old, in the written word. This workshop demonstrates how dramatic reading is a multi-sensory activity that can be used in language classes. Overall, the workshop is an example of what participants are expected to achieve with their individual reading projects: a dramatic reading with one or more language elements developed into activities that encourage student participation and learning.

Goals

The participants will leave with these insights:

- Multi-sensory lessons are fun; dramatic reading engages sight and hearing but can also engage taste, smell and touch.
- Dramatic reading is often more engaging than 'normal' reading.
- Language learners can rely on their 'community' and discuss and analyse ideas before a teacher tells them something.
- Students learn from their own insights.
- Demonstration and modelling are useful teaching tools.
- Repetition works.

Content and process

Using three or four stories presented in various ways, the workshop illustrates elements of dramatic reading:

- use of sounds (instruments, voice, hands);
- use of motions (facial expressions, natural gestures, planned movements to add audience interaction and mark changes and actions in story);
- use of setting (classroom arrangement, ways of holding and showing book, other realia);

- use of voice (intonation, making sounds, changing voices for different characters);
- audience awareness;
- use of pacing (pauses, speed, rhythm).

Participants engage as learners in stories being read aloud. Activities encourage multiple verbal repetition, active listening to multiple repetitions of target phrases and materials, discriminating listening for particular details, reproducing particular lexical items, and responding to visual and verbal cues.

At the end of the workshop, the Story Reading Project is introduced in detail and participants select a children's book to work with for the duration of the training. Some participants are unsatisfied with the choices available. We use this as a 'teachable moment', sharing our own criteria for selecting books appropriate for EFL environments. We have found that using our criteria, participants are able to find books on their own.

Reflective questions

What is dramatic reading? What dramatic reading techniques have you used in your classrooms? What do students gain from dramatic reading? What did you learn from the workshop? What book did you choose and why? What parts of your textbook or curriculum can be supported by the story you are working with?

Assignment

Participants are asked to read their story at least three times before the next day. We ask participants to bring their storybooks, and any materials they are working on, to all class meetings and workshops in order to use them in the creation of their materials portfolio. We suggest they make a photocopy of their storybooks, or type them out to use for taking notes in workshops.

Pronunciation workshop 1: stress, rhythm, and intonation – rationale

Pronunciation needs vary among groups of learners but most face challenges at both the segmental and suprasegmental levels (Celce-Murcia et al., 2010). Pronunciation is a teachable skill, and 'comprehensibility' and 'intelligibility' rather than native-like pronunciation are reasonable goals for instruction (Derwing, 2010).

Goals

The participants will: develop a deeper understanding of stress, rhythm, and intonation of English; become aware of gaps in their own production; identify areas of desired improvement; and learn techniques and strategies to help them reach their goals. Furthermore, they will experience a range of pronunciation instruction techniques that may be adaptable to their teaching, including: an overview of pronunciation instruction as it relates to English as an international language (Jenkins, 2007); inductive techniques for introducing pronunciation points, drills and exercises for initially practising a point; connecting language in pronunciation lessons to real world and other meaningful contexts; and helping learners develop strategies for improving their pronunciation as autonomous learners.

Content and process

In this workshop, participants complete the following:

- listen to language examples;
- identify patterns and rules to describe these patterns;
- practice repeating examples using drills;
- apply rules to new examples;
- practise the language point in a longer discourse.

Reflective questions

Give an overview of the process and types of activities used in this workshop. Which steps (and in what sequence) might be most effective for your learners? Which activities might you adapt for your learners? What other activities would you add? What other pronunciation points are central to helping your target learners reach their goals? What techniques/strategies would be most appropriate for teaching these to them? How can you help your students become autonomous learners of English pronunciation? What materials are you adding to your portfolio based on this pronunciation workshop?

Assignment

Following the same sequence used to complete exercises during the workshop, participants mark a photocopy of their storybooks by drawing lines between rhythm groups, underlining content words, and drawing pitch lines over focus words. They practise reading it aloud, and then record it, listen to their recording, rerecord if necessary, and submit final recordings to workshop leaders for feedback. Participants also design one or more pronunciation activities for their materials portfolio.

Practice

Meaningful practice is key to providing participants with the repetition necessary to automatise language and skills that they are learning (Brown, 2007: 64–66). The Story Reading Project has a natural context for repetition and practice built into it, so that, as each language learning or teaching issue is addressed, the participants are required to return to their storybooks and re-encounter the materials with new tools and the need to repeat the words, phrases, and sentences. Each time a concept or technique is introduced for either learners or teachers, we explore how it will affect the storybook reading and project.

Other workshops provide participants with intense structured and unstructured practice of the target language, specifically in oral skills with a focus on pronunciation. Participants practise both in and out of class, sometimes individually and other times with tutors, fellow participants, or with instructors. Participants are often inspired by their improvement and find interesting ways to practise. For example, some participants use video to record their instructors or tutors reading the storybooks, and then listen to this recording and imitate the pronunciation and prosody of native speakers.

Final presentation

In the last week of the programme, participants conduct 20-minute lessons in which they read their stories using all they have learnt. Before this, each participant has a 20-minute session with a trainer, who listens to the reading and gives feedback on pronunciation, intonation, expression, and pacing. The participants also bring their lesson plans and support materials which the trainer reviews, offering direction as needed.

Participants are encouraged to develop formal lesson plans with objectives and activities reflecting principled language teaching and appropriate use of storybook materials. The storybook can be used at various stages in a learning cycle: it can be used to introduce a concept; reinforce a concept; recycle vocabulary and ideas; or to provide a rewarding experience for the learners. Throughout, the teacher is responsible for shaping learners' interactions with materials, and can use the experience to teach language specifically or to aim for more general comprehension. Because of the flexibility these materials offer, the project allows participants to develop materials and lessons in any number of ways as long as the final product incorporates the story reading, which is the first requirement of the presentation. The second requirement of the presentation is that the lesson should aim for maximum audience participation during the reading of the storybook. Finally, it is expected that lesson plans will show evidence of principled, communicative language teaching, and reflect the application of what was learnt in the programme as appropriate for the materials they are developing.

On the day of the presentation, participants are divided into 'classes' of about ten participants. As a teacher participant presents, his or her fellow participants act as students. There is also a small audience of observers, including programme instructors, faculty in our intensive English programme, and interested university graduate students.

This brings us back to Anderson, introduced at the beginning of the chapter. In his final presentation, Anderson introduces materials that he has developed for the storybook *Pete's a Pizza*. Anderson's lesson includes a dramatic reading of the story during which students demonstrate active listening by chanting phrases from the book and learning accompanying actions for key vocabulary. He shows a short video on making pizza, which illustrates and recycles the vocabulary used in his storybook. He focuses on the pronunciation of vocalic /r/ followed by /l/ in words such as 'twirling'. He has students pantomime making a pizza with various toppings. He brings in art materials to support a language activity in which students freely use the vocabulary of the lesson. Anderson's lesson is reflective of the overall creativity of the groups of teachers we work with. They have developed everything from vocabulary card games, to video interviews about pertinent themes, to songs using phrases from the storybooks, to TPR activities – their choices influenced by the language and themes in their storybook and the needs of their target learners.

Feedback

It is imperative to design feedback that is communicative and encouraging. Brown (2007: 472) argues that effective assessment of language learning involves 'authentic, interesting, appropriately challenging…learning opportunities designed for learners' best performances and for optimal feedback'. In communicative language teaching, evaluation of learners' progress should take place through tasks that are interactive and meaningful.

In all our workshops, we demonstrate and encourage efforts at effective feedback: encouraging; noting what is effective, useful, fun, and inspiring; and offering suggestions or ideas for future directions. After the final presentation each presenter elicits comments. Giving effective feedback is the final task participants engage in. A faculty leader moderates, helping find ways to phrase a comment so that it is a critique rather than a criticism, rephrasing comments and modelling appropriate interaction between peers. The participants offer their comments verbally, and sometimes in writing; the faculty leader always gives verbal comments as well as written comments. These presentations are filmed for self-evaluation purposes.

Implications

The time constraints placed on short-term training programmes poses problems for teachers needing help with both language and teaching skills. The challenge of helping teachers develop confidence in their language abilities while training them in teaching skills in such programmes led us to develop a flexible project addressing the needs of both participants and educators. Although the project we describe in this chapter is the version we use in a four-week, fully staffed programme in the US, this approach is highly adaptable

to a variety of settings, cultures, target language proficiency levels of participants, grade levels, final products, and materials developed.

For example, we use a similar approach with a two-week programme in South
Korea, working with secondary school teachers who have vastly divergent
English language abilities. We replace the storybooks with readers' theatre
because it is more age appropriate for those teaching middle and high school
students. In readers' theatre, learners dramatically perform a play in small
groups while holding and reading from scripts. Props, minimal costuming, and
sets (including lighting, music) can be used to add theatrical effect. Readers'
theatre engages learners in a context that helps them develop in all skill areas
while engaging in real communication (Lengeling, 1996). Furthermore, it works
well for groups with differing proficiency levels and provides all participants
with experiences that are 'cognitively challenging, socioculturally rewarding,
and affectively appealing' (Liu, 2000: 360).

Like our storybook project, participants apply what they are learning in the
workshops to their final project, in this case a performance of the readers' theatre
script. The readers' theatre workshops vary from the storybook workshops in
topic and number; workshops include pronunciation, dramatic and expressive
reading, and vocabulary development with the focus on a group production.
Rather than developing a lesson plan to take back to their classroom, the participants experience the full process of readers' theatre as language learners.

Before the final presentation, each performance group is assigned a rehearsal
time and a 'coach' (a faculty trainer) who provides feedback on pronunciation,
voice, pacing, and expression. For the culminating event, all participants
attend and serve as audience for each group's performance. For readers' theatre,
the audience's reaction during the performance is the feedback. Do they laugh?
Groan? Scream? In appropriate places? This is the measure of communicative
success for the performers. We also film the plays so participants can view their
performances.

Readers' theatre was also successful in a longer eight-week programme with
Brazilian secondary teachers who worked with the same scripts as the Korean
teachers in the two-week programme, but experienced more workshops and the
use of technology for recording and feedback. As one participant commented,
'I'm sure that it [readers' theatre] can be adapted to our students and they'd
certainly benefit from that as much as we did. I loved it! It's a great way to have
fun and practice our pronunciation.'

Conclusion

After completing the Storybook Reading Project, participants in our training
programmes have portfolios of materials supporting their storybooks and
knowledge of how to continue developing their own supplemental materials

in the future. They also have an overwhelmingly positive response to the experience. The feedback we receive often focuses on participants' perceptions of significant language development (specifically in areas of vocabulary and pronunciation); learning within a positive atmosphere; feeling motivated to work hard; facing a challenging project but building confidence through scaffolded tasks while creating concrete products; and pleasure in interacting positively and intensely with colleagues. 'It was one of the most interesting ways of having fun and learning all together', commented one of our participants. 'I have never participated of such interesting and simple strategy to practise vocabulary, pronunciation and intonation', wrote another. 'When doing it we integrate speaking, reading, listening and writing. We were able to practise more, developing confidence and fluency, correct some pronunciation and intonation. We had a great time together!' Participants also comment on how much they appreciate the freedom to play with expression and intonation, and how much they enjoyed watching others present.

In other words, they have experienced communicative language learning. Our intent is to inspire them to find ways to bring this experience to learners in their classes. Nothing is more satisfying, however, than our participants' comments on how much this activity affects their confidence, which is also apparent in their presentations and the way they elicit and discuss the feedback they receive. 'Not only did it provide us with the opportunity to practise and improve our pronunciation, but also to become more aware of certain pronunciation issues that we should work on and are likely to pass unnoticed in day to day conversation.' The Story Reading Project gives these participants the tools and confidence to work on their own language skills and those of their students.

Engagement priorities

1. The approach described in this chapter recommends using storybooks for elementary school teachers and readers' theatre for secondary teachers as the texts around which participants develop materials for their classes. What are the strengths and weaknesses of these materials? What other types of texts might be successful?
2. Using and developing materials that are not part of the established curricula is challenging for teachers, but can also provide opportunities to understand how classroom materials can be supplemented and enhanced. What criteria might you consider when choosing and developing materials for a language class? How could you make supplemental materials work in any given curriculum?
3. The authors discuss briefly their goal of creating a community of language teaching peers. What are the benefits of this type of community for

understanding, using and creating materials? What steps could you take to create a support system among teachers?

4. The Story Reading Project gives many opportunities to use materials to practise and repeat target language. What materials, projects and/or activities can you think of that incorporate this kind of practice?

Notes

1. *Pete's A Pizza* by William Steig (2004).
2. The evidence here is based on native speakers learning to read their first language. At this time, we are not aware of research which has separated out ELLs and documented how reading aloud affects their oral language production and reading comprehension. The Story Reading Project has been developed over several years and programmes and, to date, anecdotal evidence is overwhelming for improved oral production, increased reading fluency and confidence in language use.
3. Additional workshops conducted concurrently with the Story Reading Project workshops focus on, among other topics, history of language teaching, classroom management, reading strategies, creative writing, oral skills activities, and grammar games.

References

Braine, G. (2010). *Nonnative Speaker English Teachers: Research, Pedagogy, and Professional Development*. New York: Routledge.

Brown, H. D. (2007). *Teaching by Principles: An Interactive Approach to Language Pedagogy*, 3rd Edition. White Plains, NY: Pearson Longman.

Butler, Y. G. (2007). How are nonnative-English-speaking teachers perceived by young learners? *TESOL Quarterly*, 41(4): 731–755.

Celce-Murcia, M., Brinton, B., Goodwin, J. and Griner, B. (2010). *Teaching Pronunciation: A Course Book and Reference Guide*, 2nd Edition. New York: Cambridge University Press.

Cullen, R. (2002). The use of lesson transcripts for developing teachers' classroom language. In Trappes-Lomax, H. and Ferguson, G. (eds), *Language in Language Teacher Education*. Philadelphia: John Benjamins Publishing Company, pp. 219–235.

Derwing, T. M. (2010). Utopian goals for pronunciation teaching. In Levis, J. and LeVelle, K. (eds), *Proceedings of the 1st Pronunciation in Second Language Learning and Teaching Conference*, Iowa State University, September 2009. Ames, IA: Iowa State University, pp. 24–37).

Jenkins, J. (2007). *English as a Lingua Franca: Attitude and Identity*. Oxford: Oxford University Press.

Johnston, B. (2009). Collaborative teacher development. In Burns, A. and Richards, J. (eds), *The Cambridge Guide to Second Language Teacher Education*. New York: Cambridge University Press, pp. 241–249.

Kamhi-Stein, L. (2009). Teacher preparation and nonnative English-speaking educators. In Burns, A. and Richards, J. (eds), *The Cambridge Guide to Second Language Teacher Education*. New York: Cambridge University Press, pp. 91–101.

Lavender, S. (2002). Towards a framework for language improvement within short in-service development programmes. In Trappes-Lomax, H. and Ferguson, G. (eds), *Language in Language Teacher Education*. Philadelphia: John Benjamins Publishing Company, pp. 237–253.

Lengeling, M., Casey, M. and Mills, L. (1996). The use of reader's theater in the EFL curriculum (Mexico). *English Teaching Forum. US State Dept.* Available at http://eca.state. gov/forum/vols/vol34/no3/p84.htm [Accessed 31/3/12].

Liu, J. (2000). The power of reader's theater: from reading to writing. *ELT Journal,* 54(4): 354–361.

National Reading Panel (2000). Chapter 3: Fluency. *Report of the National Reading Panel: Teaching Children to Read Reports of the Subgroups,* April. Available at http://www.nichd. nih.gov/publications/nrp/report.cfm [Accessed 31/3/12].

O'Donoghue, C. and Hales, T. (2002). What was that you said? trainee generated language awareness. In Trappes-Lomax, H. and Ferguson, G. (eds), *Language in Language Teacher Education*. Philadelphia: John Benjamins Publishing Company, pp. 173–186.

Penner-Wilger, M. (2008). *Reading fluency: a bridge from decoding to comprehension,* AutoSkill International Inc. February. Available at http://eps.schoolspecialty.com/ downloads/other/acad-read/fluency_research.pdf [Accessed 31/3/12].

Rasinski, T. V. (1989). Fluency for everyone: incorporating fluency instruction in the classroom. *The Reading Teacher,* 43: 690–693.

Stoller, F. (2006). Establishing a theoretical foundation for project-based learning in second and foreign language contexts. In Beckett, G. H. and Miller, P. C. (eds), *Project-Based Second and Foreign Language Education: Past, Present, and Future*. Greenwich, CT: Information Age Publishing, pp. 19–40.

Tomlinson, B. (2010). Principles of effective materials development. In Harwood, N. (ed.), *English Language Teaching Materials: Theory and Practice*. New York: Cambridge University Press, pp. 81–108.

14
Teaching Pre-service EFL Teachers to Analyse and Adapt Published Materials: An Experience from Brazil

Eliane H. Augusto-Navarro, Luciana C. de Oliveira and Denise M. de Abreu-e-Lima

Introduction

An important component of teacher education is preparing pre-service teachers to understand the theory of language as well as the principles of teaching-learning that underlie the textbooks they will use. This comprehension may lead to better preparation for teachers to critically evaluate teaching materials so that they can adapt them effectively to the needs and wants of their students, as proposed by Hutchinson and Waters (1987). However, as pointed out by Harwood (2010), little, if any, attention seems to be given to this important aspect in ESL/EFL teacher education programmes. As a consequence, many teachers tend to be consumers of appealing-looking textbooks without being aware that there are several important considerations to take into account before deciding on teaching materials, especially: who one's target students are; what they need or are interested in regarding their target language; how much time they have to reach their primary goals.

This gap in teacher education seems to be directly related to the history of second/foreign language (SL/FL) teaching materials as a field of study. In his recent state-of-the-art article on materials development for language learning and teaching, Tomlinson (2012: 144) states: 'Given how important language learning materials are, it is surprising how little attention they have received until recently in the literature in applied linguistics.' He goes on to comment that only in the mid-1990s did materials development begin to receive attention as a field.

Teaching materials serve a crucial role in organising, and hopefully stimulating and facilitating, the teaching-learning process. Based on this consideration and aligned with our observations of teacher candidates presenting their teaching practice units without a clear rationale, we realised that there should be a course in our EFL undergraduate teacher education programme to deal specifically with EFL teaching materials analysis. In this chapter we describe how we have organised and delivered a course to prepare EFL teachers to make more *informed choices* (Larsen-Freeman, 1983) in relation to adopting, adapting, and designing EFL teaching materials. The course 'Evaluation and Design of Teaching Materials in EFL' was created in 2007 with the main goals of giving teacher candidates the opportunity to:

- study teaching materials from a theoretical and practical perspective;
- recognise methodological thoughts and approaches underlying textbooks;
- design instruments of needs/wants analysis and understand results from them, considering consequent adaptions that should be made in commercial textbook activities;
- design tailor-made teaching activities based on a variety of resources (especially real life-like ones);
- analyse teaching materials through written and oral presentations;
- evaluate and discuss teaching material analysis proposed by colleagues, reflecting on reasons for choosing given teaching materials and activities.

The course introduces some theoretical concepts about teaching materials and contemporary views of grammar teaching-learning in ESL/EFL, as this topic is constantly being raised as a concern among our teacher candidates. Bringing theoretical studies and opportunities for reflection about their own practice has proved very fruitful and, as stated by Graves (1996: 2):

> Helping teachers understand how to make use of their own experience as well the theories of others raises questions about the relationship between theory and practice, which is a fundamental question for teacher educators.

Teaching context

The Brazilian context of pre-service language teacher education has common characteristics with other global contexts as well as some unique features. One of the common characteristics is the need to provide effective preparation to develop pre-service teachers' language proficiency in the language they will eventually teach. A unique feature in Brazil relates to how teacher candidates are admitted into language teacher education programmes. Upon graduation from high school, students take entrance exams in order to be admitted to undergraduate programmes. Different universities give different entrance exams and public universities receive the highest number of candidates because they offer high quality education free of charge. Candidates applying to these universities may therefore apply for a less popular degree, such as Language

Teacher Education, rather than their preferred but more popular choice, such as Law or Journalism, where there is more competition. Although most candidates do want to be teachers, there may be some students who simply want to get a degree from a high quality university, even when the career is not the one they had planned to follow. Some subsequently fall in love with teaching and go on to seek a career in education, while others do not get so involved with the objectives of the programme and end up working in areas outside teaching where language knowledge is important. Many language teacher education programmes, specifically the ones that certify teachers of English as a foreign language (EFL), teach English in the same way one would teach students who want to learn the language for any other purpose, such as tourism or business, or for general communication purposes. The fact that these programmes are teaching the language for future teachers has been neglected (see Abreu-e-Lima, de Oliveira and Augusto-Navarro, 2008 for a more detailed description of these issues).

The five-year language teacher education programme 'Languages and Literatures' certifies Portuguese (L1) and EFL teachers in Brazil at the Federal University of São Carlos (UFSCar), a public university in the central part of the state of São Paulo. The university is recognised as an excellent higher education centre and receives students from all over the country, but mostly from the state of São Paulo.

The Department of Languages and Literatures at UFSCar has provided language support for other undergraduate and graduate programmes at the university since the 1970s and the programme on Language and Literature Teacher Education (*Letras*, as it is called in Brazil) was established in 1996. Today, besides *Letras*, the department offers a bachelor's degree in Linguistics and is connected to a graduate programme in Linguistics, created in 2005, and another one in Literature, created in 2011. The goal of the Language and Literature undergraduate programme is to prepare students to be teachers of both language and literature. The programme certifies teachers to teach Portuguese and offers two tracks, English and Spanish. Students who are on the English language track will have a degree that will certify them to teach Brazilian Portuguese as a first language, English as a foreign language, Portuguese/Brazilian literature, and English/North American literature. Some of our students have never taught while others are in-service teachers. While one goal of the English programme is to develop student proficiency in English so that they can work as English teachers, more importantly, professors working in this programme are conscious that they are preparing future teachers of the language, and as a consequence, pedagogical issues are a major concern.

Because language pedagogy is a key component of our programme, a course focusing on evaluating, adapting, and designing teaching materials is particularly relevant for practising and future EFL teachers. The context for the experience reported in this chapter is the elective course 'Evaluation and Design of Teaching Materials in EFL.' The average number of students in a regular language class is 20, but in these elective classes the tendency is to have groups of five to 12 students, as in the course described here. Since the class is elective, teacher candidates make the choice based on their motivation to study teaching materials. This course is offered to prospective EFL teachers who are at least on their third year in the five-year Language and Literature programme, whose ages range from 19 to 25 years. The total amount of time for the class is 60 hours and there are two meetings a week throughout the semester (generally March to June). Most of the teacher candidates who take it have at least some teaching experience, either in private language institutes (extra-curricular courses that charge a fee for EFL classes and hire undergraduate and graduate students as teachers) and/or through university outreach programmes.

Theoretical framework

Among the various aspects involved in language teaching, and consequently in learning to teach, analysing teaching materials is a task that directly involves many others. As discussed by Tomlinson (2010, 2011), decisions about choosing or designing teaching materials should be based on principles and what factors teachers believe will affect the learning of their students, as well as why and how these should be considered in the teaching materials. He exemplifies this by listing his own basic learning principles (Tomlinson, 2011: 7): (1) learners should be 'exposed to rich, meaningful and comprehensible input'; (2) 'to maximize their exposure to language in use' learners need to be affectively and cognitively engaged; (3) 'learners who achieve positive affect are much more likely to achieve communicative competence'; (4) language learners 'can benefit from using those mental resources which they typically utilise when acquiring and using their L1'; (5) 'language learners can benefit from noticing salient features of the input and from discovering how they are used'; and (6) 'learners need opportunities to use language to try to achieve communicative purposes'.

Having the principles presented by Tomlinson as an example, we can understand that an interaction between theories, combined with reflection about one's own practice will determine one's learning (and resulting teaching) principles. We can, for instance, relate the principles listed by Tomlinson to Krashen's input hypothesis (1985), Schmidt's noticing hypothesis (1990) and Swain's output hypothesis (1993), among others.

We would argue that a key aspect of teacher education is to provide teacher candidates with opportunities to: (1) study key theories in language learning, so that they can form foundations for developing their choices; (2) identify how theories are represented in teaching materials, to support them in establishing awareness of how theories are represented in practical activities; and (3) reflect on how effective the analysed materials might or might not be for a given group of learners, so that they become aware that contextual factors should be carefully considered.

Tomlinson (2010: 97) advocates an important concept: 'The materials need to be written in such a way that the teacher can make use of them as a resource and not have to follow them as a script.' However, even if a given material is designed in this particular way, if the teacher who adopts it has not been educated to understand this principle, or has not been given the opportunity to reflect on when, why, and how to proceed with necessary adaptations and additions, the author's work might be in vain.

In addition to the importance of educating teachers to analyse teaching materials is the idea that, as pointed out by Harwood (2010: 4), 'even well-known textbook writers concede [that] no pre-prepared materials can ever meet the needs of any given class precisely; some level of adaptation will be necessary'. However, teachers are not naturally gifted with being able to perform such desirable adaptations. Experience will contribute to this task, but a smoother, shorter, and more appropriate path towards principled decisions may be constructed through opportunities for theoretical and practical reflections throughout the teacher education process.

The range of factors to consider in teaching materials for language learning is far from limited and the task of preparing teachers to analyse or evaluate them is neither simple nor straightforward. Among the many issues raised by Tomlinson (2012) are: evaluation (predictive and retrospective); criteria (general – essential features of any good teaching-learning material – and specific – context-related criteria); validity (interaction between psychological, pedagogical, process, and content), among others. Nevertheless, no matter how complex the many aspects involved in learning to teach can be, teacher educators have to choose a starting point, also making principled decisions about how to approach each subject. Regarding teaching materials, we would say that the starting point should be making both prospective and practising teachers aware that, as pointed out by Graves (1996: 5), when discussing course design: 'There is no set procedure to follow that will guarantee a successful course because each teacher and each teacher's situation is different. Put another way, there is no answer to give, but there is an answer to find.' Therefore it is essential to help teacher candidates to be aware that they should look for their own answers regarding appropriate practices in each of their contexts.

It is widely recognised that we tend to repeat the same practices we have undergone as learners, so teachers who used to have classes where their teachers would consistently follow textbooks may tend to do the same. However, Borg (2003) claims that although student teachers' individual experiences have an important role to play in their practice, 'formal education will contribute to their cognition and practices, especially if previous cognition is revisited'. Giving teachers the opportunity to reflect on which teaching-learning practices they believe to be effective, and requiring them to give supporting theoretical and practical reasons for their choices, is a possible way to revisit beliefs and prepare them for critical reflection.

While we, as teacher educators, cannot tell prospective teachers which are the best practices, we can certainly provide them with the tools to explore possibilities that are based on insightful reasons and are not merely intuitive. Respecting learners' profiles and maximising learning possibilities in each environment is what responsible teaching is about.

A course to prepare teacher candidates to reflect on EFL teaching materials

In the course 'Evaluation and Design of Teaching Materials in EFL,' teacher candidates are introduced to basic concepts underlying teaching materials. They read and discuss questions regarding what they understand by language, how they think languages are learnt, and the importance of considering their potential target groups and students' backgrounds, interests, needs, and teaching-learning contexts. Considering the many aspects involved in teaching materials, and based on the assumption that these teacher candidates should have a clear focus to relate theory to practice, we have chosen to prepare them to consider how grammar is approached in different teaching materials and why.

We have selected grammar as the focus for analysis because we share Larsen-Freeman's (2003: 10) point that 'it [grammar] is the vortex around which many controversies in language teaching have swirled'. In addition, given the constant debate around the question of whether (and how) to focus on form in language classes, grammar is a topic that teacher candidates tend to be more apt, or at least willing, to discuss. Grammar constitutes a rich topic for raising teacher candidates' awareness and preparing them to revisit preconceived concepts in the light of the relationship between theory and practice. However, it is important to note that although the focus is on grammar, the analysis and reflection skills that these prospective teachers develop can help them make principled decisions about how to teach other parts of a textbook as well.

Course description

The course is developed through a sequenced combination of reading and discussing theories of language. During the last third of the 60-hour long course, teacher candidates work on their final assignment, preparing and presenting a critical analysis of a textbook or course pack. They can choose the materials they want to analyse based on their previous experience with, or preference for, a target group of learners.

In this section, we present a description and comments about how the course unfolds. The sequence is as follows:

a. eliciting teacher candidates' views on teaching materials and grammar;
b. preparing students for individual reading of theoretical texts and writing of main points based on guiding questions provided by the teacher educator;
c. providing opportunities for pair work to share understandings and doubts;
d. conducting whole class discussions about theory comprehension and practical applications for teaching (materials and practice);
e. requiring and assisting teacher candidates to perform and present their teaching material analysis and their proposals for desirable adaptations;
f. offering peer and tutor feedback on the analysis and presentation;
g. recording teacher candidates' points of view at the end of the process to give them an explicit opportunity for reflection on their concepts, and to provide teacher educators with elements to review and enrich their practice.

Raising teacher candidates' awareness of teaching materials and grammar

Teacher candidates' points of view regarding grammar in EFL and teaching materials are addressed at two points during the course, in a pre- and post-interview. The first is prior to their reading of the indicated theoretical texts and the second is upon the conclusion of the course[1]. The first interview has been developed with the purpose of identifying the teacher candidates' understanding of language, language learning, grammar and its role in language teaching-learning, and teaching materials. This gives the candidates an opportunity to reflect on the issues and the teacher educator has some information to consider in the development of the course. It provides the opportunity for considering previous beliefs, which is likely to make the theoretical study more effective, as suggested by Borg (2003).

The first course interview repeatedly reveals that there is no common view of the value of explicit grammar instruction among teacher candidates. At the same time, even the ones who recognise the value of studying grammar in EFL do not seem to be familiar with those theoretical views of grammar instruction that see it as a natural part of communication. Often, our prospective teachers do not see the possibilities for integrating grammar and communication before they take this course.

Reading theoretical texts and writing a summary of main points

At the beginning of the course theoretical perspectives related to teaching materials are discussed, based on Tomlinson, Dat, Masuhara, and Rubdy (2001). More recently texts from Harwood's (2010) book have been added, including Tomlinson's (2010) text about principles for effective materials development. However, the central point of discussion and analysis in this course is how grammar is defined in theoretical studies that defend the integration of focus on form with communication.

Larsen-Freeman (2003) and Batstone (1994) form the theoretical basis for introducing the theory of grammar in our classes. We try to bear in mind the end result of producing practical teaching materials out of the concept of *grammaring*, a term which Larsen-Freeman coined to represent grammar's dynamism and the fact that mastering it is a concurrent skill. This term is related to Batstone's proposal of filling the critical gap between product and process perspectives in grammar teaching with a complementary and integrated approach, which he calls *teaching grammar as skill*.

Students receive some guiding questions prior to their reading of the texts, and they have to write a summary of the main points at each reading. They must bring their summary to refer to during class discussions. Typically they read two chapters a week (one after each class), and the sequence is Harwood (2010), Tomlinson et al. (2001), Tomlinson (2010), Batstone (1994), and Larsen-Freeman (2003). This gives them a sense of the importance of teaching materials, the principles behind them, different approaches to teaching ESL/EFL grammar, and the skill of developing grammar integrated with communication (grammaring).

Sharing understandings and questions through pair work and whole class discussion

After the assigned text has been read, discussions about the theory and its practical applications for teaching are conducted in class. On these occasions teacher candidates have some time to work in class, with a partner, on the questions they had received the previous class (sometimes there are others that they raise themselves). The partners read each other's summaries, compare them and discuss their questions and understanding before a whole class discussion.

Presenting teaching materials analysis: proposing desirable adaptations

At the end of the semester teacher candidates have to present, in pairs, an analysis of a particular textbook or course pack, focusing on identifying the target group for the teaching material, considering how the grammar is approached, and proposing what adaptations should be made. Each pair can choose the teaching materials that they want to analyse. Since many of them already have teaching jobs, they commonly choose materials from their work in school.

The choice of pair work relies on the fact that it gives more confidence to the teacher candidates, especially the ones who have never taught. This way they have an opportunity to learn from each other while planning and delivering their analysis, and reflecting on post-presentation feedback. Research on collaborative teaching often claims that collaborators have a lot to learn from each other. Stewart and Perry (2005), for instance, comment that in partnerships there is an opportunity for teacher growth and creativity development. Similarly,

Augusto-Navarro et al. (2011) argue that even a very experienced teacher can gain new insights by co-planning and co-delivering classes with new teachers.

The pairs meet with the teacher educator to discuss their initial choices and ideas and later to show their work progress. At these meetings the teacher candidates are questioned about the reasons behind their choice of teaching materials and the adaptations they would implement. This creates one more opportunity to discuss the relationship between theory and previewed practice. As pointed out by Watkins (2010: 370): 'English language teaching is exceptionally diverse in terms of both types of learners and teaching contexts, making any notion of a "correct" or "best" way to teach impossible to pin down. The best any teacher can hope for is to find appropriate ways to teach in the context in which they find themselves.' This shows our teacher candidates that continuous reflection on their students and other aspects is key in language teaching.

In the presentations of the teaching materials analysis, as shown in the examples in Figures 14.1 and 14.2, teaching candidates provide theoretical support, that is, they present appropriate quotations from the theory so the proposed adaptations are consistent. The following examples show how a pair of teacher candidates carefully considered a unit of instruction in a textbook to modify the content by considering their target group of young adult Brazilian students learning EFL twice a week in a private language institute.

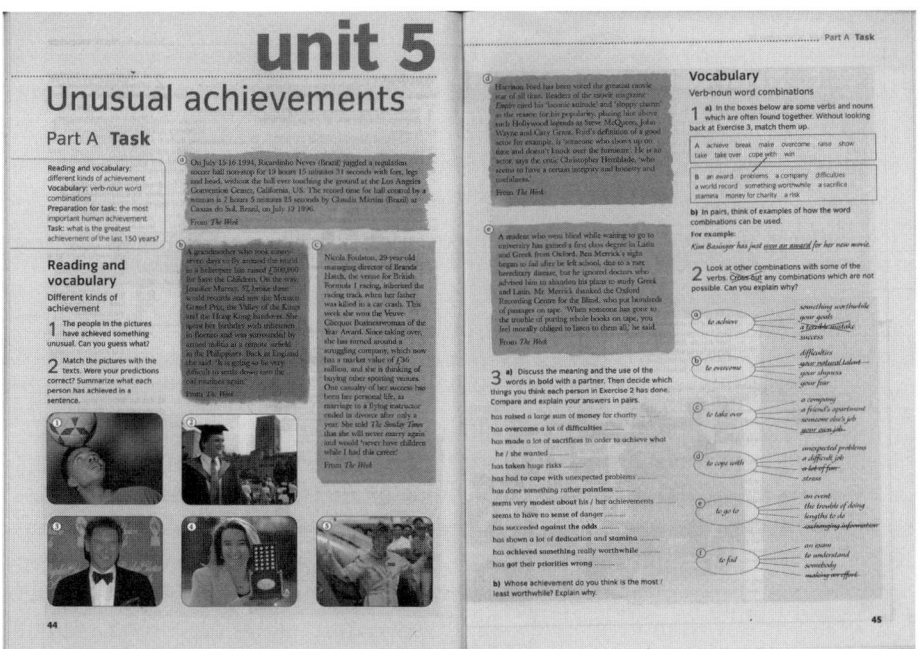

Figure 14.1   Example 1 of teaching material and suggestions by teacher candidates

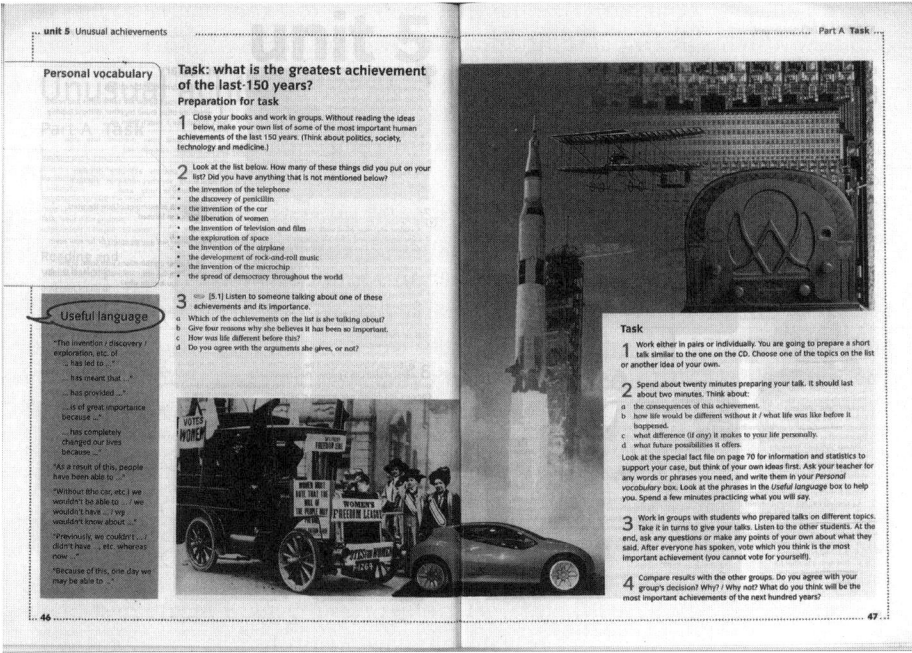

Figure 14.2   Example 2 of teaching material and suggestions by teacher candidates

Examples:

Material used for reflection: Step Ahead (Cunningham and Moor, 2005), Unit chosen: Unit 5: Unusual achievements.

Summary presented by teacher candidates:

The book is divided into six units, which are divided into: (1) Skills and vocabulary; (2) Task; (3) Language focus, (4) Writing; (5) Further skills and vocabulary.

In Unit 5, the sub-sections are:

1. Reading and vocabulary: different kinds of achievements. Vocabulary: verb–noun word combinations (cope with problems, etc.)
2. Preparation for task: the most important human achievement? (listening). Task: What is the greatest achievement of the last 150 years? (extended speaking)
3. (a) Perfect aspect in the past, present and future. (b) More about the present perfect and present perfect continuous. Pronunciation: contradictions and weak forms with more than one auxiliary. Writing skills: describing a movie or book you have enjoyed
4. Follow-up task: your proudest achievement. Wordspot: up.

The teacher candidates who presented the analysis in Figure 14.1 were the most inexperienced teachers – we will call them Laura and Maria. Laura had never taught EFL and Maria had been teaching for three months in her first teaching experience in a private language institute, where the book *Step Ahead* is used. Their analysis and propositions do not show any major new ideas, but they try to connect their analysis to the theory they had been studying in the teacher education course, trying to indicate the reasons for their choices.

When analysing the first page, we can observe that the student teachers indicate that students following this book might be asked to work in pairs instead of individually in activity 1. When referring to activity 3 they propose that the students might be invited to reflect about language choices and the reasons for them, introducing students to language forms and to thinking about why a given structure had been chosen. According to Laura and Maria, EFL learners should be asked: '3 (a) When in time did those facts occur? and (b) Which elements did you use to identify it?' They justify their proposal by quoting Larsen-Freeman's assertion about the importance of students understanding reasons for language choices, but they are previewing focused noticing, a concept studied throughout the semester.

Even with very little experience and worrying excessively about making learners' choice central to the EFL teaching material that they analysed, these teacher candidates were able to give the reasons for their choices and revealed some professional analysis based on their teacher education process.

Offering peer and tutor feedback on the analysis and presentation

All these presentations are video recorded and presenters can make a copy of their own, if they wish. At the time of the presentations the teacher educator hands out a form with rubrics to guide peer evaluation of both the presentation and the analysis. On the form, besides spaces for grading the work (such as excellent, good, poor) there is a space for providing any comments each evaluator judges relevant.

The aim of this practice is to offer opportunities for reflection to both presenters and observers. Reporting on her study of collegial observation for teacher development, Gebhard (1999), cited in Gray (2012), states that the goal of collegial observation is to observe other colleagues and in the process 'construct and reconstruct our own knowledge about teaching and thereby learn more about our teaching attitudes, beliefs and classroom practices'. We feel that these opportunities provided for teacher candidates are crucial for their development as future teachers.

Similarly, Richards (1998: 147) points out that peer observation may create 'a valuable opportunity for teachers to develop a critically reflective stance on their own teaching', but he cautions that teachers should see each other as 'co-researchers, collaborating for each other's benefit'. We would say that there should be such opportunities, whenever possible, in most courses taught on teacher education programmes.

Recording teacher candidates' points of view at the end of the process

As previously mentioned, upon the conclusion of the course teacher candidates are interviewed in the laboratory to express their views on what they understand by grammar and its role in language teaching-learning. This post-course interview has been developed with the purpose of verifying any influence that theoretical studies might have had on prospective teachers' evaluation of the studied themes. There are two main reasons for this practice, one that relates to the teacher candidates and another that relates to our roles as teacher educators. It offers teacher candidates a moment to reflect explicitly on their views of the course themes, including any changes that have taken place during the course. As teacher educators this practice helps us to understand the results of our own practice, so we can make necessary changes when re-offering the course. We have redesigned our own teaching in response to data collected in the interview with our teacher candidates as we discuss in the next section.

Outcomes and implications for teachers and teacher educators

The experience reported in this chapter has generated different kinds of awareness in all parties involved, including the teacher educators. As an example of such awareness, in the final interview of the semester every teacher candidate at some point reveals their concerns about considering who their students are when reviewing and preparing teaching materials. We believe that this is a direct result of our emphasis, while discussing the selected theoretical texts, on the idea that who our students are and their reasons for studying the language should always be a primary concern. Some even quote Larsen-Freeman's (2003: 4) assertion: 'We are, after all, teaching students, not just teaching language'. This kind of attitude motivates us to continue improving our course each time.

We have realised that updates should be made after every course. After the second course, we introduced the pre- and post-course interviews to raise teacher candidates' cognition of teaching materials and grammar. An important change deriving from the interviews was the realisation that offering teacher candidates more practical examples of activities that would fit the theory was very important, as they complained they lacked practical examples. More examples were included from the third course on. Another change was the inclusion of more theoretical texts about teaching materials *per se*, because we noticed that they could theoretically base their discussions about grammar but relied more on perception to talk about teaching materials. As a result, some texts from Harwood (2010) have recently been assigned as mandatory reading. In short, the outcomes of this experience have changed over the years. The course has been offered once a year since 2007 and we have been learning, and aiming to teach it more appropriately, each time.

There are important implications of our work as teacher educators that we think should be shared with other professionals in the area. The most prominent of them are summarised in Table 14.1.

Table 14.1 shows a summary of the main points that seem to have created the richest opportunities for professional growth, both for our students (teacher

Table 14.1   Recommended practices from a discipline in Teacher Education

Recommendations	Reasons
(1) Give teacher candidates an opportunity to explore their beliefs about the topic to be discussed in the course.	(1a) It will give teacher candidates a moment to think about the topic; (1b) Teacher educators will be better prepared to consider students' beliefs and prepare them to revisit their preconceived ideas.
(2) Provide opportunities for teacher candidates to present their comprehension of the course topic,,in both written and oral forms. They should have set occasions to show and discuss their work development with you.	(2a) It will provide teacher candidates with the time to reflect on their understanding and the reasons why, as they will have to expose them to the class audience; (2b) They will have the opportunity for intensive discussion with their instructor and to receive focused feedback.
(3) Include peer observation session(s) and whole group feedback. Give teacher candidates rubrics and discuss these with them prior to observation. Provide room for personal comments.	(3a) Receiving feedback from a larger audience than just the teacher educator will contribute to revealing both positive aspects and aspects that need to be reviewed in teacher candidates' work ; (3b) Observers will have a chance to reflect on their own practice while observing and using the rubics to evaluate their colleagues' practice.
(4) Organise the whole group feedback in a summary and deliver it to the observed student(s).	(4a) Receiving feedback that is organised will make comprehension easier and the feedback more likely to be considered; (4b) Organising whole group feedback will provide the teacher educator with one more chance to see how the whole group has understood the themes studied.

Continued

Table 14. 1   Continued

Recommendations	Reasons
(5) Record teacher candidates' beliefs about the topics addressed throughout the course.	(5a) It will give teacher candidates an extra opportunity to reflect on their educational process and its effects on their cognition about teaching and learning;
	(5b) As a teacher educator, the information gathered in this practice will provide you with tools of inquiry about your practice and contribute to the reviewing and, hopefully, improvement of your own practice.

candidates) and for ourselves as teacher educators. Therefore we would advise other teacher educators to consider them when preparing their courses.

Conclusion

In this chapter we have described our experience in designing, delivering, and reflecting on a course on teaching materials analysis in an undergraduate programme in EFL teacher education in Brazil. We have justified the importance of the topic because of both the key role played by teaching materials in the teaching-learning process and the lack of awareness among teacher candidates that teaching materials should not be followed as scripts, since each group of (language) learners and their learning contexts has to be closely considered.

Based on the outcomes of our repeated practice and reflection, we have proposed some recommendations (summarised in Table 14.1) to other professionals involved in the process of EFL/ESL language teacher education in similar settings. We do not mean to provide a recipe to be followed, as we are aware that teaching is far more complex than merely establishing a relationship between theory and practice. Each new context should generate new inquiry questions and particular ways to reach appropriate results, as many studies have demonstrated. Nevertheless, guiding prospective teachers to be more aware of what theoretical studies present, so they can reflect on what would work best in their context with their target groups of students, may be an important aspect of a teacher education course focused on the evaluation and production of teaching materials.

Furthermore, by asking teacher candidates to reflect on the relationship between the theories studied and their own practice, and by raising questions that will help them look for and identify aspects that need closer attention and possible research questions to reflect on the continuum theory–practice–theory, awareness should be generated to ensure they make more informed choices.

Acknowledgements

The first author acknowledges the financial support received from *Fundação de Amparo à Pesquisa do Estado de São Paulo* (FAPESP) (Proc. 2012/03944–7).

Engagement priorities

1. Based on this chapter, how do teaching contexts and the special needs of students influence materials selection and design?
2. What are some special considerations for EFL teachers in materials design and production?
3. How can language teachers be better prepared to evaluate and design their own materials in your specific context? Discuss some possible topics that could be included in a methods course related to developing and adapting materials.
4. Are textbooks published by major companies better than teacher-designed materials for specific learners? Why or why not?

Note

1. The interviews take place in the language laboratory. The teacher educator reads the questions into a microphone and each teacher candidate listens to it individually in their private headphone cabin. They record their individual answer and this generates a file related to the cabin number. Later the teacher educator can save each file from her control table.

References

Abreu-e-Lima, D. M., de Oliveira, L. C. and Augusto-Navarro, E. H. (2008). Focusing on teaching from the get-go: an experience from Brazil. In Carroll, M. (ed.), *Developing a New Curriculum for Adult Learners*. Alexandria, VA: TESOL, pp. 177–198.
Augusto-Navarro, E. H., Kawachi, C. J., Campos-Gonella, C. and Terenzi, D. (2011). Collaboratively teaching at undergraduate level: teacher learning through analytical team-teaching. *Signum: estudos da linguagem*, Londrina, 14(1): 37–56. Available at http://www.uel.br/revistas/uel/index.php/signum/article/view/8509/9272).
Batstone, R. (1994). *Grammar*. Oxford: Oxford University Press.
Borg, S. (2003). Teacher cognition in language teaching: a review of research on what language teachers think, know, believe, and do. *Language Teaching*, 36(2): 81–109.
Cunningham, S. and Moor, P. (2005). *Step Ahead I* (Project by Ana Maria Cristina Cuder). New York: Longman CNA.

Graves, K. (1996). Teachers as course developers. In Graves, K. (ed.), *Teachers as Course Developers*. New York: Cambridge University Press, pp. 1–11.

Gray, S. M. (2012). From principles to practice: collegial observation for teacher development. *TESOL Journal*, 3(2): 231–255.

Harwood, N. (2010). Issues in materials development. In Harwood, N. (ed.), *English Language Teaching Materials: Theory and Practice*. Cambridge, UK: Cambridge University Press, pp. 3–30.

Hutchinson, T. and Waters, A. (1987). *English for Specific Purposes*. Cambridge, UK: Cambridge University Press.

Krashen, S. (1985). *The Input Hypothesis: Issues and Implications*. London, UK: Longman.

Larsen-Freeman, D. (1983). Training teachers or educating a teacher. In Alatis, J. E., Stern, H. H. and Strevens, P. (eds), *Georgetown Round Table on Languages and Linguistics*. Georgetown: Georgetown University Press, pp. 264–274.

Larsen-Freeman, D. (2003). *Teaching Language: From Grammar to Grammaring*. Boston: Heinle & Heinle.

Richards, J. C. (1998). Through other eyes: revisiting classroom observation. In Richards, J. C. (ed.), *Beyond Training*. Cambridge, UK: Cambridge University Press, pp. 141–152.

Schmidt, R. (1990). The role of consciousness in second language learning. *Applied Linguistics*, 11(1): 17–46.

Stewart, T. and Perry, B. (2005). Interdisciplinary team teaching as a model for teacher development. *TESL-EJ*, 9(2): 1–17.

Swain, M. (1993). The output hypothesis: just speaking and writing aren't enough. *Canadian Modern Language Review*, 50(1): 158–164.

Tomlinson, B. (2010). Principles of effective materials development. In Harwood, N. (ed.), *English Language Teaching Materials: Theory and Practice*.Cambridge, UK: Cambridge University Press, pp. 81–108.

Tomlinson, B. (2011). Introduction: principles and procedures of materials development. In Tomlinson, B. (ed.), *Materials Development in Language Teaching*. Cambridge, UK: Cambridge University Press, pp. 1–31.

Tomlinson, B. (2012). Materials development for language learning and teaching. *Language Teaching*, 45(2): 143–179.

Tomlinson, B., Dat, B., Masuhara, H. and Rubdy, R. (2001). EFL courses for adults. *ELT Journal*, 55(1): 80–101.

Watkins, P. (2010). Evaluating the effectiveness learning to teach English as an introduction to ELT. In Brian, B. and Masuhara, H. (eds), *Research for Materials Development in Language Learning: Evidence for Best Practice*. London: Continuum International Publishing, pp. 369–380.

15

Factors Influencing Japanese Teachers' Adoption of Communication-oriented Textbooks

Simon Humphries

Overview

Textbooks are one of the main tools of the trade in language teaching (Littlejohn, 2011). One reason for their popularity is that they provide a concrete set of guidelines and activities for teachers to follow, as such it is often maintained that they can facilitate curricular change because they help teachers to 'fully understand and "routinize" change' (Hutchinson and Torres, 1994: 323). However, the idea of the textbook as agent of change (Hutchinson and Torres, 1994) can be problematic when considered against the broader context of language learning and teaching.

This chapter outlines a context of change in Japan in which new textbooks were introduced into a rural technical college (*kosen*). Although the textbooks were innovative in this context, the teachers received no training to help them adapt. The question therefore arose: What factors promote or inhibit the appropriate use of an innovative textbook? Through studying these factors, we can consider what measures can be taken to support teachers and what training can be given to help the transition to textbooks that require new pedagogical approaches.

Teaching context

From the late eighties onwards, the Japanese Ministry of Education, Culture, Sports, Science and Technology (MEXT) announced policies aimed at improving the communicative competence of secondary school students, culminating in the 'Action Plan to Cultivate Japanese with English Abilities' (MEXT, 2003).

Key areas of the Action Plan included:

- development of students' communicative competencies through activities promoting the use of English;

- criterion-based assessment for students and teachers;
- English classes in primary schools (compulsory from 2011);
- listening component for the national Centre Test from 2006 (many universities use this test to select candidates);
- funding for a five-year in-service teacher training programme.

Despite the government's emphasis on improving students' oral skills and communicative competencies through using English to communicate, Japanese teachers of English (JTEs) tended to continue the *yakudoku* (grammar translation) tradition (Kikuchi and Browne, 2009). In general, *yakudoku* is: (a) teacher-centred and highly structured; (b) predominantly in Japanese (English output tends to be limited to repetition); and (c) focused on translating a written text from English to Japanese.

Japanese technical college: the *kosen*

The *kosen* described in this chapter is located in a rural area of the Kii Peninsula on Japan's main Honshu Island. In contrast to students in regular Japanese high schools who study for three years (aged 16–18) and may take English examinations to enter university, *kosen* students study for an additional two years for an associate degree in their engineering major. Upon graduation from the five-year course, *kosen* students have three options: they can seek employment; study for an in-house degree; or transfer into the third year of a university course without sitting an English entrance examination. Although general English is taught in the *kosen*, vocational engineering subjects take precedence.

From 2007, the *kosen* joined the Japan Accreditation Board for Engineering Education (JABEE), which sets certification criteria for bachelor's degrees in engineering (JABEE, 2008). Although JABEE sets the standards for tertiary-level courses, the *kosen* adopted the same objectives for secondary-level syllabi. Some of JABEE's engineering policies overlapped with MEXT's visions, such as internationalisation, for which students need to acquire 'basic skills for international communication' and the communicative language teaching (CLT) learner-centred values: 'an ability to carry on learning on an independent and sustainable basis' (JABEE, 2008: 2).

In line with JABEE recommendations, a new English curriculum was implemented for Grades 11 and 12, which led to changes in assessment and textbooks from 2007. The Grade 10 students, unaffected by the change in assessment, continued to use a MEXT-mandated textbook called *Vivid English Course (New Edition) I* (Minamimura, T., Asai, M., Ishihara, Y., Itoh, T., Iwamoto, K., Goi, C., Torio, N. Harada, Y. Miyagawa, K. Miyamoto, T. Watanabe, K. and Rockenbach, B. 2006). However, Grades 11 and 12 used new CLT-oriented textbooks: *On the Go* (Gershon, Mares, and Walker, 2004a) and *On the Move* (Gershon, Mares, and Walker, 2004b).

There are substantial differences between the old and new textbooks as outlined in Table 15.1.

Although CLT has existed in various forms since the late 1970s, this approach was new for the potential adopters – the teachers in the *kosen* – therefore, it could be regarded as an educational innovation in this context.

Theoretical background

Drawing upon examples from the introduction of CLT in Japan, various factors emerge that influence the successful adoption of an innovative textbook (see Table 15.2). By successful adoption, I mean use of the textbook in the way that the authors intended. (Practitioners who feel that they successfully adapt new textbooks to suit their context may dispute this interpretation.)

Table 15.1   Textbook comparison

Vivid	**On the Go and On the Move**
Teacher-centred	Learner-centred
Emphasis on reading comprehension	Emphasis on listening and speaking
Overt grammatical usage instruction	Focus on communicative situations
Japanese publisher, aimed at Japanese high schools	British publisher, aimed at a variety of institutions in East Asia
Instructions and explanations in Japanese	Only glossary and 'phrase book' contain Japanese
Low output, highly structured exercises	Meaning-focused exercises, designed to encourage students to creatively share information and opinions

Table 15.2   Factors influencing the use of innovative textbooks

Category	Example
Sociocultural traditions	Local cultural values may differ from BANA values
Teacher's confidence	The teacher may feel that he or she lacks the sociolinguistic competence
Training vs. experience	Teachers may reject training in favour of using their experience
External factors	Teachers may perceive external tests as more important than government policies
School level factors	The culture of the school
Classroom factors	Students' attitudes
The textbook itself	The textbook might not do what it claims to do

Sociocultural traditions

Teaching methods are not free of values. Curriculum planners and textbook writers design their syllabi and materials on the basis of their social practices and interests (Pennycook, 1994). When schools introduce textbooks that contain values from a different worldview, teachers and students may struggle to adapt to new forms of study and new social roles. CLT and internationally-published textbooks that claim to follow this approach tend to incorporate cultural norms from private language providers in Britain, Australasia and North America (BANA) (Holliday, 1994). As a result, a cultural mismatch can occur when CLT-oriented textbooks are exported from 'interpretation-based' BANA countries to 'transmission-based' regions (Wedell, 2003). Although countries are diverse and continually evolving, East Asian countries generally incorporate transmission-based learning through a shared Confucian heritage (Carless, 2012), where teachers and elders are regarded as sources of wisdom. Japan's *yakudoku* tradition fits into this transmission paradigm and is a well-rooted cultural norm.

Junior JTEs conform to the teaching approaches of their seniors. This finding is supported by a survey of 422 novice teachers, which showed that the majority (61 per cent) named elder teachers as their main source of advice (Sato and Asanuma, 2000). Following peer on peer observations, teachers tended to avoid critiquing senior colleagues, which could hinder change; however, younger teachers received critical feedback, which would encourage them to follow the established practices of the school (Sato and Kleinsasser, 2004).

Confidence

True change can be a stressful process, as people need to relinquish what they are accustomed to in order to risk failure in a new venture. This stress is compounded for teachers, who know that students may evaluate the quality of their teaching. If teachers do not appear to know how to teach, there is a risk that they can lose the respect of the students and, as a result, lose control of the classroom. It is therefore often safer for teachers to maintain the status quo and many may lack the confidence to change. In the case of non-native teachers of English introducing CLT, they may perceive deficiencies in their spoken English ability, as well as their strategic or sociolinguistic competence and their understanding of suitable methods (Li, 1998).

In Japan, a MEXT survey indicated that fewer than half the secondary school teachers had attained the national proficiency targets (a TOEFL score of 550 or the equivalent on other tests) (Nishino and Watanabe, 2008). These JTEs might fear making mistakes in front of their students, because this can tarnish their authority (Nishino and Watanabe, 2008). Moreover, JTEs seem to lack confidence in the students. They are reluctant to use too much English, because they fear that the students will not understand and that they could lose control of the class (Sakui, 2007).

Training vs. experience

Several studies have indicated that many JTEs feel uncertain about how to follow the government-mandated communicative goals; therefore, they tend to 'fall back on how they themselves were taught in school as a student' (Kikuchi and Browne, 2009: 175). Hino (1988) agrees that JTEs are poorly trained and lack knowledge of alternative methods; therefore, they turn to *yakudoku* methods, because they require no training to use.

Regarding pre-service training, Japanese universities tend to focus on theory without integrating it into reflective practice (Kizuka, 2006). This lack of focus on practice is reflected in the teaching practicum, which only lasts for approximately two weeks during which 'trainees do not have sufficient time to reflect on their own teaching together with [their] mentors' (Kizuka, 2006: 57).

In-service training has been poorly funded. Although MEXT's 2003 Action Plan provided funds for in-service training, at the end of the five-year period mentioned in the Plan, the funds dried up (Kikuchi and Browne, 2009). Moreover, many MEXT-organised conferences and seminars have been poorly attended (Lamie, 2004). One reason for the poor attendance could be the transmission-based nature of the training, which tends to preach theories originating from BANA, but fails to address local problems (Nagasawa, 2004).

External factors

Teachers are influenced by factors from outside the school in how they must teach. Local influences include parents and boards of education, for example. At national level, the government may influence teaching approaches through their policy documents and curricula, while the performance of teachers may be assessed using agencies like Ofsted in the UK.

MEXT's communicative policies have largely failed to change teaching practices in Japan. Instead, university entrance examinations form the most powerful external factor influencing teachers, students and textbooks. Studies of English entrance examinations for prestigious universities have revealed an enduring emphasis on reading comprehension and lexico-grammatical knowledge. Rather than testing creative English output, most exercises are multiple-choice and translation (Kikuchi, 2006). The pressure to prepare students to pass examinations for prestigious universities, combined with a lack of training in alternative approaches, causes teachers to fall back on their test preparation experience as students. Therefore, they continue to use *yakudoku* rather than risk adopting communicative policies.

School

Schools can influence a teacher's capacity to develop and deal with change in two ways. Firstly, the working conditions mean teachers may have various administrative duties and after-school extra-curricular activities, which reduce their time for marking and preparation and may squeeze out any time remaining for professional development. Secondly, school cultures may contain norms that influence a teacher's enthusiasm to discuss new approaches and find solutions to methodological problems.

Japanese teachers tend to follow a culture of *kizuna*, where they routinely and constantly consult each other in shared offices. The culture of *kizuna*, combined with the Confucian-influenced respect for older teachers, means that new teachers are soon socialised into school routines and the practices of senior teachers are reinforced. In one school, teachers felt no practical need to attend workshops, because 'new or innovative ideas seemed not to be a necessity' (Sato and Kleinsasser, 2004: 812).

Classroom

Classroom factors include issues such as the physical attributes of the room, the contact hours, the class size, and the students. Traditionally, classrooms tend to be organised with desks facing the teacher and the blackboard, which favours transmission-style education. Multimedia equipment, or the lack of it, can also influence the variety of learning approaches. Most importantly, the number of students in the class and their age, gender, expectations, proficiency levels, and behaviour, influence teaching approaches.

In Japan, many teachers feel that they need smaller classes (the maximum is 40 students) and more contact hours to maintain control of students and balance new activities with the perceived need for entrance examination preparation. Government surveys of attitudes to English classes have indicated that, in comparison to other subjects, more students struggle to follow the content and over time there were steeper decreases in motivation (MEXT, 2011). Moreover, students tend to prefer quiet passive study because they fear making mistakes in front of the teacher or their friends (Taguchi, 2002). Attempts to implement learner-centred CLT approaches require new role expectations and a new set of norms, which can lead to disruption for both teachers and students – especially if seen as a diversion from the students' perceived 'real study' for entrance examinations (Sakui, 2007).

The textbook

So far, this chapter has focused on issues that affect how teachers mediate changes in methodology that may be inherent in the new textbooks. However, the ease of use of the actual textbooks for the teachers and students will ultimately decide if they are adopted successfully. Moreover, from the perspective of the policymakers, textbooks need to be introduced that accurately reflect their goals.

All public secondary school teachers in Japan must use textbooks authorised by MEXT and they have indicated that textbooks are the main influence on their teaching practice (Wada, 2002). However, rather than follow the government's CLT guidelines, these textbooks support the *yakudoku* approach, with extensive information in Japanese that teachers can transmit to students and a focus on selected language structures (Humphries, 2013). Moreover, students have limited opportunities to use English creatively because most exercises are highly structured and low output (Humphries, 2013).

Mediating the textbook

As mentioned earlier, the *kosen* introduced new textbooks which required a fundamental change in teaching approach compared to the standard MEXT-mandated textbooks used previously. However, the teachers received no training for the new approach. The opportunity therefore arose to explore, in the absence of teacher training, the factors that promoted or inhibited the appropriate use of an innovative textbook.

Four *kosen* JTEs volunteered to participate in the study: Akira, Bonda, Chikara, and Daiki (pseudonyms). They all taught Grades 10 (ages 15–16) and 11 (ages 16–17), which facilitated a comparison of the influence of the two different types of textbooks on their attitudes and practices. The participants' details appear in Table 15.3.

The data collection consisted of classroom observations and semi-structured interviews during a six-week period. For each teacher, I observed four periods of 45 minutes per grade. In other words, there were eight periods per teacher, totalling 32 periods. During the observations, I collected data using fieldnotes and video recording. An independent bilingual Japanese transcribed and translated the video footage. For the interviews, topics arose through the process of constant comparison (Glaser and Strauss, 1967) of data from classroom observations. I collected interview data using fieldnotes and audio recording.

Table 15.3 Participant background information

	Akira	**Bonda**	**Chikara**	**Daiki**
Age	55	43	55	41
Full-time/part-time (rank)	Part-time (lecturer)	Full-time (assoc. professor)	Full-time (professor)	Part-time (lecturer)
Years teaching at this college	1	16	6	5
Class (proficiency)	A (lower-middle)	B (lowest)	C (highest)	D (lower-middle)
Education	MA Theology	MA English Literature	MA Education	BA English Literature

Table 15.4   Factors in the study

Category	Example
Sociocultural factors	All the teachers predominantly used *yakudoku*
Uncertainty	The teachers tended to externalise their feelings of uncertainty
Limited training	Only one teacher valued his training but struggled to apply it
Negligible external influences	None of the teachers felt any pressure from external sources
Internal *laissez-faire*	No pressure to conform but some teachers wanted guidance
Student issues	Even the highest proficiency learners seemed to prefer silent deskwork
Unsuitable materials	The teachers struggled to explain sociocultural differences

Factors influencing textbook use

Several factors arose that mediated the teachers' use of the new textbooks: sociocultural factors, uncertainty, limited training, negligible external influences, internal *laissez-faire*, student issues, and unsuitable materials (Table 15.4).

Sociocultural factors

All the participants used the traditional *yakudoku* teaching approach with the new textbooks. Akira, Bonda, and Daiki guided students through the materials, selecting students to answer orally, and then writing the responses on the blackboard for the whole class to copy. For both textbooks, the teachers used most of their instruction time to translate sections of extended text into Japanese. In the case of *On the Go*, the participants changed the emphasis from listening comprehension to the translation of the listening transcript.

Chikara used more variety in his teaching approach because he was the only teacher who attempted speaking pairwork and listening comprehension. However, he also tended to avoid textbook sections that would require students to create original utterances. Instead, he was inclined to select highly structured speaking exercises.

Uncertainty

All the teachers had feelings of uncertainty, but they externalised these feelings to blame the students, textbooks, training, and lack of support from the *kosen*, which are described later. Only Daiki indicated that he lacked confidence in his own capacity to conduct communicative classes:

> *An ne* communication *no mokuteki wo tassei saseyouto omottara* English teacher *no* skill *ga* skill level *ga yappa, takaku nakya dameyato omouwa. Bokuga yattemo*

anma kawan nainda (To accomplish communicative aims, we need to increase the skill level of English teachers. Even if I try, nothing will change).

Limited training

Chikara was the only teacher who discussed the positive aspects of his training. He held an MA in English Education and said that he attended conferences and read methodology books in an effort to find new methods to improve his teaching. However, he explained that the students struggled to understand some of his linguistic explanations and they had tended to waste time when he had tried to introduce some autonomous learning approaches. For example, he abandoned an attempt to introduce extended reading in the library because they chatted and fell asleep.

Chikara's colleagues did not indicate the same degree of enthusiasm for training. Bonda had studied English literature up to MA level, but described the limited study style: 'the only thing I can remember is always translation'. His undergraduate English literature course included 'four or five subjects to get a teacher's licence'. However, when asked if he could remember the titles of the subjects, he joked that he had forgotten them, because they were 'just credit[s]'. Regarding in-service training, Bonda attended an annual conference organised for teachers from the *kosen* and schools attached to the same parent university. However, he explained that these gatherings were 'no use', because the schoolteachers had different goals from *kosen* teachers: 'High school is just cramming to succeed in the [university entrance] examination.'

Unlike his colleagues, Akira was not principally a teacher, his main career was as a Christian pastor. Rather than education or English, he had studied theology to MA level in Scotland, but he explained that teaching qualifications were not necessary in the *kosen*: 'You can teach without being trained to be a teacher. I didn't have any teacher training course.' Instead, Akira asserted that his experience prepared him for English language teaching. He felt sociolinguistically competent from living in the United Kingdom. Moreover, he believed that he could transfer skills from the church, 'preaching is communicating', but conceded *kosen* students were far less inclined to listen than his congregation.

Daiki, like Bonda, took teaching licence credits while studying an undergraduate course in English literature. He could remember a theory related to English-only instruction, but explained that he could not apply it in the *kosen*, because the students were too 'noisy'.

Daiki gave contrasting views regarding continual professional development. From one perspective, he seemed to eschew new ideas, 'my own way, no theory'. However, he also expressed some regret that he had not studied new approaches and asked during an interview, 'please teach me how to teach English'.

Due to the limited influence of training, the teachers' memories of the instruction they received at school could be the most important factor influencing their approach at the *kosen*. However, none of them could remember their schooldays. Instead, Bonda and Chikara recalled studying at home using *mondaishu,* textbooks that contain practice questions from previous university entrance examinations.

Negligible external influences

None of the participants claimed to notice any influence from external sources. As described earlier, the *kosen* teachers did not need to prepare students for English university entrance examinations; moreover, the policies of JABEE and MEXT appeared to be remote and all the participants tended to question the relevance of either organisation to their own classes. Bonda joked that they were out of touch with reality: 'I don't care. I think it's an ideal thing of teaching English, but in reality it's almost impossible [laughs].' Akira showed his disdain for MEXT's policies by stating, 'I tend to ignore [laughs].'

Chikara, who had taught at a high school during most of his career, claimed to take more notice of MEXT, but he noted the discrepancy between the proclamations and the publications that it permitted: 'what they [MEXT] decide, write there and what they allow publishers to describe in the textbooks is really quite distant'. He blamed the lack of change on the entrance examinations.

Internal laissez-faire

According to Daiki there was 'no pressure' from colleagues or management to conform to any teaching approaches and the other participants shared this opinion. However, Akira described the uncertainty caused by the lack of guidance. As the newest English teacher he explained that it had been a 'struggle to find out what to do in the course of the classes'. Akira explained that he received help from another part-time teacher, but her advice focused on administrative issues rather than methodology: 'She was giving me [advice about] how to run, do things, not how to teach the students.'

Although departmental meetings could have provided a forum for discussing classroom issues, Daiki asserted that the gatherings had not been useful because they did not have any targets. Chikara agreed that a vacuum had been created due to the lack of study for entrance tests. However, rather than suggest internal options such as criteria based on the textbooks, he focused instead on the need for a new external test.

Student issues

During the interviews, the teachers professed that student behaviour hindered the implementation of communicative activities. The students' conduct during the observations tended to support these claims. Three main student-related issues arose in both interviews and observations: sleeping, disrespect, and quiet passivity.

During each observation some students slept at some point, leading Daiki to claim that 'school is their sleeping place'. In addition, Daiki also faced mockery, but he treated it as good-humoured banter: 'I think they are…good person[s], but not good students.'

In contrast, Akira felt that he faced a 'battle' with some of his rudest students.

> It's really bad. So before you start teaching there's a battle going on, you know, how mentally making them turn around to listen to you to the class, but you know some kids are not interested in listening at all.

Although Akira and Daiki faced a few disruptive individuals, most of the students in all the teachers' classes tended to be quiet and passive. Even Chikara, who taught the highest proficiency students, noted that they preferred silent individual deskwork, which partly explained his preference for highly structured activities. On the few occasions that he nominated students to answer unscripted questions, they either stayed silent, gave quiet single-word English utterances, or responded in Japanese.

The teachers gave two reasons for these student issues. Firstly, the students seemed unmotivated due to the lack of pressure from external assessment. Instead, Akira asserted that students did the minimum necessary 'just to pass, not so much to study…just to get through the course'. Secondly, the teachers felt that the students' low proficiency caused a lack of confidence. Bonda asserted 'students [are] not confident about English, so yeah often they read [in] a very small voice'. Due to their reluctance to talk, Bonda tried a strategy where he stood next to each speaker to guide him or her to the correct answer, 'to cheer them up'. However, he felt uncertain: 'I don't know if it's effective to their skilling up or not [pause] but I think I can only do this way.'

Unsuitable materials

Apart from Daiki, who explained that he struggled to use the new textbooks because they did not contain grammatical usage drills and explanations, the participants preferred to focus on a textbook's unsuitability for the students. They described three issues.

Firstly, the students lacked the required sociocultural knowledge. Chikara claimed that it was easier for the students to understand the contexts in *Vivid* than the foreign locations in the new textbooks: 'I must use background knowledge, cultural matters, without these things, sometimes it's quite difficult for them to understand.' Secondly, the nature of the activities in the new textbooks, which focused on listening and speaking, may have caused some difficulties. Akira stated: 'I suppose they're not so familiar with English, they don't never mind about talking, they cannot even listen to a conversation.' Chikara added that listening 'is a very difficult aspect of studying' and asserted that the Japanese culture inhibited the students because 'they don't have to listen to English or speak it'. Thirdly, the new textbooks may have lacked relevance.

Akira hinted that his students lacked the ambition to follow the travel-related dreams in the textbooks, because they 'just want a job, enjoy life and type of thing'.

Implications

Based on the issues arising from attempts at curricular change in Japan and from the introduction of innovative textbooks in the *kosen*, implications for effective change can be discussed from two perspectives: policymaking and relevant training.

Policymaking

Policymaking decisions can occur at various levels from national (such as MEXT) to institutional (such as the *kosen* management). Before introducing new policies, two initial factors should be considered. Firstly, teachers need appropriate working conditions (small class sizes, adequate class contact hours, time for reflection and professional development, and adequate facilities). Secondly, although benefits may arise from implementing changes based on language learning theories, policymakers must also consider the suitability for local contexts. Changes introduced without listening to advice from teachers regarding feasibility are less likely to garner support.

After considering these two initial factors, policies will be more successful if they are co-ordinated with three supporting components: materials, assessment, and training (see Figure 15.1).

As described earlier, in Japan the perceived need to focus on reading, grammar, and translation skills for university entrance tests influences teaching and learning. Teachers can use the same *yakudoku* test preparation

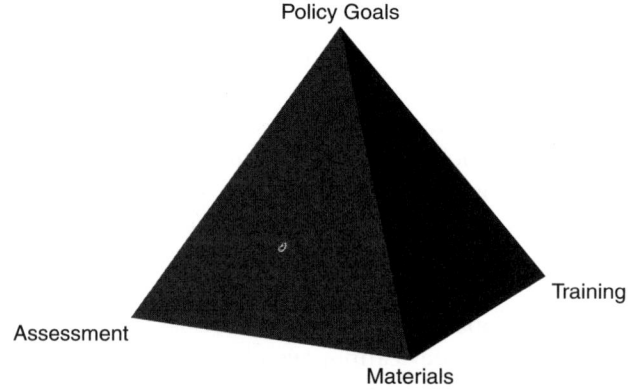

Figure 15.1   Factors supporting policy change

approach that they experienced during their own schooldays; therefore, they rely on experience and feel less need for in-service training. Moreover, although publishers of the MEXT-mandated textbooks need to pay lip service to the government's communicative aims, they can sell more books by satisfying the demand for reading- and grammar-focused exercises. Although the *kosen* differed because communicative materials were introduced and the students did not need to study for English entrance examinations, a lack of direction existed. The teachers found it difficult to motivate students without the examination incentive and their lack of confidence in some of the approaches in the new textbooks caused instructors to fall back on a form of *yakudoku*.

Relevant training

Training needs to be relevant to the issues that teachers face in their classrooms. Areas highlighted in this study in which teachers need support are: methodology, textbook selection, foreign sociocultural topics, student issues, and instructional language proficiency (Table 15.5).

Methodology

Many training courses, such as the ones in Japan, feature lectures and presentations preaching theories originating from BANA cultures. It is ironic that interpretation-based, learner-centred approaches are explained to teachers in a transmission-based style, and no surprise that teachers then struggle to understand and implement what they hear. We need workshops where teachers can practise using new materials and discuss issues of methodology with colleagues and teacher trainers. From such hands-on practice and problem-focused discussions, teachers can feel more confident about adopting changes that work in their context. Moreover, the experience of an interpretation-based approach to professional development can provide a model for teachers to change from transmission-based instruction to learner-centred alternatives.

Table 15.5 Recommendations for teacher training to support change

Category	Example
Methodology	Workshops focusing on the materials that facilitate discussion of methodological problems
Textbook selection	Help teachers to analyse textbooks
Foreign sociocultural topics	Students themselves can research foreign cultures
Student issues	Help teachers develop strategies to develop students' intrinsic motivation
Instructional language proficiency	Train teachers to use the target language and/or vernacular effectively

Textbook selection

Teachers may find the process of textbook selection time consuming; however, selecting the correct textbook can save time in the long run because it reduces the need to adapt activities and create supplementary materials. Various frameworks exist for choosing textbooks, as reviewed by McGrath (2002). Moreover, Littlejohn (2011) has a powerful framework for unpacking underlying textbook approaches so that teachers can challenge the claims of the publisher/author. Training in materials analysis and evaluation can also help teachers to make principled decisions about the use of textbooks and the design and creation of their own supplementary activities.

Foreign sociocultural topics

Unlike the MEXT-mandated textbooks, which tend to contain general topics Japanese students can easily relate to, the new textbooks in the *kosen* contain foreign sociocultural situations that the teachers sometimes struggled to explain. However, culture influences language and a desire to learn about overseas communities can stimulate language learning. Helping teachers to learn about foreign cultures could be one solution, but training courses should also focus on raising awareness of exploratory learning; in other words, using approaches that encourage students to research and present their findings about cultural differences. Depending on the students' English proficiency level, such exploratory study could be done in their first language – possibly in coordination with another subject such as social studies.

Student issues

Low student confidence and motivation can create barriers to change because teachers may opt for the safety of continuing past practices to avoid uncomfortable periods of silence or a loss of control. In normal Japanese schools, change seems to be hindered by students' preference to study using traditional methods for university entrance tests. However, *kosen* students lacked this extrinsic motivation to study English for tests and they had few opportunities to use the language outside the classroom. The resulting behavioural problems caused uncertainty for the teachers. Teachers need training in classroom management and, more importantly, training in techniques to engender intrinsic motivation.

Instructional language proficiency

In this study, only Daiki indicated that he lacked adequate English ability. The other three teachers expressed their opinions fluently in English during the interviews. Nevertheless, classes tended to be dominated by the teacher talking in Japanese. Rather than setting benchmarks based on external examinations such as TOEIC and TOEFL, it would be preferable for training courses to focus on developing the teacher's ability to use English for instructional purposes. Alternatively, using the first language can help comprehension and form solidarity between teacher and learners, so training can also focus on finding the optimal balance between English and the vernacular (Macaro, 2009).

In summary, effective change is unlikely if new textbooks are introduced without considering other factors, such as: sociocultural conditions; level of teacher confidence; quality of training; the impact from external, school level and classroom forces; and the suitability of the textbook itself. Policymakers can improve teaching conditions and ensure that the materials, assessment, and training support the change. Training can focus on methodology, textbook selection, foreign sociocultural topics, student issues, and instructional language proficiency.

Engagement priorities

1. The teachers at the *kosen* adapted the new textbooks to suit their teaching preferences. Think about the textbooks you use. What types of activity do you tend to (a) disregard, (b) use in more depth, (c) alter, and (d) supplement? What does this tell you about your teaching preferences?
2. Curricular change tends to be viewed from a top-down perspective. Policymakers order changes for teachers to implement. Studies then focus on how the teachers mediate the changes. This approach seems to view the learners as passive receivers of change. Try spending a few minutes at the end of your classroom activities to gather student feedback. What advantages and disadvantages are there to asking students for their opinions?
3. MEXT-authorised textbooks do not tend to follow the CLT claims made by the publisher. Read the claims made by the publishers of the textbook that you use and analyse it using a framework such as Littlejohn (2011). To what degree does the textbook actually support its claims? Why might it diverge from the claims? How might you improve the textbook?

References

Carless, D. R. (2012). *Task-Based Language Teaching in Confucian-Heritage Settings: Prospects and Challenges*. Paper presented at the TBLT in Asia Conference.

Gershon, S., Mares, C. and Walker, R. (2004a). *On the Go: English Skills for Global Communication*. Hong Kong: Pearson Education Asia Limited.

Gershon, S., Mares, C. and Walker, R. (2004b). *On the Move: English Skills for Global Communication*. Hong Kong: Pearson Education Asia Limited.

Glaser, B. G. and Strauss, A. (1967). *The Discovery of Grounded Theory: Strategies for Qualitative Research*. London: Aldine Transaction.

Hino, N. (1988). *Yakudoku*: Japan's dominant tradition in foreign language learning. *JALT Journal*, 10(1 and 2): 45–55.

Holliday, A. (1994). The house of TESEP and the communicative approach: the special needs of state English language education. *ELT Journal,* 48(1): 3–11.

Humphries, S. (2013). Western-published versus MEXT-mandated: a comparative textbook analysis. *Doshisha Studies in English,* 90: 217–238.

Hutchinson, T. and Torres, E. (1994). The textbook as agent of change. *ELT Journal,* 48(4): 315–328.

JABEE. (2008). Criteria for accrediting Japanese engineering education programs leading to Bachelor's Degree [Homepage]. Available at http://www.jabee.org/english/OpenHomePage/Criteria_Bachelor_2008_1020.pdf [Accessed 21/1/08].

Kikuchi, K. (2006). Revisiting English entrance examinations at Japanese universities after a decade. *JALT Journal,* 28(1): 77–96.

Kikuchi, K. and Browne, C. (2009). English educational policy for high schools in Japan: ideals vs. reality. *RELC Journal,* 40(2): 172–191.

Kizuka, M. (2006). Professionalism in English Language Education in Japan. *ELTED,* 9(1): 55–62.

Lamie, J. M. (2004). Presenting a model of change. *Language Teaching Research,* 8(2): 115–142.

Li, D. (1998). 'It's always more difficult than you plan or imagine': Teachers' perceived difficulties in introducing the communicative approach in South Korea. *TESOL Quarterly,* 32(4): 677–703.

Littlejohn, A. (2011). The analysis of language teaching materials: inside the Trojan Horse. In Tomlinson, B. (ed.), *Materials Development in Language Teaching,* 2nd Edition. Cambridge: Cambridge University Press, pp. 179–211.

Macaro, E. (2009). Teacher use of codeswitching in the second language classroom: exploring 'optimal' use. In Turnbull, M. and Dailey-O'Cain, J. (eds), *First Language Use in Second and Foreign Language Learning.* Bristol: Multilingual Matters, pp. 35–49.

McGrath, I. (2002). *Materials Evaluation and Design for Language Teaching.* Edinburgh: Edinburgh University Press.

MEXT (Ministry of Education, Culture, Sports, Science and Technology) (2003) Regarding the establishment of an action plan to cultivate 'Japanese with English abilities' [Webpage]. Available at http://www.gifu-net.ed.jp/kyoka/eigo/CommunicativeEnglish/Regarding%20the%20Establishment%20of%20an%20Action%20Plan%20to%20Cultivate%20%A1%C8Japanese%20with%20English%20Abilities%A1%C9.htm [Accessed 20/9/12].

MEXT (Ministry of Education, Culture, Sports, Science and Technology) (2011). Five Proposals and Specific Measures for Developing Proficiency in English for International Communication.[Webpage]. Available at http://www.mext.go.jp/english/elsec/1319701.htm.

Minamimura, T., Asai, M., Ishihara, Y., Itoh, T., Iwamoto, K., Goi, C., Torio, N., Harada, Y., Miyagawa, K., Miyamoto, T., Watanabe, K. and Rockenbach, B. (2006). *Vivid English Course (New Edition) I.* Tokyo: Daiichi Gakushusha.

Nagasawa, K. (2004). Teacher training and development. In Makarova, V. and Rogers, T. S. (eds), *English Language Teaching: The Case of Japan.* Munich: Lincom, pp. 280–295.

Nishino, T. and Watanabe, M. (2008). Communication-oriented policies versus classroom realities in Japan. *TESOL Quarterly,* 42(1): 133–138.

Pennycook, A. (1994). *The Cultural Politics of English As an International Language.* London: Longman.

Sakui, K. (2007). Classroom management in Japanese EFL classrooms. *JALT Journal,* 29(1): 41–58.

Sato, M. and Asanuma, S. (2000). Japan. In Morris, P. and Williamson, J. (eds), *Teacher Education in the Asia-Pacific Region: A Comparative Study*. New York: Garland, pp. 107–131.

Sato, K. and Kleinsasser, R. (2004). Beliefs, practices and interactions of teachers in a Japanese high school English department. *Teaching and Teacher Education*, 20: 797–816.

Taguchi, N. (2002). Implementing oral communication classes in upper secondary schools: a case study [30 paragraphs]. *The Language Teacher* [Online Journal], 26(12) December. Available at http://www.jalt-publications.org/old_tlt/articles/2002/12/taguchi [Accessed 2/3/12].

Wada, M. (2002). Teacher education for curricular innovation in Japan. In Savignon, S. J. (ed.), *Interpreting Communicative Language Teaching: Contexts and Concerns in Teacher Education*. New Haven: Yale University Press, pp. 31–40.

Wedell, M. (2003). Giving TESOL change a chance: supporting key players in the curriculum change process. *System*, 31: 439–456.

16
Materials in ELT: Looking Ahead

Kathleen Graves and Sue Garton

The chapters in this volume have been written against the background of the growth of English as a global language. Nine of the fifteen contributors, representing Albania, Algeria, Argentina, Bahrain, Bangladesh, Brazil, Ghana, Japan, and Thailand, point out that English is being taught in these countries because globalisation has made it the language of economic and social access and participation. Although the role of English in people's actual access to economic and social opportunities is highly problematic (see Coleman, 2011), its status as an international language (EIL), or global lingua franca (ELF), is well established. As such, the importance of English has resulted in policy decisions in countries around the world such as: lowering the age of compulsory English in schools; the provision of school subjects in English; and the required use of materials that may not match the teacher's background. These policies have created huge challenges to their implementation from the standpoint of materials development, of teaching and teacher preparation, of learner-readiness, and of available resources, particularly technology. These challenges are a cause for concern, since difficulties in implementing the policies undermine the teaching workforce and simply do not produce the desired results. As Wedell puts it,

> national policy makers seem generally to have given insufficient thought to existing socio-economic and educational/cultural realities, when considering hoped-for curriculum outcomes. Teachers have thus often failed to enable learners to achieve them. (2008: 635)

This volume offers an exploration of the educational and cultural realities for practitioners as they attempt both successfully and unsuccessfully to use, adapt, and develop materials at the ground level in the classroom. These accounts suggest three broad themes to consider as we sketch future developments and lines of inquiry within the field: the content of materials for English as a globalised language; teachers' effective use of materials; and the affordances of technology for language learning.

The content of materials for English as a globalised language

How does one develop materials for English as a globalised, heterogeneous language that is learnt locally in largely homogeneous populations? A globalised English is different from English learnt as a *foreign* language, in the sense of studying the language, literature, and culture of a foreign country with the aim of travelling to or living in the country or interacting with people of that country. Today's learners are being educated to participate in discourse communities in which English will be used as a lingua franca with other users of English as an L2 as well as with native speakers (Modiano, 2009; Ur, 2010). In fact, English is already part of many learners' daily lives, as al Majthoob points out in describing Bahrain (Chapter 4), where English pervades the media, is part of the linguistic landscape, and is necessary in local government and business communication.

The distinction between English as a globalised language and as a foreign language is important for understanding classroom materials because much of their content is still based on an EFL view. For example, representations of the BANA (Britain, Australasia and North America) countries tend to dominate materials, not only in materials produced in those countries for a global market, but even in countries like Algeria that develop their own school materials (Messekher, Chapter 5). Despite the recognition that there are more speakers of world English varieties than of BANA 'native speaker' varieties (Jenkins, 2003), a glance through most coursebooks will show that the 'native-speaker' is still the preferred voice on audio recordings.

For materials developers, teaching English as a globalised language raises questions about the future content of materials. Whose English and whose culture are to be represented in language learning materials? Which texts, contexts, and people? Should materials represent local people, concerns, contexts, practices, and topics of interest because these will be more familiar to learners? Or should materials represent a range of global contexts and speakers in order to provide a variety of perspectives? Contributors to this volume suggest that both are necessary.

Localising materials offers the benefit of familiarity. López-Barrios and Debat (Chapter 3) make the case that localising materials connects them to the learners' world and matches local practices and curriculum. Rahman and Cotter (Chapter 10) describe how user feedback on cell phone language learning materials resulted in recording fluent Bangladeshi speakers of English rather than less familiar British speakers, as well as choosing topics that were more relevant to their users. Familiarity is also a factor for teachers. As Humphries (Chapter 15) points out, one reason that the teachers in his study did not follow the CLT-based textbook was that they 'contained foreign sociocultural situations that the teachers sometimes struggled to explain' (p. 266).

Localising content enables learners to talk and write about their own experiences, concerns, and culture through English. Providing global content gives a platform for learning about other perspectives and becoming interculturally competent. While López-Barrios and Debat, and Messekher support some degree of localisation in materials, they also make the case that exploring sociocultural and sociolinguistic differences are an important part of learning a new language. Materials can provide opportunities for learners to explore these differences and so develop a broader global awareness. López-Barrios and Debat suggest that 'Learners go beyond mere surface impressions and engage in activities that challenge stereotypes and alter their world view' (p. 44). Messekher argues that the intent should not be to alter a student's worldview, but to show them that there are other worldviews.

Looking to the future it is important to consider sociocultural differences not only as differences between BANA cultures and the cultures of the learners but also as differences between the cultures of people who use English as an L2. According to Sharifian (2009) what is needed is 'meta-cultural competence' because:

> in EIL communicative events, speakers are likely to draw on their L1 systems of cultural conceptualisations, perhaps not always realising they are doing so. Since in such contexts English, a common language, is being used for communication, speakers may too easily assume that they mean the same thing when they use the same or similar words. (ibid.: 251)

Thus materials will need to provide opportunities for learners to become aware that the ways in which they use English represent values and assumptions drawn from their L1 systems of cultural conceptualisations, which may not be shared by another user of English with a different L1. Further, they will need to learn how to identify and address potential misunderstandings when they occur.

Teachers and learners may welcome more localisation of the content of materials, but materials designed to develop intercultural or meta-cultural competence will only be effective if teachers see their point. The majority of English teachers have themselves learnt English as a second or additional language. While this means that they are ideal role models for their learners, many have been prepared to teach English as a *foreign* language in the sense described earlier; they are prepared to teach the English of a BANA country, not a globalised language. Moreover, the ideology of English as a foreign language holds the native speaker as the norm, which implies that the non-native has a deficit to overcome (Amin and Kubota, 2004.) So, while teachers may experience English as a global language, they probably haven't learnt or been taught to teach it in that way and are unlikely to perceive themselves as role models. As teachers are central to the effective use of materials, any changes in the orientation of materials will need to make sense to them.

Teachers' effective use of materials

The effectiveness of classroom materials ultimately depends on how they are used by teacher and learners and how that use enables learners to become competent in the language, however competence is defined. As the orchestrators of classroom practice, teachers play a critical role in how materials are used, which, in turn, depends on the teacher's understanding of and skill in using them. Humphries (Chapter 15) outlines a range of factors that affect a teacher's use of materials including: understanding of language and how it is learnt, and of learners; the teacher's own experience of learning and confidence in English; and contextual factors such as the culture of the school and perceptions of the purposes for learning English. When teachers are asked or required to use materials that do not match their expertise, experience, and beliefs, they may not use the materials in the ways intended and the expected results are not likely to be achieved. (See Chapter 1 for a discussion of teachers' responses to communicative methodology in coursebooks and Chapters 6 and 15 for examples.)

Mismatches between the intended use of materials and how they are actually used are exacerbated when teachers are required to use materials they feel do not take into account the realities of their classroom. A recurring theme in the volume is the need to get teachers' input and feedback about the materials they use – at policy level, at development level, and at school level. Seargeant and Erling's (2011: 16) suggestion that not only teachers, but also learners and community members should be consulted by policy makers applies to materials as well:

> What is needed for ELT to be transformational, then, is an ongoing dialogue between practitioners (that is learners, teachers, and the surrounding community) and policy makers which will enable a dialectic which can tailor English language education to the local needs of communities attempting to engage fully in a rapidly globalising world.

Teachers have 'funds of knowledge' – to borrow Moll and his colleagues' term[1] – about students and classrooms that can help developers design materials to meet their needs even more effectively. This knowledge includes how to manage a classroom, understanding learner's backgrounds, and understanding the teacher's role. For example, the teacher in Seferaj's study (Chapter 6) gives well-thought out reasons for eschewing pair work/fluency activities with her 36 students and instead focusing on accuracy through teacher-student exchanges. She has clear ideas about her role and authority, what she can give the students, and what her students' parents expect of her as a teacher. Looking to the future, materials developers and policy makers need to avail themselves of the wisdom and experiences of teachers – and through them, learners, in order for materials to better reflect and meet local needs.

Even when there is a good fit between the materials and the classroom, the teacher will still need to make adjustments for her particular learners. Bosompems' study (Chapter 7) found that novice teachers were reluctant to adapt materials because they did not feel it was permissible to make changes to the curriculum. Teachers need to learn that adapting is something good teachers do. As Bosompem puts it, 'not only is it acceptable to adapt a textbook but vital to do so in order to meet the particular needs of students in a particular context' (p. 115). Knowing how and why to adapt is another matter. Adaptation may take a variety of forms, as described by both Richards (Chapter 2) and Bosompem. Teachers need to be aware of different ways to adapt, and the reasons for adapting. This will facilitate what Richards calls 'creative teaching rather than textbook dominated teaching' (p. 34).

Adaptation is based on understanding students, context, and materials and Nuangpolmak (Chapter 8) provides an excellent example. The author problematised the gaps between the coursebook and the students' proficiency levels on the one hand, and the coursebook and the syllabus aims on the other. She then designed multilevel writing tasks aimed at different levels, thus meeting the needs of her learners. These same writing tasks gave students the opportunity for choice and self-direction, thus fostering autonomy, which was one of the syllabus aims. To accomplish these steps, she needed to: understand her learners' backgrounds, language proficiency, and motivation; understand the aims of the syllabus; and analyse the extent to which the course book fitted the learners so she could help them achieve the aims.

A second striking example of adaptation is Igielski's (Chapter 9) modification and supplementation of the core textbook in her primary classroom. Her context, the US, is the only one in the volume that does not fit straightforwardly in the discussion of English as a globalised language. The US is an ESL context in the conventional sense that the language and culture of English are clearly dominant and 'minority' students are expected to function socially and academically in English. Igielski problematises the dominance of English by exploring ways to value her students' language and backgrounds. She chooses additional materials, in both English and the students' L1, that reflect their experiences. She invites perspectives on curriculum themes that are different from those of the dominant culture. She draws on her learners' funds of knowledge to create a culturally rich classroom that makes her students visible in the curriculum.

In summary, the effective use of materials depends on the teacher's understanding of the materials, on the fit with their beliefs, expertise, and experience, and on their ability to adapt the materials to their particular learners. One implication for the future is that published materials should, as a matter of course, include suggestions for different ways to adapt the content and tasks in classroom contexts. Another is that teacher accounts of their reasoning and experience of adaptation need to be part of the discourse in materials development and evaluation.

Teacher education

The need to educate teachers to understand and learn how to use materials is a corollary of the need for teacher input into the materials they use. A number of contributors to this volume note the paucity of courses in materials design and evaluation in teacher preparation programmes. While adding such courses is an important step, this volume makes it clear that an individual course is not enough. Analysis of coursebooks and how to use and adapt them needs to be threaded through all teacher preparation courses, including those that focus on core areas such as second language acquisition, methodology, and linguistics. To do otherwise ignores the reality that teachers use materials on a daily basis in teaching and helps to perpetuate the separation between what is taught in teacher education programmes and what teachers experience in the classroom.

One of those rare pre-service materials evaluation courses is the focus of Augusto-Navarro, de Oliveira and Abreu-e-Lima's chapter (Chapter 14). They outline three aspects to a critical understanding of materials that are the foundation for the course: learning key theories of language as a foundation for their choices; identifying how theories are represented in materials; and analysing how effective specific materials might be for a given group of learners. Their course focuses on grammar, hence the emphasis on theories of language. All the chapters in this volume written by practitioners about their development and use of materials (Chapters 4, 8, 9, 10, 11, 12, 13 and 14) provide clear evidence of these three aspects in practice; they all have strong theoretical frameworks, which they link to the materials and to their learners.

A critical understanding of materials is a first step in educating teachers so that they can use them effectively in the classroom. However, if teachers have not themselves had successful experiences of the approach on which materials are based, such as interactive group work in communicative tasks, they are unlikely to have confidence in their ability to implement the approach (Butler, 2005; Li, 1998). Put another way, in order to effectively teach something, teachers need to have had a successful experience of it. Bandura's concept of self-efficacy (1997) may be useful here. An individual's perceived self-efficacy is 'a judgment of one's ability to organise and execute given types of performances' (Bandura, 1997: 21). He identifies four sources of self-efficacy,[2] two of which are enactive mastery experiences and vicarious experiences. In enactive mastery experiences, a teacher enacts the complex tasks involved in the practice or innovation. In vicarious experiences, the teacher observes peers enacting a successful experience. Tibbitts and Pashby's (Chapter 13) approach to educating Korean primary teachers to use authentic materials for storytelling includes both 'enactive mastery' and 'vicarious' experiences. In addition, their approach includes a third type of experience, that of being a learner. As learners, the teachers experience the trainers' storytelling. Building on this experience, they then teach stories to their peers and participate as learners in their peers' storytelling. They thus have successful experiences in using materials in innovative ways, both as learners and teachers, as well as experiences observing others.

Looking to the future, in addition to learning how to critically analyse materials throughout their courses, teachers in teacher preparation programmes need to have experiences with the approaches the materials are based on. This means that teacher educators need to provide those experiences, not simply talk about them. When teachers can critically analyse materials in terms of theoretical frameworks, their learners' needs, and their own practice, they will be equipped to use and adapt materials effectively. Moreover, they will be in a position to engage in substantive dialogue with both policy makers and materials developers about the types of materials that are most likely to help learners learn.

The affordances of technology for language learning

Technology as a means for learners to direct their own learning is a salient feature of the learning experiences described in the chapters on technology (Rahman and Cotter, Chapter 10; Pereira, Chapter 11; Maggi, Cherubin and Pascual, Chapter 12). Whether they use a language program on a mobile phone, engage in reading and writing fiction via a program on a computer, or brainstorm and display information on an interactive whiteboard, learners are in charge of the activities of learning. Where their experiences differ is in the role that language plays in their learning. The cell phone users use technology as a means, with English as an end. The interactive fiction writers and science researchers use English as a means, with new content as an end.

In Bangladesh, the learners use the technology – the program on their cell phones – to listen to, answer questions about, and practise English dialogue. The aim is for the learners to gain confidence and develop communication skills that they can then use for their own purposes.

The students in Portugal and Italy use the technology – including IF programs, Google docs, the Internet – to carry out interactive activities in English. Technology *and* English are the means for reading and writing fiction and learning science. English is not the explicit end, but is a tool or means for learning or interacting with the content. Technology, by providing students with access to content as well as platforms for decision-making and co-construction of content, supports individual autonomy and group collaboration. Technology thus enables students to direct the course of their learning.

Students do not learn to use the technology in English without support. In each of these classrooms teachers play a critical role that makes the autonomy afforded by technology possible. They select and adapt materials and design tasks to support and guide students. Interestingly, although there is no teacher present for the cell phone users, a modification made in response to learner feedback was the addition of a teacher's voice to provide a similar sense of support and guidance to the learners.

The difference in the way technology is used in Bangladesh and Europe underscores, to some extent, the divide between countries where technology is readily available and those where it is not. The European students function in a world where using technology interactively with others, through social media and other tools, is commonplace. For them, technology is one arena where the globalisation of English is evident; they are likely to use technology in more than one language, including English (Chien, 2012). A large number of today's students are what Chien has called 'digital English natives', people who have grown up using English to a greater or lesser extent with various forms of technology in their daily lives. Since technology permeates these students' lives, materials developers and language educators need to consider how language education can make best use of it. While the lack of access to technology is a very real issue, it is likely to become less so over time as both access to and use of technology spreads. A more important issue may be that many educators lag behind their students in understanding how to use technology and thus do not know how to make it part of classroom practice.

In summary, technology provides new paths to language learning. It affords greater autonomy to students than print materials because, in terms of content, it gives students access to varied, authentic, spoken, and written sources of English; in terms of process, it provides interactive tools for constructing and co-constructing knowledge in English. The content available through technology and its potential for interactivity and knowledge construction may, ultimately, provide the most promising basis for learning English as a globalised language.

Conclusion

This is a time of transition in ELT and therefore a time with the potential for change and innovation. According to Modiano:

> while there is agreement that English is now 'global' and as such is best defined as a heterogeneous entity, few practitioners have as yet been able to

devise methods and curricula that can act as a basis for teaching with such an understanding as the guiding principle. (2009: 59)

The challenge that Modiano defines for teaching a language that is used globally but learnt in local contexts, must, by its nature, be addressed in those contexts. The contributors to this volume have explored, from a variety of local perspectives, the complexity of what is involved in successfully meeting this challenge. Moreover, they have shown how local solutions can have relevance across continents and contexts and have thus provided a sense of the future of materials in ELT.

Notes

1. Moll, L.C., Amanti, C., Neff, D. and Gonzalez, N. Funds of knowledge for teaching: Using a qualitative approach to connect homes and classrooms. *Theory Into Practice* 31(2): 132–141.
2. In addition to enactive mastery experiences and vicarious experiences, the other sources of self-efficacy are verbal persuasion and physiological and affective states (Bandura, 1997).

References

Amin, N. and Kubota, R. (2004). Native speaker discourses: power and resistance in postcolonial teaching of English to speakers of other languages. In Ninnes, P. and Mehta, S. (eds), *Reimagining Comparative Education: Postfoundational Ideas and Applications for Critical Times*. New York: Routledge, pp. 107–128.

Bandura, A. (1997). *Self-Efficacy: The Exercise of Control*. New York: Worth Publishers.

Butler, Y. G. (2005). Comparative perspectives towards communicative activities among elementary school teachers in South Korea, Japan and Taiwan. *Language Teaching Research,* 9(4): 423–446.

Chien, Y. H. (2012). *Life in the 21st Century: A Study of Pre-service Teachers' Uses of Technology and English*. Unpublished Doctoral Dissertation: University of Michigan.

Coleman, H. (ed.) (2011). *Dreams and Realities: Developing Countries and the English Language*. London: British Council.

Jenkins, J. (2003) *World Englishes*. London: Routledge.

Li, D. F. (1998). 'It's always more difficult than you plan and imagine': Teachers' perceived difficulties in introducing the communicative approach in South Korea. *TESOL Quarterly, 32*(4): 677–703.

Modiano, M. (2009). EIL, Native-speakerism and the failure of European ELT. In Sharifian, F. (ed.), *English As an International Language*. Bristol: Multilingual Matters, pp. 58–80.

Seargeant, P. and Erling, E. J. (2011) The discourse of 'English as a language for international development: policy assumptions and practical challenges. In Coleman, H. (ed.), *Dreams and Realities: Developing Countries and the English Language*. London: British Council, pp. 248–268.

Sharifian, F. (2009). Cultural conceptualizations in English as an International Language. In Sharifian, F. (ed.), *English As an International Language*. Bristol: Multilingual Matters, pp. 242–253.

Wedell, M. (2008). Developing a capacity to make 'English for Everyone' worthwhile: reconsidering outcomes and how to start achieving them. *International Journal of Educational Development,* 28: 628–639.

Ur, P. (2010). English As a Lingua Franca: A Teacher's Perspective. Cadernos de Letras (UFRJ) 27. Available at http://www.letras.ufrj.br/anglo_germanicas/cadernos/numeros/122010/textos/cl301220100penny.pdf [Accessed 25/5/13].

Suggested Reading

Aarseth, E. (1997). *Cybertext: Perspectives on Ergodic Literature*. Baltimore, MD: Johns Hopkins University Press.
The definitive scholarly work on digital literature. A dense read, but seminal in its defining of ergodic literature, which includes Interactive Fiction.

Beckett, G.H. and Miller, P.C. (eds) (2006). *Project-Based Second and Foreign Language Education: Past, Present, and Future*. Greenwich, CT: Information Age Publishing.
Bridges the gap between research and practice in the area of project-based learning and teaching and provides examples of its implementation in a variety of language learning contexts.

Coleman, H. (ed.) (2011). *Dreams and Realities: Developing Countries and the English Language*. London: British Council.
Provides insights on the complex dynamics of language policy and practice, and the current debate on the discourse of English as a global tool for development. The contributors analyse a range of English language projects in Asia and Africa in the light of this discourse. The link to m-learning in Bangladesh may be perceived through this critical stance on the 'dreams' and the 'realities' of English learning in the region.

Cummins, J. and Davison, C. (2007). *International Handbook of English Language Teaching*. New York: Springer.
Provides a comprehensive examination of policy, practice, research and theory related to ELT in international contexts.

Dalton-Puffer, C. and Smit, U. (eds) (2007) *Critical Perspectives in CLIL Classroom Discourse*. Frankfurt: Peter Lang.
Content and language integrated learning (CLIL), classroom discourse, discourse analysis, pragmatics, bilingual education.

Freeman, D.E. and Freeman, Y.S. (2007). *English Language Learners: The Essential Guide*. New York, NY: Scholastic.
This text is an essential reference tool, particularly the sections that focus on drawing on students' primary language and culture, and how to develop rich academic language in the classroom context.

Gay, G. (2002). Preparing for culturally responsive teaching. *Journal of Teacher Education*, 53(2): 106–116.
Gay defines and explores the term culturally responsive teaching. In this article and her book (2000), she stresses the need for teachers to move beyond respect and recognition towards the development of their own knowledge base about the cultural diversity present in their classroom. Her work draws on the strengths that students bring in service of learning.

Gonzalez, N. and Moll, L. (2002). Cruzando el puente: building bridges to funds of knowledge. *Educational Policy*, 16(4): 623–641.
Utilizing students' funds of knowledge is a major component in teaching for social justice and equity. This article explores in great depth the importance of validating one's students' identities, specifically in terms of language, both within the content and within the classroom community.

Graves, M. (2008). *Teaching Individual Words: One Size does not Fit All*. New York: Teachers College Press.

Graves introduces techniques and strategies for rich vocabulary instruction, which can be used in any language teaching context to enhance a variety of materials.

Gray, J. (2010). *The Construction of English: Culture, Consumerism and Promotion in the ELT Global Coursebook.* London: Palgrave Macmillan.

A critical examination of global ELT coursebooks and the values and interests they often reflect. A number of well-known coursebooks are subject to critical scrutiny. It is a thought provoking reading for English teachers and teacher educators as to how culture is depicted and taught.

GSMA Development Fund (2012). *Shaping the Future: Realising the Potential of Informal Learning Through Mobile.* London: GSMA.

All content development needs to be relevant to the learners it is trying to reach. This report shows how research into the needs, interests, ambitions of young people in emerging markets as well as research into how they use technology and for what purpose can help shape mobile learning content for the future.

Harwood, N. (ed.) (2010) *English Language Teaching Materials, Theory and Practice.* Cambridge Language Education Series editor Jack C. Richards. NY: Cambridge University Press.

Explores issues related to the design, implementation, and evaluation of materials in language programs, including an interesting introduction that raises important issues related to materials development and design.

Jackson-Mead, K. and Wheeler, J.R. (eds) (2011). *IF Theory Reader.* Transcript on Press: Boston, MA. Available at: http://www.lulu.com/items/volume_71/11643000/11643447/1/print/10228464_IFTheoryBookv2.pdf. [Accessed 28/03/2012.]

A very interesting collection of essays on the theory and design of Interactive Fiction written by many of its most acclaimed authors.

Kashtan, Aaron (2009). Because It's Not There: Verbal Visuality and the Threat of Graphics in Interactive Fiction. Proceedings of the Digital Arts and Culture Conference, 2009 – After Media: Embodiment and Context. Retrieved 8 January 2011, from http://escholarship.org/uc/item/58c9373m.pdf

An excellent article on the staying power of text in Interactive Fiction amidst our current graphics-dominated world.

Linse, C. (2005). *Practical English Language Teaching: Young Learners.* New York: McGraw-Hill

A rich and reflective, but also simple resource. It covers everything you need to work with young learners in EFL and ESL.

López Barrios, M. and Villanueva de Debat, E. (2006). Minding the needs of the Argentine learner: Global textbooks and their adapted versions for the local context. *Folio,* 10(2): 14–16.

The authors apply the framework from their chapter to the analysis of the international and localised versions of two EFL coursebooks.

Masuhara, Hitomi and Tomlinson, Brian (eds) (2010) *Research for Materials Development in Language Learning: Evidence for Best Practice.* London: Continuum.

Qu Jiangfiong and Tan Bee Tin's chapter evaluates three coursebooks used in China from the perspective of the cultures of learning reflected in them. Other chapters in the same book report on research on different types of materials used in varied contexts.

McGrath, I. (2002). *Materials Evaluation and Design for Language Teaching.* Edinburgh: Edinburgh University Press.

This has the advantage of being a single-authored volume rather than a collection of articles. Topics covered include choosing, evaluating and adapting textbooks and designing other forms of materials. It offers practical ideas on how teachers can adapt and supplement textbooks and suggestions for teachers who wish to prepare their own materials.

Mehisto, P., Frigols, M.J. and Marsh, D. (2008). *Uncovering CLIL*. MacMillan

Provides interesting ideas on successful CLIL planning and teaching strategies.

Montgomery, W. (2001). Creating culturally responsive, inclusive classrooms. *The Council for Exceptional Children*, 33(4): 4–10.

This article is accessible and explicit about responsive methods and materials. The author examines "culturally complex atmospheres" and provides reflection tools that a teacher can use in researching her classroom, particularly in the primary grades.

Nault, D. (2006). Going global: rethinking culture teaching in ELT contexts. *Language, Culture and Curriculum*, 19(3): 314–328.

This article encourages teachers to think about which culture they teach in the age of globalization where US and British cultures cannot be the unique target cultures anymore. Culture and ELT should meet students' needs and be more international and inclusive to promote linguistic and cultural awareness.

Pachler, N. and Redondo, A. (2006). *A Practical Guide to Teaching Modern Foreign Languages in the Secondary School*. New York: Routledge.

Discusses key pedagogical issues and seeks to help teachers in their early professional development to develop their key skills, knowledge and understanding of ELT.

Prensky, M. (2006). *Don't Bother Me Mom, I'm Learning!: How Computer and Video Games are Preparing your Kids for Twenty-first Century Success and How You Can Help!* St. Paul, MN: Paragon House.

Prensky's follow up book to the incredibly influential 'Digital Game-based Learning' (2001) is better argued and more convincing at promoting the learning affordances of video games.

Reilly, J, and V. Reilly (2005) *Writing with Children*. UK: Oxford University Press.

A practical resource for teachers who wish to guide children to become confident writers whether in EFL, ESL or EAL. The introduction highlights everything the teacher needs to know about how children learn to write.

Richards, Jack C. (2006). *Communicative Language Teaching Today*. Available at www.cambridge.org/other.../Richards-Communicative-Language.pdf.

This document gives a general introduction to CLT with many examples to demonstrate CLT key concepts.

Richardson, J. (2009) *The Next Steps in Guided Reading: Focused Assessments and Targeted Lessons for Helping Every Student Become a Batter Reader*. USA: Scholastic

A useful tool to help teachers meet the diverse needs of learners. It has the essential components of effective guided reading lessons and the use of guided writing to support the reading process.

Savova, L. (ed.) (2009) *Using Textbooks Effectively*. Washington DC: TESOL.

A useful collection of articles covering very different territory from the Tomlinson collections. Topics covered include textbooks for different skill areas, authenticity in textbook language, and evaluating textbooks.

Seegert, A. (2009). Doing there vs. being there: performing presence in Interactive Fiction. *Journal of Gaming & Virtual Worlds*, 1(1): 23–37. Available at http://www.ingentaconnect.com/content/intellect/jgvw/2009/00000001/00000001;jsessionid=asjvstqxq qua.victoria. [Accessed 28/03/2012.]

An interesting article that argues for the existence of the sense of 'performing presence' in text-based Interactive Fiction games (the sense of actually performing actions in a textual virtual world).

Tomlinson, B. (ed.) (2003). *Developing Materials for Language Teaching.* London: Continuum.

Gives a comprehensive introduction to the many aspects of materials development for language teaching. The chapters, written by both teachers and researchers, discuss theories of materials design but also provide concepts and approaches that teachers can use to apply these theories. The book helps teachers to develop the ability to evaluate, select, adapt and/or create materials that are appropriate to their local context and relevant to their learners' needs.

Tomlinson, B. (ed.) (2008). *English Language Learning Materials: A Critical Review.* London, UK: Continuum.

This edited volume provides an informed and critical review of the materials used in ELT, with a focus on specific learners and contexts around the world. It is especially relevant for those interested in research in materials development that has practical applications.

Tomlinson, B. (ed.) (2011) *Materials Development in Language Teaching,* 2nd Edition. Cambridge: Cambridge University Press.

A good overview of issues involved in the design and evaluation of different types of materials including textbooks. Included are the role of corpora, materials writing processes, and the role of technology.

Trappes-Lomax, H. and Ferguson, G. (eds) (2002). *Language in Language Teacher Education.* Philadelphia: John Benjamins Publishing Company.

Considers a variety of approaches for incorporating the building of language skills into programmes for pre- and in-service language teachers.

Wardley S. (2012). *Learning from Web 2.0.* Computer Sciences Corporation.

Explores the use of open source technology for classroom activities.

Wedell, M. (2009). *Planning for Educational Change,* 1st Edition. London: Continuum

Wedell is a powerful voice on the issue of planning and managing educational innovation and change. He illustrates the theory and practice of change through several case studies. His "questions to consider" are designed to encourage critical reflection while his own answers and approaches focus on implementation processes that are sensitive to local contextual realities.

Wright, A. (1995). *Storytelling with Children.* Oxford: Oxford University Press.

Contains extensive materials and lessons designed to bring stories to life while building fluency in listening and other language skill areas.

Whitton, N. (2010). *Learning with Digital Games.* New York: Routledge.

A very accessible and comprehensive guide to digital game-based learning, which looks at the advantages and disadvantages of using DGBL in higher-learning.

Index

Printed and bound by CPI Group (UK) Ltd, Croydon, CR0 4YY